Saint Joseph
As Seen by Mystics and Historians

(by Gasnier—*Joseph the Silent*, from p. 9)

In poetic language, Francis Jammes says: "O my dear ones, I promise you that he who goes about like one of the common herd, like one of us, with his tools on his shoulder and a smile in his beard...he will never abandon you."

HAIL, BLESSED JOSEPH!

(by Doze—*St. Joseph: Shadow*, from pp. 14, 53 & 69)

A holy Jesuit, Fr. Jacquinot, the exact contemporary of Monsieur Jean-Jacques Olier, founder of the Society of St. Sulpice and of the first seminaries in France, and Pastor of St. Sulpice in 1657, cried out: "Beautiful sun, father of the day, hasten your course, quickly bring this happy hour into its day, during which all the oracles of the saints must be fulfilled, who promise us that, as we near the end of time, the glories of St. Joseph will be magnificently displayed; who assure us that God Himself will draw the curtain and tear the veil that, until now, has kept us from seeing, out in the open, the wonders of the sanctuary of St. Joseph's soul; who predict that the Holy Spirit will constantly operate in the hearts of the faithful to move them to exalt the glory of this most holy person."

Father Bossuet's voice in France in 1656, proclaimed a profound text on St. Joseph. The whole sermon was so beautiful that the queen mother wished to hear it again on March 19, 1659, which fell on a Wednesday, and the impression was unforgettable. Bossuet was again chosen by the Court, two years later, on this great March 19, 1661, when France was consecrated to St. Joseph at the insistence of the young queen, who had come from Spain the previous year; it was on this occasion, while speaking of St. Joseph, that Fr. Bossuet pronounced these prophetic words: "What is most illustrious in the Church, is that which is most hidden."

(*Favorite Prayers to St. Joseph*, from p. 26)

Let us remember the great prophecy of Father Isidore Isolanis, O.P.: "The sound of victory will be heard, when the faithful recognize the sanctity of Saint Joseph."

This book is a compilation of what has been written about Saint Joseph by leading mystics and historians. The dignity of Saint Joseph becomes obvious, to an even awesome degree, as one reads what the experts reveal. As we become increasingly aware of the greatness and power of Saint Joseph, we are inclined, and with confident expectation, to humbly supplicate in all things, "Saint Joseph, pray for us."

Editor, Dr. Rosalie A. Turton.

The imprimatur is important in books that deal strictly with matters of faith and morals. This text does not require it.

Most Reverand Michael J. Sheridan
Auxiliary Bishop of St. Louis
February 24, 2000

1st printing, March, 2000 — 15,000 copies
Printed in the U.S.A.
by The 101 Foundation, Inc.

Books available from:

The 101 Foundation, Inc.
P.O. Box 151
Asbury, NJ 08802-0151
Phone: 908-689 8792
Fax: 908-689 1957
www.101foundation.com
email: 101@101foundation.com

ISBN: 1-890137-38-3

Table of Contents:

Chapter #   Page #

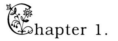

Chapter 1.

St. Joseph's Birth, Lineage, And Childhood

(by Agreda—*City (Conception)*, from p. 576,
(Transfixion), from p. 162)

On the day on which our Princess Mary completed the fourteenth year of Her life, the men who at that time in the city of Jerusalem were descendants of the tribe of Juda and the race of David, gathered together in the Temple. The Sovereign Lady was also of that lineage. Among the number was Joseph, a native of Nazareth, then living in Jerusalem, for he was one of the descendants of the royal race of David.

All the vast perfection of his virtues and graces were conferred upon Saint Joseph for the purpose of making of him a worthy protector and spouse of Her, whom God selected as His Mother. According to this standard, and according to the love of God for His most holy Mother, is to be measured the holiness of Saint Joseph; from my understanding of this matter, if there had been in the world another man more perfect and more worthy, the Lord would have chosen this other one for the spouse of His Mother. Since he was chosen by God, Saint Joseph was, no doubt, the most perfect man upon earth. Having created and destined him for such a high end, it is certain that God, in His almighty power, prepared and perfected him in proportion to the exaltedness of his end.

The more angelic and holy he grew to be, so much the more worthy was he to be the spouse of most holy Mary, the depository and treasure-house of Heavenly sacraments. He was to be a miracle of holiness, as he really was. This marvelous holiness commenced with the formation of his body in the womb of his mother. He was sanctified in the womb of his mother seven months after his conception, and the leaven of sin was destroyed in him for the whole course of his life, never having felt any impure or disorderly movement.

The holy child Joseph was born most beautiful and perfect of body, and caused in his parents and in his relations an extraordinary delight, something like that caused by the birth of Saint John the Baptist, though the cause of it was more hidden. The Lord hastened in him the use of his reason, perfecting it in his third year, endowing it with infused science and augmenting his soul with new graces and virtues.

He was of a kind disposition, loving, affable, sincere, showing inclinations not only holy but angelic, growing in virtue and perfection and advancing toward his espousal with most holy Mary by an altogether irreproachable life. For the confirmation and increase of his good qualities was then added the intercession of the Blessed Lady. The Lord listened to Her prayer and permitted Her to see what great effects His right hand wrought in the mind and spirit of the patriarch Saint Joseph. They were so copious, that they cannot be described in human words. God infused into Joseph's soul the most perfect habits of all the virtues and gifts. He balanced anew all his faculties and filled him with grace, confirming it in a most admirable manner.

(*Ante-Nicene*, from p. 391)

Joseph speaking: "...my father Jacob...

(by Baij—*Life of*, from pp. 1, 12, 16, 23, 35, 39 & 46)

Since God had destined glorious St. Joseph to be the spouse of the Mother of His Only-Begotten Son, He wanted him to have many characteristics in common with Her, such as lineage, and place of birth, but most of all He wanted him to resemble Her in the realm of virtue.

Joseph's father was born in Nazareth, his mother in Bethlehem. After their marriage, they remained for the rest of their lifetime in Nazareth. His father's name was Jacob, his mother's name was Rachel. Both distinguished themselves by leading very holy lives; they had in common nobility of birth (both were of the family of David) as well as the practice of virtue. God permitted that their marriage should, for a time, prove to be unfruitful, for He wished Joseph to be a child obtained through prayerful entreaty.

An angel spoke to each of his parents in their dreams. It was disclosed that the child would have the happy privilege of seeing the promised Messiah and associating with Him, and it was incumbent upon them to rear him with special foresight and diligence. They were to call him "Joseph," and were not to divulge this "secret of the King," not even to their child, but were to speak about it between themselves, for their own spiritual consolation.

At his circumcision, he was given the use of reason and many other spiritual gifts. He previously was freed of the stain of original sin, which by its presence would have made him radically displeasing to God. At his Presentation, they brought substantial gifts for the Temple, considerably more than was customary, as a token of their gratitude for this God-given blessing of such a child.

In addition to his regular guardian angel, Joseph had another angel assigned to him by God, who was to speak to him often in his dreams, and who was also to instruct him in all those things which would be required of him, in order that he might become ever more pleasing to God.

Whenever Joseph was carried about by his mother, and found himself to be in a place where he could see the open sky, he would gaze steadfastly up at the Heavens. His joy and exultation showed that all his happiness and treasure lay up above.

Satan tried many times to attack Joseph, but he would often unite fasting to his prayers, and as a result, the enemy found himself deprived of his powers. Satan always found himself vanquished and beaten, for Joseph's prayers were very powerful. The angel, who had been assigned to speak to Joseph in his dreams, continually advised him as to what was incumbent upon him to do in order to overcome the infernal demon, and Joseph never failed to carry out the admonitions of the angel.

Joseph's first words were "My God." That is what the angel had taught him. His parents heard it with amazement. He often renewed his donation of himself to God, a repetition of that initial act which he had made at the time of his Presentation in the Temple.

Once he was able to walk unhampered, Joseph often went and hid himself in order to pray. With uplifted hands, he would offer thanks to God for having heaped so many benefits upon him. He would remain on his knees for hours at a time. His words were still somewhat stammering, but came from a heart inflamed with love for God. His parents and his angel told him about the coming of the Messiah, and Joseph sent forth fervent appeals to God, asking Him to deign to shorten the time of waiting. Thenceforward, he applied all his prayers to this intention.

He soon advanced to the reading of the Sacred Scriptures, and especially the Davidic Psalms, all of which his father explained to him. All his available time was taken up either by prayer, by reading, or by reflection upon the things he had read, and he set for himself a definite time for each.

In spite of his extreme youthfulness, Joseph was never seen to be angry or impatient. He always maintained a cheerful and peaceful demeanor, although God often permitted him to be mistreated by other people of the house during the absences of his parents. The youngster accepted all with patience and cheerfulness. Even though he was still so very young, Joseph was never occupied with childish things and preferred to remain in seclusion within his own home.

Joseph, now seven years of age, continued on in this way, and preserved undiminished the luster of his innocence, so much so, that he never caused the slightest displeasure to his parents. All his actions were exceedingly pleasing to God. His deportment was so humble and obedient that his parents could not help but wonder at it.

The angel spoke again to Joseph, telling him that God had decreed that he was to be the recipient of a very great and sublime favor. The angel confessed his own ignorance as to what this favor might be. He declared that for the present, he was informing him of the fact, primarily for the purpose of moving him to make entreaty to God for it, and to make himself worthy of it by the practice of virtue. Inasmuch as God is much pleased when He is petitioned, and wants prayers and entreaties to precede the rendering of great graces and favors, Joseph was attentive to the message of the angel, but made no attempt to discover the nature of the signal grace in question.

On the other hand, he supplicated God with all the powers of his soul and with a special earnestness, first, for the favor that He would hasten the coming of the Messiah, and secondly, that He would deign to grant him the favor foretold by his angel. He also besought God for many other graces, but especially for these two which lay so close to his heart. At the

Paschal season, he prepared himself for the solemnity with fasting and prayer, because that was what the angel had taught him to do. Joseph was never to be seen going about the city to gander at new and strange things, as one is accustomed to do at that age. Nor did he ever look for a companion.

He held in great esteem those who served in the Temple, and was very subservient towards them. Consequently, he was very much liked by the priests. One and all, they held him in special regard, both because of the generous alms which he was wont to distribute, and because they observed in him the loftiest of dispositions.

One day, as he was praying in the Temple with greater fervor than usual, Joseph perceived within himself the Voice of God, which assured him that these prayers were pleasing to Him, and that all his petitions would be granted. God also assured him of His great love, and invited him to respond to His advances. So great was Joseph's joy upon hearing these words, that he went into an ecstacy. For hours he remained immovable. He was enjoying the incomparable sweetness and delight of the Divine Spirit.

He became increasingly enkindled and inflamed with divine love. He did not wish to hear anyone speak of anything else except God and His divine perfections. He longed fervently to find a true friend with similar appreciations, to whom he could unburden himself. When it appeared that he would not be able to find such a one, he asked God to send him one.

Joseph gave continual thanks to God for all the benefits given to him, and offered himself up completely to God. Joseph never wished to discuss, or even to hear about, the current events or developments in the town. He alleged that it interfered with the concentration which he found so necessary for maintaining his contact with God and for studying the Scriptures. Hence, such matters, or anything else that might arouse a useless curiosity, were never mentioned in his presence.

Joseph always undertook to do anything he knew would please God. Among other things, Joseph had received a special faculty for giving effective assistance to the afflicted. Whenever he conversed with such people, his attitude and treatment somehow always managed to produce an alleviation of sorrow. Of course, he always had recourse to God, and pleaded fervently for comfort in behalf of those with whom he had to deal. His ability to ease the burden of the oppressed became known throughout the locality, and brought many to his home to listen to him and to obtain his assistance.

Joseph was 18 when his parents died. The angel appeared to Joseph and advised him to leave his native village and go to Jerusalem. The next morning Joseph made ready to depart. He gathered a few clothes into a small bundle and then betook himself to prayer to beseech God to stand by him on his journey, saying: "My God, You see that I am about to leave my home to go to Jerusalem, in order to accomplish there Your divine will. I am leaving as a poor man—a beggar. Even though I am now much poorer than before, I am content because I believe it pleases You to have me to be so.

"I place myself entirely into Your loving Fatherly arms."

(by Binet—*Divine Favors*, from p. 8)

The Evangelists would appear to give Joseph two fathers; but the contradiction is only apparent. St. Luke says he was the son of Heli, who, however died childless; while St. Matthew calls him the son of Jacob, because, according to several commentators, Jacob, brother of Heli, espoused his sister-in law Esta as the Law of Moses commanded, by whom he had Joseph, who was thus the son of Jacob by nature, and the son of Heli according to the law.

It is the pious belief of some authors that St. Joseph was sanctified in his mother's womb. Suarez does not go so far. Still we must allow that the partisans of this opinion support it by solid reasons, which have a great appearance of truth.

In the genealogy of Joseph, St. Matthew shows him to be descended in a direct line from 14 patriarchs, beginning with Abraham, until David; from 14 kings after David, until the transmigration of the Jews to Babylon; and from 14 princes or chiefs of the people, after the transmigration of Babylon, until Jesus Christ. Why did the Holy Spirit inspire this long enumeration? Doubtless, among other reasons, to show that the descendant of so many great men was also the heir of their noble qualities and royal virtues.

All the perfections distributed among so many princes were united in St. Joseph. The liberal hand of the Creator poured forth in profusion all qualities of body and soul upon this great saint, so as to make him worthy of espousing the Queen of Angels and men, of being the supposed father of the little Messias, and of being teacher of the Divine Apprentice, Who, during 18 years, deigned to work under his direction in the humble workshop at Nazareth.

(by Chorpenning—*Just Man,* from pp. 111 & 213)

Like the Patriarch Joseph, St. Joseph, the husband of Mary, was handsome. St. Joseph was of noble lineage, a most perfect soul, created to be the spouse of the most beautiful Woman of all women, the culmination and the last of the Old Testament patriarchs, most of whom were extremely handsome such as Abraham, Jacob, Joseph, David, Solomon, and so on. Why must we think that St. Joseph was ugly? Usually the most handsome are always those of noble descent, and the most perfect souls have dominion over their faculties and passions.

Being of the finest ancestry in the world, Joseph was born into poverty. Since Joseph was of noble descent, he was not born with a natural inclination to manual labor.

(by Cristiani—*The Father of Jesus,* from p. 29)

St. Justin, who was a native of Palestine, assures us that Saint Joseph was born in Bethlehem.

11.

(by Emmerich—*Life of Jesus, Vol. 1,* from p. 182)

Joseph was the third of six brothers. I think there were also some daughters in the family. His parents dwelt in a large mansion outside of Bethlehem, with a large courtyard or garden in front of the house. It was the ancient birthplace of David, but in Joseph's time, only the principal walls were in existence. His father's name was Jacob.

Joseph was perhaps eight years old. He was very different from his brothers, very talented, and he learned quickly. The other boys used to play all kinds of tricks on him and knock him around at will. Sometimes, when kneeling in prayer in the colonnade that ran around the courtyard, his face to the wall, his brothers would push him over. Once I saw one of them, when Joseph was thus praying, kick him in the back; but Joseph appeared not to notice it. The others repeated his blows, until at last Joseph fell to the ground. Then I saw that he had been absorbed in God. But he did not revenge himself; he merely turned away quietly and sought another secluded spot.

The hostility of his brothers at last went so far that, when 18, Joseph fled from his father's house by night. I saw him in Lebona carrying on carpentry. He worked for his living in a very poor family. His parents believed that he had been kidnapped, but his brothers discovered him, and then he was again persecuted. Joseph, however, would not leave the poor people nor desist from the humble occupation, of which his family was ashamed.

Joseph lived very piously and humbly, loved and esteemed by all. At last he worked for a man in Tiberias, at which place he lived alone near the water.

Joseph's parents were long since dead, and his brothers scattered; only two of them still dwelt in Bethlehem. The paternal mansion had passed into other hands, and the whole family had rapidly declined.

Joseph was deeply pious; he prayed much for the coming of the Messiah. I noticed, too, his great reserve in the presence of females. Shortly before his call to Jerusalem for his espousals with Mary, he entertained the idea of fitting up a more secluded oratory in his dwelling. But an angel appeared to him in prayer, and told him not to do it; that, as in ancient times, the Patriarch Joseph became, by God's appointment, the administrator of the Egyptian granaries, so now to him was the granary of Redemption to be wedded. In his humility Joseph could not comprehend the meaning of this, and so he betook himself to prayer. At last he was summoned to Jerusalem to be espoused to the Blessed Virgin.

(by Fitzmyer—*Saint Joseph's Day*, from pp. 2 & 10)

The name Joseph means "May Yahweh add." As in most male names in the Old Testament, the name is related to the birth of the child just born. The mother or father, delighted over the birth of the child, exclaims, "May God add (another one)," i.e., another one like the one just born. From Matt. 1:16 we learn that the father of Saint Joseph was named Jacob, but we do not know his mother's name. In any case, she and Jacob must have been overjoyed at his birth, and so they named him.

13.

Neither the Church's teaching authority nor theologians have ever maintained that the necessary formal effect of biblical inspiration is historicity. That they are inspired does not make them historical. If items or details in them are judged to be historical, they are so for reasons other than their inspiration. The infancy narratives have been inspired to teach Christians saving truths, i.e., truths necessary for their salvation, such as that Jesus was born as the "Savior" of mankind, or that He was born as "Lord and Messiah." They have not been composed under divine inspiration to guarantee the historicity of what may have only been intended to have symbolic meaning.

(by Gasnier—*Joseph the Silent*, from pp. 25 & 183)

When we consider the forty generations enumerated in Joseph's genealogical table, we realize they cover two thousand years of history. It is said that all the glory, valor, faith, and piety of that great people of Israel culminated in Jesus, the Heir of the divine promises.

God, in being born into this world, chose as His father the heir of 19 kings in order to teach kings that their blood carried with it a special responsibility. But this descendant of kings, who would never have thought of making anything of his noble origin, lived in poverty that the world might learn that in the kingdom of Heaven, poverty is the highest nobility, and, when accepted without repining, it will be a means of assuring a share in the riches of God.

Joseph never forgot from whence he was. He called his forbearers to mind at times, not through pride, but in order to remember each one to whom he owed a debt of gratitude. In his veins ran the blood of Abraham, whose living faith and total obedience had won for him an everlasting posterity; the blood of Jesse, of whom Isaias had said "a branch shall spring forth from his root."

Many legal documents bore witness to the chain of generations by which he was linked to the prophet-king. Solomon was an ancestor glorious among rulers, whose wisdom was known to the ends of the earth, who had built the great Temple in Jerusalem; Roboam, whose yoke the Ten Tribes had thrown off; Josaphat, the saint; Achaz, to whom Elias had foretold the Virgin conception; Ezechias, brought back miraculously from the gates of death; Jechonias, the last of the Kings of Juda; Zorobabel, who had led the people home from captivity, and many, many more.

There are those who think St. Joseph was sanctified from his birth. If some saints, they say, have had that privilege—Jeremias, John the Baptist, for example—could it have been withheld from the spouse of Mary, predestined as he was to surpass all those others? That is the opinion held by Gerson, St. Alphonsus Liguori, and many other theologians. They hold that the mission of the adopted father of Jesus, which placed him so near the Redeemer, made it necessary that he be sanctified before his birth.

All that can be absolutely affirmed is that Joseph, confirmed in grace after his marriage to Mary, profiting from the constant companionship of Her Who was conceived Immaculate, having never resisted the call of grace, saw that supernatural treasure ever growing in his soul. He had been able, in so far as man is capable thereof, of raising himself to so high a degree of perfection that sin had no part in him.

(by Gill—*Saint Joseph, A,* from pp. 3, 8, 16, & 64)

The parents of Mary are spoken of as being of a fairly prosperous condition of life, and our Lady, Herself, as Heiress to their property and owner of the Holy House.

It is sufficient to ask who was Heli? Now, as can be established from several passages in Scripture, Heli is by abbreviation Heliakim, and Heliakim, the synonym of Joachim. Joachim, according to the universal and constant tradition, was the father of Mary and the father-in-law of Joseph. By marrying the Daughter of Heli, Joseph became the legal heir and son of Heli, so that St. Luke, by basing his genealogical table on the latter, has, in reality, given the paternal descent of Mary and Jesus.

That Joseph was a near relative of Mary is held by every authority.

There was a special reason why Joseph should obey the decree of Caesar Augustus exactly, for not only was Joseph an exact observer of the law, but, as appears from the genealogies of St. Matthew and St. Luke, the *chief representative* of the royal line of David.

(by Griffin—*Saint Joseph & Third*, from p. 342)

But the name Joseph, in Hebrew, means "God will add." God adds unsuspected dimensions to the holy lives of those who do His will. He adds the one important dimension which gives meaning to everything, the divine dimension. To the humble and holy life of Joseph He added, if I may put it this way, the lives of the Virgin Mary and of Jesus, our Lord.

God does not allow Himself to be outdone in generosity. Joseph could make his own the words of Mary, his Wife: "He has looked graciously upon the lowliness of His Handmaid...because He Who is mighty, He Whose name is holy, has wrought for Me His wonders."

(by Griffin—*Saint Joseph, Theo.*, from p. 22)

The question has often been raised whether or not Saint Joseph, like Mary, was privileged by God to have been free from original sin from the first moment of his existence. Surely if there is reason to suspect that God bestowed this favor on any soul besides the Blessed Mother, the most logical one—and the only one—who comes to mind is Saint Joseph. This is prompted by the fact that he was truly married to the Mother of God and that he had a singular paternal relationship towards Christ. A strong logical case could be built up to show how fitting it would be for Saint Joseph to have been accorded such a privilege.

Nevertheless, reason, no matter how compelling, is not sufficient to prove that God actually granted this or that favor to a particular saint. We can only have certitude when it is guaranteed by Scripture or the Magisterium of the Church. Scripture says nothing of such a privilege, and more important still is the fact that the Magisterium of the Church seems clearly to rule out the possibility. In 1953, Pope Pius XII in his encyclical letter *Fulgens Corona* had this to say about the Immaculate Conception of Mary: "Mary obtained this most singular privilege, never granted to anyone else, because She was raised to the dignity of the Mother of God."

Saint John the Baptist was sanctified in his mother's womb. Is there not reason to believe that Saint Joseph must have been accorded a similar privilege? Some have not hesitated to reply in the affirmative, but the majority of theologians see no reason that justifies the claim. Once again, the only way in which we can be sure of the prenatal sanctification of Saint Joseph would be through an explicit affirmation of Sacred Scripture or the teaching of the Church. Since we would look in vain for such approval in either of those sources, the only prudent conclusion we come to is that Joseph was not sanctified until after his birth.

In simple terms it comes to this: Saint Joseph was born with original sin on his soul and was not cleansed from its stain until the time of his circumcision, as was the case with every other Jewish boy of his time.

(by Healy Thompson—*Life and,* from pp. 41, 65, 72, 82, 87, 185 & 218)

Joseph surpasses all the other saints in dignity and sanctity. As Mary, above all, was nearest to Jesus, so Joseph was nearest to Mary; and for the sake of Jesus, and also for Mary's sake, we may justly conclude that to Joseph must have been conceded a privilege second only to Hers. Thus it is that he was pre-announced in Holy Scripture, and ennobled with so high a genealogy.

Now, in order to correspond to so lofty a vocation, which, after that of the Virgin Mother, was superior to all others, whether of angels or saints, Joseph must have been sanctified in a most eminent degree, that he might be worthy to take his place in this most sublime order of the Hypostatic Union, in which Jesus held the first place and Mary the second. And indeed, we find it to be the constant doctrine of St. Thomas Aquinas, as well as of all the Fathers, that those whom God elects and designs for some great work, He also prepares and disposes, so as to fit them for its performance.

Menochius, Benedict XIII, and other doctors assert, namely, that St. Anne, the mother of our Blessed Lady and the wife of Joachim, was sister to Jacob, the father of Joseph; thus it would follow that Joseph and Mary were first cousins, and that Mary, as also Her Divine Son, was descended from King David by the double line of Solomon and Nathan; from Nathan on the paternal side, and from Solomon on the maternal.

St. Ambrose observes that as a sign of predilection, the Blessed Trinity was pleased immediately to confirm our saint in grace, so that by a special privilege he should never commit even a venial sin, a privilege which was most fitting in him, who was to be in the place of a father to the Son of God and the true spouse of His immaculate and holy Mother.

That Joseph was a first-born son there can be no doubt. For if, according to the view with which we do not agree, Jacob married the widow of Heli, who had died without children, Joseph would still be the first-born of this marriage. We abide by the opinion that Joseph was the first-born of Jacob and a young and holy spouse who had never been wedded to any other husband.

That Joseph was a first-born son we desire to establish, because under the ancient law it was esteemed an honor and a privilege to be so; and many advantages were attached to primogeniture. We can, therefore, well understand how when Esau recognized the great loss he had incurred by selling his birthright for such a trifle to his brother, he was filled with consternation and cried aloud for grief. Seeing, then, that primogeniture was an important prerogative, and that Joseph was to sum up in himself all the gifts and privileges of the patriarchs, he must have possessed the rights and advantages of a first-born son.

This being so, Joseph, was taken to Jerusalem to be presented in the Temple, and redeemed according to the prescriptions of the law. The Holy City had now virtually fallen under the domination of the Romans. All who were of the race and family of David would court obscurity and concealment through the fear inspired by jealous rulers.

Jacob had one other son besides Joseph, the same, according to the historian Eusebius and others, who is frequently mentioned in the Gospel as Cleophas, or Alpheus, and whose sons are called the brethren of our Lord, that is, His cousins. So, too, Mary, the wife of Cleophas, who is also called in the first three Gospels the mother of James and Joseph, is styled by St. John the sister of the Mother of Jesus; not that she was Her sister in the literal sense of the term, but Her sister-in-law and, indeed (as it is believed), otherwise nearly related to Her.

Joseph had an exalted intellect, his judgment was profound, his wisdom surpassed that of the wisest among men.

That Elizabeth was Mary's cousin is of faith, because we have the angel's word for it, as recorded in the Gospel. How she was thus related we learn from tradition. Jacob, the son of Mathan and father of Joseph, had two sisters, Anne, the happy mother of Mary, and Sobe, the mother of Elizabeth, so that Mary and Joseph were Elizabeth's cousins in the same degree. That Sobe should have married into the tribe of Levi need cause no surprise. The law which obliged maidens to marry in their own tribe was peculiarly stringent as regarded orphans or such as were otherwise possessed of property, in order to prevent the inheritance passing out of their tribe; but in other cases there was more license.

Hebrews were not in the habit of tracing genealogies on the female side, and that Mary, being near of kin to Joseph and of the house of David, was included in the same descent. Besides which, the genealogy given by St. Luke is by some interpreters, though not by all, considered to be Mary's, Heli being identified with Joachim, Her father.

21.

(by Joseph—*Joseph, Son of David*, from pp. 10 & 45)

The name of Joseph signifies "the growing one, the one who progresses." You may judge how great a man Joseph was. His very name suggests it, for Joseph means *increase*.

(by Keyes—*St. Anne*, from pp. 61, 69 & 74)

Regarding Mary's birthplace, 20 Popes at least have caused to be inserted or attained, in the Roman breviary, the assertion of one of the most learned fathers of the Church—St. John Damascene—who offers that the Blessed Virgin was born in Jerusalem, and only five Popes have maintained that "according to popular belief of the populace, She was born in Nazareth." One attractive little picture is captioned: "The figure of a tiny babe lies under the altar of the Grotto of the Nativity, site of Our Lady's birthplace, in St. Anne's Church, Jerusalem."

The fact that the Virgin had been dedicated to the Temple when She was three years old did not mean that She had been cloistered in it. Her father, who had an entree there, due to his father-in-law's official position, could certainly have seen Her at any time; and Her mother, universally recognized as a woman of culture and character, would very logically have been chosen to supplement the teachings of other instructors as often as she was willing to do so. Moreover, there were periods that children and parents spent together after school hours and in what then corresponded to "terms" or "semesters," just as there are now.

Joachim, Mary's father, had a brother, Jacob, much younger than himself. Jacob was the father of four children:

Joseph, (husband of the Blessed Virgin Mary),
James, (married to a sister of Cleophas and father of Thaddeus Jude),
Mary, (married to Cleophas of Alpheus, and mother of James the Less, Joseph, Simon, and Jude),
and, Salome, (married to Zebedee, and mother of James the Greater and John).

This family chart is presented by Émile Rey in his book, which has been officially approved by the Vatican, and which is accepted unconditionally by the White Fathers in charge of St. Anne's Sanctuary in Jerusalem.

(by Levy—*Joseph, the Just Man*, from p. 13)

To quote a great spiritual writer, the Rev. M. Meschler, S.J.: "This genealogy is of the highest import to St. Joseph, to his position and office, to his greatness and title to veneration; it is, first and foremost, the accepted genealogy of our saint himself. By means of it, he is proved to be the son of David and is placed in the closest relationship to the promised Messias and God-Man, if not as real father, nevertheless as legally recognized parent. Thus, too, as regards the family of David, is the prophecy fulfilled that from one of its roots the Messiah would come forth (Ps. 83:30; 1 Macch. 2:57); hence, also it is proved that the Savior is truly the Son of David, and that the whole glory of this family culminates in Him though Joseph in a very particular manner.

For Matthew calls Joseph's father Jacob (1:16); Luke however styles him Heli, a difference which can only be explained on the supposition that in view of the Law of the Levirate (where a man was bound to marry the widow of his brother who had died childless, and thus perpetuate the latter's family), Jacob was the natural father of Joseph, while Heli was his legal father."

St. Ambrose says: "We might wonder why the lineal descent of Joseph, rather than Mary, should be given, since Mary conceived Christ by the Holy Ghost, and Joseph appears to be unconnected with our Lord's birth, were it not that Holy Scripture teaches us that it was the custom to trace the descent on the male side. The personality of the male is emphasized; his dignity is maintained, even in the senate and the high places of the commonwealth. How unseemly it would be if, omitting the lineage on the father's side, that of the mother had been sought out; it would have appeared to proclaim to all the people in the world that Christ had no father!

One sees that in every place, family genealogy is traced in the male line. Do not be perplexed at the lineage of Joseph being given. As Christ was born in the flesh, He was bound to follow the custom of the flesh, and He Who came into the world had to be enrolled in the worldly manner, especially as Joseph's descent was the same as Mary's.

"But why St. Matthew should begin to reckon the descent of Christ from Abraham, while Luke traces it from Christ up to God, seems to require explanation. Luke considers that Christ's lineage should be traced to God, because God was Christ's true progenitor, either as His Father according to His real begetting, or as the Author of the mystical gift according to His rebirth in the laver of baptism.

"It was of the utmost importance that the Evangelists should record Joseph's origin, since Mary was of the same lineage, for indeed Mosaic Law forbade the marriages between the different tribes, so that the hereditary rights of one tribe might not pass into another. Therefore, giving the pedigree of Joseph attested that the Virgin Mary was of the lineage of David.

(by O'Carroll—*Joseph, Son of,* from pp. 19, 27 & 29)

"Several Fathers of the Church," says Pope Leo XIII, "have been of opinion, and the Sacred Liturgy itself confirms the fact, that the Joseph of former times, son of the patriarch Jacob, was a prototype of the person and offices of our Joseph, announcing thus by the splendor of his sanctity the greatness of the future guardian of the Holy Family."

In the case of a son-in-law, husband of an only daughter who would be heiress to the patrimony, in the second book of Esdras, we read of "Berzellai," who married the daughter of Berzellai, and took his name. This could have happened in the case of Joseph. Our Lady being an only Daughter and an Heiress, Her husband was regarded in a general way as Her father's son, entitled to use his name. Thus we also explain a difference in phrase between Matthew and Luke. The former says firmly that Jacob begot Joseph, the latter, only that Joseph was the son of Heli.

We may assume that Joseph belonged to a devout Jewish family. We can, from the general family customs, reconstruct some of the events of his early years. Eight days after his birth, he was circumcised. This ceremony brought the child into the descendants of Abraham; it was strictly obligatory. It was performed by the father of the child or by the *mohel*, a Jewish official found in every locality.

Circumcision was accompanied by name-giving and to the father alone belonged the right and duty of imposing the name. As he did so, he prayed for a blessing: "Blessed be He Who has sanctified us by His commandments, and Who has ordered us to introduce the child into the covenant of our father Abraham." Then the *mohel* and the child's mother replied: "Since he has entered into the covenant, may he also enter into the Thora and under the baldacchino of foliage, and into good works."

When the child had grown to boyhood, he was sent to the village school which was conducted by the sacristan of the synagogue, the *hazzan*. Under his care and instruction, Joseph learned to read the Hebrew letters on the parchments.

At the age of 12, the boy became a "son of the law." Henceforth, he was bound by the legal prescriptions of the law and of the ceremonial rites. He attended the religious services and went to Jerusalem for the great festivals of the Passover, Pentecost, and Tabernacles.

At the age of 12, the boy also became a "son of work," and went to learn a trade from one of the village artisans. These usually had their shops in the center of the town. Joseph exercised the trade described by the work, *techton* in Greek and *faber* in Latin.

When Joseph brought to Bethlehem his young pregnant Wife, he apparently had no relations or acquaintances there; otherwise, he would certainly have sought hospitality from them. On the other hand, Father Prat, whose authority cannot be lightly dismissed, says he had relatives in Bethlehem, but had serious reasons for not approaching them. But if we accept the plausible view that Joseph did not seek the assistance of near relatives or close friends because he had none, it seems more probable that Nazareth and not Bethlehem was his birthplace. At the time of the espousal, he was living in Nazareth because it was his native place.

(by O'Shea—*Mary and Joseph*, from pp. 6, 22, & 34)

The title, "Son of David," was held in honor all over Israel. The blood of David ennobled all his descendants, no matter how low their fortunes had fallen, and Israel held them in higher honor than even its priests of the proud House of Aaron.

Another famous personage who is credited with Davidic descent is the great Rabbi Hillel, who was chief of the Sanhedrin during part of the reign of Herod, and the most illustrious jurist of his time. But if Hillel were really descended from David, which is not at all certain, his birth was inferior to Joseph's, for his descent was not through the direct royal line going back through the kings to Solomon, the son of David and Bathsheba, the queen-mother, but to Abigail, an inferior wife of David, who was the mother of none of his kingly successors.

The descendants of David were respected as members of the first family in the land, and their pedigrees were kept as faithfully as in the days of their greatness, for the people knew that the Messiah was to be born of their stock.

King Herod was not a son of David, nor even of Hashmon, from whom Machabean priest-kings had traced their descent; in fact, he was not a true Jew at all, but an Idumean upstart who owed his crown to the patronage of the all-powerful Romans. Hence his pedigree was not to be found in the archives of Israel. He was so conscious of his ignoble descent and alien origin, that in a fit of despotic anger, he tried to set fire to the public archives.

But if both Joachim and Anna were of the House of David and the tribe of Judah, how, then, was Mary a cousin of Elizabeth, who was of the House of Aaron and the tribe of Levi? It has too often been assumed that women were not allowed to marry outside their own tribe. The prohibition (Num. 36-6. 7) refers not to all women, but to heiresses only, in order to prevent the alienation of the property of the tribe. If a woman was not the heiress of her father, she was free to marry any son of Abraham. Tradition is unanimous in declaring that Mary was an only child, and so She would be a considerable Heiress, and bound to marry within the tribe.

(by Petrisko—*St. Joseph and the Triumph,* from p. 173)

St. Joseph was born a Jew of humble and pure lineage—a lineage that had not lost the true sense of the Messiah. Among all the monarchs of the earth that have ever lived, none have such a lineage as St. Joseph. Indeed, God Himself saw to it that St. Joseph's illustrious lineage was documented in Scripture, and was, therefore uncontestable. The Gospel according to St. Matthew, descending from Abraham through David to Joseph, registers forty generations. In the Gospel of St. Luke, there is registered as many as seventy-four, as Joseph is traced back to Adam.

In this lineage, we find the great patriarchs and monarchs of the Old Testament: Abraham, Isaac, Jacob, David, and Solomon. We also find in St. Joseph's genealogy the careful fulfillment of many messianic prophecies—that Jesus should be born of the tribe of Juda, a direct descendent of David, and that He should be born of a Virgin and no earthly father.

From this we see how St. Joseph's genealogy is most glorious and how God privileged him to become most worthy of whatever was to follow, for his lineage was foretold to be messianic. He was, indeed, the illustrious son of David, and the "light of the patriarchs." He was "the just one."

(by Rondet—*St. Joseph*, from p. 4)

Joseph is of kingly family, his town is David's Bethlehem, though he lives at Nazareth (Luke 2:4).

(by Sparks—*Dominicans*, from p. 123)

Joseph and Mary were from the same tribe, that is Juda. Nuptials were not sought outside one's tribe, especially by the just, such as St. Joseph was. I would add that Joseph and Mary were also from the same family, that is, of David. Hence, Matthew, tracing the genealogy of Christ from David through Solomon, shows sufficiently the family of Mary.

(by Stramare—*Saint Joseph*, from p. 91)

If it is important to profess the Virginal conception of Jesus, it is no less important to defend the marriage of Mary and Joseph, since on it depends juridically the fatherhood of Joseph. From this, one can understand why the generations were listed according to the genealogy of Joseph.

(*The Glories of Saint Joseph*, from p. 47)

Joseph is a son of David, a close relative of the Virgin.

(by Toschi—*Joseph in the New*, from pp. 19 & 22)

The opening genealogy of Matthew is not without problems. It diverges considerably from that of Luke. There is a disagreement even over the name of Joseph's father: Jacob (Mt 1:16) or Heli (Lk 3:23), though their fathers' names are similar, Matthan and Matthat respectively. In Jewish practice, genealogical descent was not passed on only by biological fatherhood. It could also occur through adoption and be considered no less valid.

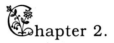

hapter 2.

Joachim and Anne

(by Agreda—*City (Conception)* from pp. 519 & 555)

The happy death of the patriarch Saint Joachim happened about a half year after his most holy Daughter Mary had entered the Temple. Hence She was three and a half years old, when She was left without an earthly father. The age of the patriarch was 69 years, divided as follows: at the age of 46 years he accepted Saint Anne as his spouse, in the 20th year of his marriage, they were blessed with most holy Mary; and the three and half years of the age of Her age at his death complete the 69 and a half years, a few days more or less.

Saint Anne lived 56 years, portioned off into the following periods; at the age of 24 she espoused Saint Joachim and she remained without issue for 20 years; then in the 44th year, she gave birth to the most holy Mary, and of the 12 years which she lived during the lifetime of Mary, three were passed in Her company, and nine during Her absence in the Temple, which altogether make 56 years.

Concerning this great and admirable woman, as I have been informed, some grave authors assert that Saint Anne was married three times, and that in each one of these marriages, she was the mother of one of the three Marys; others have the contrary opinion. The Lord has vouchsafed to me, solely on account of His goodness, great enlightenment concerning the life of this fortunate saint; yet never was it intimated to me that she was ever married except to Saint Joachim, or that she ever had any other daughter besides Mary, the Mother of Christ.

When her spouse Saint Joachim died, she was in the 48th year of her age, and the Most High selected and set her apart from the race of women, in order to make her the mother of Her, who was the Superior of all creatures, inferior only to God, and yet His Mother. Because of her having such a Daughter and of her being the grandmother of the Word made Man, all the nations may call the most fortunate Saint Anne blessed.

(by Emmerich—*Life of Blessed*, from p. 165)

For several days in succession, I have seen the Blessed Virgin with Her mother Anne, whose house is about an hour's journey away from Nazareth in the valley of Zabulon. The only woman remaining in our Lady's house in Nazareth is Anne's maidservant, who looks after St. Joseph while Mary is with Anne. For several weeks, the Blessed Virgin has been busy with preparations for the Birth of Christ. She is sewing and knitting coverlets, cloths and swaddling-bands. There is more than enough of everything. Joachim is no longer alive.

(by Emmerich—*Life of Jesus, Vol. 1*, from pp. 208, 275 & 289)

Mary and Joseph received their principal support from Anne's house as long as she lived. All expected Mary to be delivered in Anne's house, and these covers and other things were being prepared by Anne and others, partly for the birth of Mary's Child, and partly as gifts for the poor. Everything was of the best, and all abundantly and richly provided. They knew not that Mary would have to journey to Bethlehem and bear the Child there.

After the departure of the Kings, the Holy Family went over into the other cave, and I saw the Crib Cave quite empty. Everything, even the hearth, had been cleared away. Many persons going up to Bethlehem for the Sabbath called also at the Crib Cave; but when they no longer found Mary there, they went on to the city.

Saint Anne now came to Bethlehem to see the Holy Family. She had visited for eight days with her youngest sister, who had married into the tribe of Benjamin, and who lived about three hour's distance from Bethlehem, and who had several sons who later became disciples of Jesus; among them was the bridegroom of Cana.

Anne's eldest daughter, Mary Heli, was with her. She was taller than Anne and looked almost as old. Anne's second husband also was with her. He was older and taller than Joachim, was named Eliud, and was engaged at the Temple where he had something to do with the cattle intended for sacrifice. Anne had a daughter by this marriage, and she, too, was called Mary. At the time of Christ's birth, the child may have been from six to eight years old.

By her third husband, Anne had a son, who was known as the brother of Christ. There is a mystery connected with Anne's repeated marriages. She entered into them in obedience to the divine command. The grace of which she had become fruitful with Mary had not yet been exhausted. It was as if a blessing had to be consumed.

I saw the Holy Family while at Nazareth visited also by Mary Heli. She came with St. Anne, bringing with her, her grandson, a boy of about four years, the child of her daughter Mary Cleophas. I then saw the holy women sitting together, caressing the Child Jesus, and laying Him in the little boy's arms. Mary Heli lived in a little town about three hours east of Nazareth. She had a house almost as large as her mother's. Mary Heli's husband was named Cleophas. Their daughter Mary Cleophas, who had married Alpheus, lived at the other end of the town.

(by Healy Thompson—*Life And*, from pp. 104 & 118)

It may be considered as almost certain that Joseph would frequently see his holy relatives, Joachim and Anne, when they came up to keep the great feasts at Jerusalem; Anne, as we have shown on good authority, being probably the sister of Jacob, and therefore Joseph's aunt. For many years their marriage had remained unblest with any offspring, which was, as we know, considered by the Jews as more than a misfortune.

Elizabeth's exclamation, "Thus hath the Lord dealt with me in the days wherein He hath had regard to take away my reproach among men," would be sufficient proof, were such needed, that this was the general feeling. It pleased God to allow this affliction to weigh most heavily on this holy couple.

Tradition tells us that having come up from Nazareth, where they dwelt, to keep the feast of the Dedication of the Temple, and having made their offering, while they were kneeling in devout prayer, a priest named Issac, or according to others, Isachar, sternly rebuked St. Joachim in the presence of all the worshippers, for daring to present himself within the sacred precincts when the curse of God rested upon him, as shown in the sterility of his marriage.

If the youthful Joseph was present on this occasion, or, at any rate, being in Jerusalem, was cognizant of the humiliation of which his pious relatives had been the object, how must his tender heart have grieved, and how he must have exerted himself to raise their drooping spirits!

They returned to the mountains of Nazareth, but not without having both of them been favored with angelic consolation and the assurance that God had heard their prayers and accepted their oblation. Epiphanius tells us that Joachim was praying in the solitude of a mountain and Anne retired in her garden, when they each of them separately received this Divine favor. Joachim and Anne, says the historian Ludolphus, in his *Life of Jesus Christ*, having for 20 years been without offspring, had both of them promised, if their prayer was heard, to dedicate the Child which should be granted them to God.

And behold, Anne, miraculously healed of her sterility, conceived in her womb Her who was to be the delight, the life, and the joy of the whole world. Here was the commencement of a series of unprecedented prodigies. As this Infant was to be the Daughter of the Eternal Father, Mother of the Divine Son, and Spouse of the Holy Ghost, so Her beautiful soul from the first instant of its creation and infusion into the body was, through the especial grace and privilege of God, and in regard of the merits of Jesus Christ, His Son, and the Redeemer of mankind, to be preserved free from all stain of original sin, and filled with every grace, gift, and perfection of which a human creature is capable.

The Virgin was born at Nazareth on the eighth of September, in the year of the world, as is supposed, 3986, and Her happy nativity was the harbinger of joy to the whole universe. Her name, we cannot doubt, came from Heaven, and was revealed to Joachim, who gave it to Her on the eighth day after Her birth. "O name," exclaims that devout adorer of the Infant Jesus, St. Anthony of Padua, "joy to the heart, honey in the mouth, sweetest music to the ear!" And St. John Damasus, "O happy couple, Joachim and Anne, what a debt of gratitude is due to you from every creature!"

On the eighth day after her delivery, Anne accompanied by her holy spouse, must have borne in her arms this most lovely Babe to offer Her to the Lord in the Temple, and perform, according to the law, the rite of her own purification.

Scripture gives us no record of this act, but the devout mind loves to dwell upon it. For never before that day had so acceptable or pleasing an offering been made to the Most High. That sweet Infant, but a few days old, was burning with the desire to consecrate Herself entirely to God, that God Whom She already knew so clearly and loved so ardently. For even in Her mother's womb, Mary enjoyed the use of reason and of Her free will.

How could it be otherwise, since to John the Baptist this privilege was conceded, before he saw the light, in the sixth month of his existence? Her holy parents on their part, no doubt, renewed their promised consecration of the Child which had been so miraculously given to them.

According to a pious tradition, Anne possessed a flock on Mount Carmel and a house for its shepherds; and there she and Joachim would often resort with their spotless Infant. We can readily believe that it was here, on those heights of immemorial sanctity, that She, sweet Child, Who was one day to be invoked as Our Lady of Mount Carmel, besought Her parents to fulfill their vow and allow Her to go and enclose Herself with other daughters of Sion in the House of the Lord.

It must have been a very painful sacrifice to this holy couple to part with their incomparable Child, the joy and treasure of their life, but they loved God too much to refuse Him what He asked and what they had promised to Him. That the Virgin was three years old when She was presented in the Temple and devoted to the service of God is clear from the testimony of St. Evodius, successor to St. Peter of Antioch, as well as from that of St. Epiphanius, St. Jerome, St. Gregory Naziarzen, St. Basil and many others. There is, in fact, a whole catena of tradition on the subject.

It was in the month of November, when the Hebrews celebrate the solemn Dedication of the Temple, that Joachim and Anne brought the Infant Mary to give Her to God. Without objecting Her tender age, or pleading for delay, they had at once acceded to the holy desire of their most innocent Child. The sacrifice was willed by God, was pleasing to God; that was enough to cause them to bow their heads, and make the offering with all readiness of heart.

What a beautiful example does Mary here present to the young, to follow without hesitation the Voice of God calling them to a perfect life in the solitude of a cloister, without heeding for a moment the flattering allurements of the world; and what a splendid example do Joachim and Anne also offer to parents, not to oppose the religious vocation of their children, but to give them willingly to God, when it pleases Him to call them!

The Presentation of Mary in the Temple is believed to have taken place in the year of the world 3989, and on the 21st of November, the day on which the Church celebrates the feast. The enclosure in which these young maidens had their abode was beside the Temple; that it was also attached to it we may gather from the Second Book of Machabees, chapter iii. v. 39, where it is said that the young virgins ran in consternation to Onias when they beheld Eliodorus rifling the sacred building. In memory of the abode of Mary in the Temple, the Emperor Justinian I erected in the sixth century, on its southern side, a church which was called the Church of the Presentation.

It is certain, as Saint Jerome says, that the priests were not in the habit of charging themselves with the establishment of the maidens confided to them for education in the

Temple, but were wont to restore them to their parents at a suitable age, that they might provide for their marriage. But in this case they acted differently, whether from a particular inspiration, as was the opinion of St. Gregory Nazianzen, or that, the parents of the Blessed Virgin having died during Her abode in the Temple (as is generally believed), they considered that it evolved upon them to provide for this holy Maiden's future.

She was a Daughter of the house of David, and was, moreover, the Heiress of whatever had belonged to Joachim and Anne. In such cases, where the woman represented her family and inherited property, the ancient law was particularly stringent concerning her marriage with a member of her own tribe, in other cases allowing a certain latitude.

Notwithstanding Joseph's desire to eclipse himself, he had not been able so far to conceal his high sanctity and rare merits as to escape the observation of the priests who had the guardianship of the Virgin of Nazareth; at least we seem irresistibly led to this conclusion, since it was upon him that their choice fell; on him, the poor artisan, in preference to many who must have possessed higher worldly recommendations, and in spite of the exalted estimation in which they held the Heavenly-gifted Maiden, their Ward, an estimation which laid upon them the responsibility of procuring for Her the most suitable and most honorable marriage possible.

(by Keys—*St. Anne*, from p. 71)

Anne would have been almost, if not quite, at the limit of normal child-bearing age when the Blessed Virgin was born. That, and her great love for Joachim, make it unlikely that Anne would have contemplated a second marriage within less than three years of Joachim's death, which would have brought her almost to the age of 50; and though normal maternity is not unheard of at that age, it is very, very rare. As for maternity after 50 years of age, this is, of course, rarer still.

On these wholly commonplace grounds, if on no others, I decline to subscribe to the legend that Anne had three husbands. However, *The Golden Legend* of Jacques de Voranges reads as follows: "Anne is said to have had three husbands, namely Joachim, Cleophas, and Salome, and had a daughter named Mary by each of them."

(by Valtorta—*Poem, Vol. 1*, Jesus says: from p. 48)

Like a quick winter twilight when an ice-cold wind gathers clouds in the sky, the lives of My grandparents had a quick decline, after the Sun of their lives (Mary) was placed to shine before the Sacred Veil of the Temple.

I surrounded Myself with wise people, in My human kinship. Anne, Joachim, Joseph, Zacharias, and even more Elizabeth, and then the Baptist... are they not real wise people? Not to mention My Mother, the abode of wisdom.

Wisdom had inspired My grandparents how to live in a way which was agreeable to God, from their youth to their death, and like a tent protecting from the fury of the elements, Wisdom had protected them from the danger of sin. The sacred fear of God is the root of the tree of Wisdom, that thrusts its branches far and wide to reach with its top, tranquil love in its peace, peaceful love in its security, secure love in its faithfulness, faithful love in its intensity: the total, generous, effective love of saints.

Their strongest temptation: not to deny their declining lives the consolation of their Daughter's presence. *But children belong first to God and then to their parents.* Every man can say what I said to My Mother: "Do you not know that I must be busy with My Father's affairs?" And every father, every mother must learn the attitude to be maintained looking at Mary and Joseph in the Temple, at Anne and Joachim in the house of Nazareth, a house which was becoming more and more forlorn and sad, but where one thing never diminished, but increased continuously: the holiness of two hearts, the holiness of a marriage.

Because of their holiness, Anne suffered no pain in giving birth to her Child: it was the ecstasy of the bearer of the Faultless One. Neither of them suffered the throes of death, but only a weakness that fades away, as a star softly disappears when the sun rises at dawn. And if they did not have the consolation of having Me present, as Wisdom Incarnate, as Joseph had, I was invisibly present, whispering sublime words, bending over their pillows, to send them to sleep, awaiting their triumph.

Someone may ask: "Why did they not have to suffer when generating and dying, since they were children of Adam?" My answer is: "If the

Baptist, who was a son of Adam, and had been conceived with the original sin, was presanctified by Me in his mother's womb, simply because I approached her, was no grace to be granted to the mother of the Holy and Faultless One, Who had been preserved by God and bore God in Her almost divine spirit, in Her pure heart, and was never separated from Him, since She was created by the Father and was conceived in a womb, and then received into Heaven to possess God in glory forever and ever?" I also answer: "An upright conscience gives a peaceful death, and the prayers of saints will obtain such a death for you."

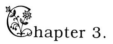hapter 3.

St. Joseph At His Betrothal

(by Agreda—*City (Conception)*, from pp. 570, 576 & 584)

The High Priest, by divine inspiration and order called together the other priests, and informed them of the will of God and the favor in which His Majesty held this Maiden, Mary of Nazareth. He told them that as She was a resident of the Temple and was now without parents, it was their duty to provide for Her and find a husband worthy of a Maiden so modest, virtuous, and of such unimpeachable conduct as was Hers in the Temple.

Moreover, as Mary was of noble lineage and as Her property and other considerations made this marriage particularly important, it was necessary to consider well to whom She was to be entrusted. He added also that Mary of Nazareth did not desire to be married; but that at the same time it would not be proper to dismiss Her from the Temple unmarried, since She was an orphan and a first-born daughter.

Saint Joseph, at his betrothal to the Blessed Virgin Mary, was 33 years old, of handsome person and pleasing countenance, but also of incomparable modesty and gravity; above all, he was most chaste in thought and conduct, and most saintly in all his inclinations. From his 12th year, he had made and kept the vow of chastity. He was related to the Virgin Mary in the third degree, and was known for the utmost purity of his life, holy, and irreprehensible in the eyes of God and of men.

The men, who at that time in the city of Jerusalem were descendants of the tribe of Juda and of the race of David, gathered together in the Temple.

All the unmarried men gathered in the Temple and they prayed to the Lord conjointly with the priests, in order to be governed by the Holy Spirit in what they were about to do. The Most High spoke to the heart of the High Priest, inspiring him to place into the hands of each one of the young men a dry stick, with the command that each ask His Majesty with a lively faith, to single out the one whom He had chosen as the spouse of Mary.

And as the sweet odor of Her virtue and nobility, the fame of Her beauty, Her possessions and Her modesty, and Her position as being the first-born in Her family was known to all of them, each one coveted the happiness of meriting Her as a Spouse.

Among them all, only the humble and most upright Joseph thought himself unworthy of such a great blessing; and remembering the vow of chastity which he had made, and resolving anew its perpetual observance, he resigned himself to God's will, leaving it all to His disposal and being filled at the same time with a veneration

and esteem greater than that of any of the
others for the most noble Maiden Mary.

While they were thus engaged in prayer, the
staff which Joseph held was seen to blossom
(thus, we often see statues of St. Joseph holding
a branch with lilies, which represent purity,
blossoming upon it), and at the same time a dove
of purest white and resplendent with admirable
light, was seen to descend and rest upon the
head of the saint, while in the interior of his
heart, God spoke: *"Joseph, My servant, Mary
shall be thy Spouse; accept Her with attentive
reverence, for She is acceptable in My eyes,
just and most pure in soul and body, and thou
shalt do all that She shall say to thee. . ."*

At this manifestation and token from Heaven,
the priests then declared Saint Joseph as the
spouse selected by God Himself for the Maiden
Mary.

Calling Her forth for Her espousal, the Chosen
One issued forth like the sun, more resplendent
than the moon, and She entered into the presence
of all with a countenance more beautiful than
that of an angel, incomparable in the charm of
Her beauty, nobility, and grace; and the priests
espoused Her to the most chaste and holy of
men, Saint Joseph.

The Heavenly Princess, more pure than the
stars of the firmament, with tearful and sorrowful
countenance, and as the Queen of Majesty, most
humble, yet uniting all perfections with Herself,
took leave of the priests, asking their blessing,
and of Her instructress and Her companions,
begging their pardon. She gave thanks to all of
them for the favors received at their hands
during Her stay in the Temple.

She betook Herself, with Her spouse Joseph,
to Nazareth, the native city of this most fortunate

married couple. Joseph, although he had been born in that place, had, by the providential disposition of circumstances, decided to live for some time in Jerusalem. Thus, it happened that he so improved his fortune as to become the spouse of Her, Whom God had chosen to be His Own Mother.

From the eighth of September, when they were espoused, until the 25th of March following, when the Incarnation of the Divine Word took place, the two spouses thus lived together, being prepared in the meanwhile for the work designated for them by the Most High.

(*Ante-Nicene*, from p. 388)

There was a man whose name was Joseph, sprung from a family of Bethlehem, a town of Judah, and the city of King David. This same man, being well furnished with wisdom and learning, was made a priest in the Temple of the Lord. He was, besides, skillful in his trade, which was that of a carpenter; and after the manner of all men, he married a wife. Moreover, he begot for himself sons and daughters, four sons, namely, and two daughters. Now these are their names—Judas, Justus, James, and Simon. The names of the two daughters were Assia and Lydia. At length, the wife of righteous Joseph, a woman intent on the divine glory in all her works, departed this life.

Now when righteous Joseph became a widower, My Mother Mary, blessed, holy, and pure, was already twelve years old. For Her parents offered

Her in the Temple when She was three years of age, and She remained in the Temple of the Lord nine years.

The priests assembled twelve old men of the tribe of Judah. And they wrote down the names of the twelve tribes of Israel. And the lot fell upon the pious old man, righteous Joseph. Then the priests answered, and said to My Blessed Mother: "Go with Joseph, and be with him till the time of Your marriage."

Righteous Joseph, therefore, received My Mother, and led Her away to his own house. And Mary found James the Less in his father's house, broken-hearted and sad on account of the loss of his mother, and She brought him up. Hence, Mary was called the Mother of James. Thereafter, Joseph left Her at home, and went away to the shop where he wrought at his trade of a carpenter. And after the holy Virgin had spent two years in his house, Her age was exactly 14 years, including the time at which he received Her.

And I chose Her of My Own Will, with concurrence of My Father, and the counsel of the Holy Spirit. And I was made Flesh in Her by a mystery which transcends the grasp of created reason. And three months after Her conception, the righteous man Joseph returned from the place where he worked at his trade; and when he found My Virgin Mother pregnant, he was greatly perplexed, and thought of sending Her away secretly. But from fear and sorrow, and the anguish of his heart, he could endure neither to eat nor drink that day.

But at midday there appeared to him in a dream the prince of the angels, the holy Gabriel, furnished with a command from My Father; and he said to him: "Joseph, Son of David, fear not to take Mary as thy Wife; for She has conceived of the Holy Spirit; and She will bring forth a Son, Whose name shall be called Jesus. He it is Who shall rule all nations with a rod of iron." Having thus spoken, the angel departed from him. And Joseph rose from his sleep, and did as the angel of the Lord had said to him; and Mary abode with him.

He lived 40 years unmarried; thereafter his wife remained under his care 49 years, and then died. A year after her death, My Mother, the Blessed Mary, was entrusted to him by the priests. She spent two years in his house, and in the third year of Her stay with Joseph, in the 15th year of Her age, She brought Me forth on earth by a mystery which no creature can penetrate or understand, except Myself, and My Father and the Holy Spirit, constituting One Essence with Myself.

(by Baij—*Life of St. Joseph*, from p. 72)

Joseph reached the age of thirty, and the time was drawing near when he was to receive his Bride and Companion. The angel advised him to pray more intently during the next month for a special gift that God wished to give to him. It never entered his mind that it might be Mary. In view of the fact that he had vowed his virginity to God, he considered that the good fortune could hardly be his.

Soon the day for the decisive selection drew near. During the night immediately preceding it, the angel again appeared to Joseph in a dream and said to him: "Be it known, Joseph, that God has most graciously accepted your fervent preparation and your ardent desires." The angel then placed into his hands a white dove, in conjunction with these words: "Accept this gift which is being presented to you by God. You shall be the guardian of Her purity. Cherish Her deeply, for She is the delight of the Heart of God: She is His most beloved and most gratifying creature. There never was and there never will be another like Her in this world." Joseph took the dove into his hands, and in the great joy over the favor that he had received, he awoke. He felt all afire with love for God, but he experienced an extraordinary peace. He was beside himself with joy, and yet he did not fully understand what was to happen.

In the Temple, our Joseph had purposely chosen a very unobtrusive spot as being more befitting to his unworthiness. Then, suddenly, he saw his branch begin to sprout and become bedecked with snow-white blossoms. Everyone around him was soon staring wonderingly at this miraculous sign. The servants of the Temple and the officiating priest announced that Joseph was the bridegroom chosen by God for the Virgin Mary.

But God wished to supplement this miraculous occurrence with another external affirmation of this chaste espousal. All those present now saw a snow-white dove descend from Heaven and settle on the head of Joseph, and they gazed in amazement at this additional testimonial from God.

In the meantime, the holy Virgin Mary was brought forth for the espousal ceremony; everyone remained to see this. She appeared with eyes downcast and Her countenance was suffused with the flush of maidenly modesty. Everyone was astonished at Her beauty, gracefulness, and singular modesty, and they all envied Joseph for his good fortune. Joseph, upon seeing Her, became enraptured, and shed tears of joy.

He was captivated every time he looked at Her. He realized, by virtue of a supernatural discernment, that his Spouse was filled with Divine Grace. He often cried out: "Oh my God! How is it that so much condescension is shown to me?"

The priest now proceeded with the ceremony that was customary in those days. During this solemn function, the holy couple beheld a flame darting forth from each of their hearts; these two flames then united into one and ascended Heavenwards. By this visible sign, God reaffirmed what He had previously given Joseph to understand, namely: that there would be a fusion of their loves, and that God would be the object of this love in their marriage.

(by Binet—*Divine Favors*, from pp. 10 & 50)

Mary was in Her 15th year; the age of Joseph is not known so exactly, tradition being silent on the subject. The opinion that he was about 80 years old is without reasonable grounds, and is not held by theologians, the most esteemed of whom think that he was neither an old man nor a youth, but in the prime of life, between thirty and forty. There are many reasons in support of this opinion, which is now generally held.

St. Bernardine of Siena says that the virginal marriage of Mary and Joseph was only contracted

on earth after having been decided in Heaven,
and that these two spouses were perfectly worthy
One of the other. Mary surpassed all men and
angels in the sovereign plenitude of Her graces;
therefore, it was necessary that, after Her, Joseph
should be the most holy human being that
existed, that had ever existed, or that should ever
exist upon earth.

According to the ancient law, whoever espouses
a queen becomes a king by the fact of his
marriage. From this, St. Leonard of Port Maurice
draws the following conclusion: Mary is Queen of
Angels and of Saints; Joseph is the spouse of
Mary, therefore, he is also King of Angels and
Saints; and consequently it is allowable to
invoke him by this title, notwithstanding that
the Church has consecrated the custom of
addressing this invocation principally to Jesus
Christ.

If St. Bernard be right in asserting that no
grace comes down from Heaven to earth but
through the munificent hands of the Mother of
God; if there be no kind of celestial blessing
which She has not obtained for one or the other
of Her servants; must we not believe that She will
have done more for Her spouse and the guardian
angel of Her virginity than for all other human
beings?

(by Biver—*Père Lamy*, from p. 97)

Speaking of the third visit of the holy Patriarch
to Père Lamy: "St. Joseph is not just a simple
working man, as they are too much inclined to
depict him. That is only one side of this holy

personage, but he was very well versed in the Psalms, and knew the Holy Scripture. St. Peter was, in the same way, quite a cultured man. St. Joseph had personal merits of intelligence. The merits of holiness gilded all the other qualities. He was fit to live in the company of the Blessed Virgin, and the Blessed Virgin was well-educated from the school of Jerusalem, the Temple school. She had natural virtues, but also scientific qualifications, and St. Joseph understood Her. He was of one mind with Her.

(by Burkey—*Brindisi*, from pp. 265, 270 & 276)

A true marriage had been duly and validly contracted between them, even though it never was consummated. The marriage of these two Virgins was lawful because it was divinely revealed that they should marry. God said in speaking of Adam, "It is not good for man to be alone." Such was also His mind from all eternity with regard to the most Blessed Virgin. Therefore, He arranged for Her to be espoused to a man like to Herself in holiness.

Not without a mystery was the angel sent to a Virgin espoused to a man, of the house of David, named Joseph. This happened that human matrimony might be an image of the divine; that, as St. Paul said, the matrimony of Adam and Eve might stand forth a symbol of Christ's marriage with the Church.

Whereas Joseph of Egypt of the Old Testament was chaste, refusing the passionate love of his master's wife, St. Joseph's chastity is all the more wonderful. In his case, he had a Wife of his own, a most beautiful and gracious young Woman. Yet he willed to preserve perpetual chastity. Such wonderful chastity appears even greater if, as was the case with Joseph the Patriarch, St. Joseph was also a young man. The people thought that Jesus was the naturally generated Son of Joseph, a fact which is hardly credible if Joseph were an old man.

As Booz did not know Ruth who slept with him during the night (cf. Ru 4, 13), nor did David Abisag (cf. 3 Kg 1, 1-4), neither did Blessed Joseph know the most holy Virgin. For just as God brought it about that Pharaoh and Abimelech did not touch Sara, the Patriarch Abraham's wife (cf. Gn 12, 14-20 and 26, 7-11), He also saw to it that the Blessed Joseph would not touch the holy Virgin, the Spouse of the Most High.

Lawrence likens Mary to the very beautiful Bethsabee, Solomon's mother. The Supreme King of Heaven longed for Her, so He killed Joseph, Her husband, since he was (like) Urias. He, Joseph, was dead to the world through a vow of chastity. At first Joseph refrained out of a love of virtue; afterwards it was because he knew God had chosen Her for His Own Spouse.

(by Chorpenning—*Just Man*, from pp. 73, 93, 111, 116 & 204)

The priests did not dare to decide Mary's state of life without first consulting with God in prayer. God ordained that all the marriageable young men of Mary's tribe who were in Jerusalem should come to the Temple, and that

He would miraculously make known to whom Mary should be given as Wife. When the suitors came together, Joseph's staff flowered and a white dove appeared over him, as Germanus and other authors testify.

Because theirs was a true marriage, the angel called the Virgin "Wife" (Matthew 1:20), meaning that She was married to, was watched over by, and was the Woman and Spouse of Joseph. And Joseph is said to be Mary's true husband and spouse because conjugal intercourse is not of the essence of marriage, as scholastic doctors prove.

St. Thomas Aquinas stated that it was a true and perfect marriage, in that the twofold perfection of marriage was present: consent of the nuptial bond, and the upbringing of the Child.

Although St. Epiphanius says that Joseph was 80 years of age at the time of his espousal to Mary, most other authors believe that he was between 40 and 50 years old, an age that would have made him like a father to the Virgin. The evidence marshalled for this opinion is that Joseph was chosen to support Mary by the work of his hands, to accompany Her on journeys, and to defend Her from temerarious judgment and from anyone thinking that She had a Child but no husband.

Joseph would not have been able to do these things if he had been very old. Learned authors interpret these words of the Prophet Isaiah in view of Joseph's youth and handsomeness: "The bridegroom will rejoice in his Bride, and the young man will marry the Virgin" (Isaiah 62:5). This verse refers to Joseph and Mary. And if in paintings, Joseph is portrayed as an old man, it is because he was a wise and prudent man of mature judgment. It is also to prevent weak and dull-witted people from thinking, when they would see two persons of such youth and beauty together, that this couple would not be able to live together with the most ineffable purity, forgetting that Joseph was most chaste, that chastity is of greater value for purity than advanced age, and that Joseph's chastity sufficed for him to be in the Virgin's company, although he may not have been an old man.

St. Bernard has remarked, no man born who saw the Virgin's most beautiful face ever had a lewd thought, and those who were not pure were restrained, according to the sovereign chastity with which She was endowed. And is that too much to believe, for St. Cecilia made her husband Valerian a virgin, and St. Agnes destroyed immodesty in a house of prostitution? St. Jerome compares the Virgin to a cedar that puts serpents to flight. Thus chastity makes sensual temptations flee, and thus it was not improper that Joseph would live in the Virgin's company, although he was not of advanced age.

When the Patriarch Joseph entered any city, all the women ran to the walls and windows to see him pass by, admiring his great handsomeness. When St. Joseph would enter a place with the Christ Child in his arms, all Heaven would become a window, with the angels in awe at God being carried in the arms of a carpenter and at such great humility on the part of the Creator and so great a favor bestowed on a creature.

The characterization of Joseph as aged is challenged in the Renaissance. This characterization is flawed on three counts. First, Joseph would have had to have been sufficiently vigorous and robust to support Mary and Jesus by the work of his hands, to travel with Them, and to defend Them. Second, this characterization destroys the very truths that it was invented to safeguard: "If Joseph had been so old that he was physically incapable of generating Jesus, then Mary would have appeared as an adulteress in the public eye, and Jesus would have been suspected as an illegitimate Son!" Third, this legend neglected to take into account that, having chosen Joseph, God would have endowed him with the grace necessary of his office, and God's grace was a help in preserving Joseph's virginity far greater than any natural limitations of an aging body.

Francisco Oacheco prescribes that in portraying the espousal, Mary should be depicted as being 14 years of age, and Joseph a little more than 30. Modern scholars believe that Joseph was even younger. The customs of the time were that Joseph should have been in his middle teens when he was espoused to our Lady. Mary in Her turn would be two to three years younger than Her virginal husband.

For Fr. Gracian, St. Joseph epitomizes human wholeness—the integration and harmony of the inner and outer self: the saint's self-control, discipline, chastity, wisdom, prudence, and maturity are manifested by his gracefulness, attractiveness, and handsomeness.

I regard as certain what Venerable Bede says: "It is an old trick of heretics to mix their errors with the sound doctrine of the saint, just as tavern keepers mix water and wine, as Isaiah says (Isaiah 1:22). The heretics introduced into their teaching the idea that Joseph had been an old man and had been married previously. Bede believed that the early Fathers of the Church, who were the actual authors, did not hold this opinion.

(by Chorpenning—*The Holy Family*, from p. 29)

In his instruction on marriage, St. Francis de Sales explains that because God, with unseen Hand ties the marriage bond and gives husband and wife to one another: "They should cherish each other with a completely holy, completely sacred, and completely divine love." The bishop tells married people that: "The primary effect of this love is an indissoluble union of your hearts, not of bodies. Marriage is true holy friendship. Husband and wife are to be friends, to enjoy a mutual love that results in the reciprocal perfection of both parties realized day by day over the course of a lifetime." The Holy Family is the example par excellence of magnanimous love.

(by Cristiani—*The Father of Jesus*, from p. 20)

In Jewish practice, a betrothal was equivalent to marriage and gave the betrothed couple all the rights of marriage.

(by De Domenico—*True Devotion*, from p. 8)

Twelve Reasons for the Marriage—St. Thomas gives 12 reasons, gathered from the Fathers of the Church, that show the importance and necessity of the marriage of the Blessed Virgin and St. Joseph for the Incarnation and Birth of Christ. First, there are four reasons given for the marriage for the sake of Christ.—First, lest they consider Him illegitimate. Second, that His genealogy might be traced through the male line according to the custom. Third, for the safety of the Child, lest the devil and his followers plot against Him, Who would be born of a Virgin. Fourth, that He would be fostered by Joseph.

It was fitting for the sake of the Virgin for three reasons.—First, lest they stone Her for having a Child out of wedlock. Second, that She should be protected from ill fame. Third, that Joseph might administer to Her wants.

It was also fitting for our sake.—First, Joseph is a witness that Jesus is born of a Virgin. Second, the Blessed Virgin's words regarding Her virginity are more credible, Third, virgins would not be able to use the ill fame of our Lady as an excuse for their fall from virtue. Fourth, the marriage is a type of Christ and His Bride, the virgin Church. Fifth, both virginity and marriage are honored in the One Person, the Mother of the Lord, contrary to those heretics that disparage one or the other. While these reasons support the need for the marriage, they also show the importance and the necessity of the role of St. Joseph in God's plan.

The Necessity of Marriage in God's Plan— While the above reasons of the Fathers explain the unique necessity of the marriage of Joseph and Mary, it is important to see that the basic reason for their marriage lies ultimately in the necessity of marriage itself in God's plan. It is only in marriage that parents can fully carry out their rights and responsibilities toward their children. The child also has a right to the care and attention of both his or her parents in his complete upbringing. This can only be fully accomplished when the parents have made a permanent and indissoluble commitment to one another.

Also, since work must be done in order to support the family, two parents are better able to give attention to the love and care of the child than only one, and also are better able to provide for the child's needs. In addition, a woman tends to contribute to a child's development in one way, while a man contributes to that development in a complementary way. Thus, the child develops in a balanced way, experiencing the love of a man and a woman. Further, the child learns the meaning of commitment from his or her parents' marriage, and thus how to be a responsible person.

Since without marriage the child tends to remain with the mother only, the idea of father is a weak one in the child's mind, and even can be a cause of bitterness and sorrow. This in turn makes it very difficult to approach God as a Father. Moreover, in this situation, the mother may tend not to be a good role model for the daughter. Similarly, boys have no role model at all, and so, have no idea of what it means to be a man. It was necessary, then, that Jesus be received into a marriage, not only that He might receive the benefits of having both parents to care for Him, but also that He might give the strongest witness for family life in the Divine Plan.

(by Deiss—*Joseph, Mary, Jesus*, from p. 26)

In Scripture, neither shall we learn anything concerning the wedding ceremony. In Jesus' time, it lasted seven days. The principal rite was the leading of the bride into her husband's house. The cortege formed in the evening and proceeded among songs, dances, blessings, and congratulations.

(by Doyle—*Espousals of Mary and Joseph*, from p. 1)

Approximately 2000 years ago, in the city of Jerusalem, a young couple, Mary and Joseph, came together for their espousals. The espousal was the beginning of married life for a righteous Jewish couple. In Hebrew, the word is "Kiddushin," closely related to "Kadosh," meaning "holy," with the idea that each spouse is consecrated, set apart exclusively, for the other.

Ordinarily, the espousal was arranged between the father of the bride and the future husband, always with the young woman's consent. If it is true that Mary grew up in the Temple of Jerusalem, and that Her parents were deceased at the time of the espousal (She was between 12—14 years of age), then the ceremony could have taken place in the Temple, as many artists depict; otherwise it took place in the home of the bride.

Joseph was probably 18 or a little older when he was espoused to Mary, for it was very rare that a Jewish man remain single after the age of 22. Why then do so many artists portray Joseph as an old man? The Church in the East followed the tradition, based on the Apocryphal Gospels, that Joseph had been married previously and had several grown children (the brothers and sisters of Jesus).

Although the earliest artistic renderings of St. Joseph (from the catacombs, for example), show him to be a young man, later images depicted him to be quite old because of heretical teachings, which denied the perpetual virginity of Mary. Many Western artists were influenced by this tradition. The consensus of theologians in the Latin church, however, for the past 1,500 years, has taught, that St. Joseph maintained his virginal integrity throughout his entire life, due to the grace of his unique vocation.

What happened at the ceremony? In front of two witnesses, the bridegroom, upon completing financial arrangements regarding the dowry, gave the bride a small coin and said: "By this you are betrothed to me." Did Joseph give Mary a ring? Some scholars say that this was a Roman custom, not Jewish. However, in Perugia, Italy, in their Cathedral Church is a ring, which they and many others believe is the one given to Mary by Joseph. If Joseph did give Mary a wedding ring, these are the words he might have said: "Here is the ring that unites You to me in the sight of God, according to the Mosiac Rite." It was also customary for the groom to give the bride a gift such as linen, oil, or dried fruit.

Once the espousal ceremony was over, the couple, now truly husband and wife, would separate, usually for up to one year. She would return to her family and he would find work in order to save enough money for the day of the wedding ceremony. At this second step of Jewish marriage, the groom would accompany his wife to his house in a procession of lively singing and dancing. This celebration, like the one at Cana of Galilee, might last up to a week. No wonder they needed 120 gallons of wine!

It is interesting that on this occasion, the wife would give her husband two gifts, which she made with her own hands at the spindle and loom during the waiting period: a prayer shawl and a burial shroud. Every Jewish maiden wanted a husband who was prayerful and aware of his mortality.

(by Doze—*St. Joseph: Shadow*, from p. 14)

One of the most astonishing witnesses of this period is Jean Gerson, a gentleman of note, the Chancellor of the University of Paris, who used his leisure time to write Latin verses on Joseph, and who wrote about the marriage of Joseph and Mary. For him, as for the other authors of these times, Joseph was a young man, active, of perfect purity, eminently holy, and certainly sanctified in his mother's womb as St. John the Baptist would be. The author was convinced that he is spiritually present in Heaven: "As for his body," he added, "I do not know."

63.

(by Emmerich—*Life of Blessed*, from p. 128)

The Blessed Virgin lived with other virgins in the Temple under the care of pious matrons. The maidens employed themselves with embroidery and other forms of decoration of carpets and vestments, and also with the cleaning of these vestments and of the vessels used in the Temple. They had little cells, from which they could see into the Temple, and here they prayed and meditated.

When these maidens were grown up, they were given in marriage. Their parents, in dedicating them to the Temple, had offered them entirely to God, and the devout and more spiritual Israelites had for a long time believed that the marriage of one of these virgins would one day contribute to the coming of the promised Messias.

When the Blessed Virgin had reached the age of 14 and was to be dismissed from the Temple with seven other maidens to be married, I saw that Her mother Anne had come to visit Her there. Joachim was no longer alive and Anne had, by God's command, married again. When our Lady was told that She must now leave the Temple and be married, I saw Her explaining to the priests, in great distress of heart, that it was Her desire to never leave the Temple, that She had betrothed Herself to God alone, and did not wish to be married. She was, however, told that it must be so.

Then a Voice spoke to Her and She received a revelation which comforted Her and gave Her strength to consent to Her marriage.

(by Emmerich—*Life of Jesus, Vol. 1*, from p. 186)

The priest prayed sitting before a roll of writings, and in a vision, his hand was placed upon that verse in the Prophet Isaias (Is. 11:1) in which it is written that there shall come forth a rod out of the root of Jesse and a flower shall rise up out of his root. Thereupon, I saw that all the unmarried men in the country of the House of David were summoned to the Temple. Then the High Priest gave to each of the suitors a branch which was to be held in the hand during the offering of prayer and sacrifice.

After that, all the branches were laid in the Holy of Holies with the understanding that he whose branch should blossom was to be Mary's husband. They all failed to blossom. After this, I saw the priests hunting through different rolls of writing in their search for another descendant of the House of David, one that had not presented himself among the suitors for Mary's hand. And there they found that, among the six brothers of Bethlehem, one was unknown and ignored. They sought him out and so discovered Joseph's retreat, six miles from Jerusalem, near Samaria.

There Joseph dwelt alone in a humble house near the water, and carried on the trade of a carpenter under another master. He was told to go up to the Temple. He went, accordingly, arrayed in his best. A branch was given him. As he was about to lay it upon the altar, it blossomed on top into a white flower like a lily. At the same time, I saw a light like the Holy Spirit hovering over him. He was then led to Mary, who was in Her chamber, and She accepted him as Her spouse.

The espousals took place, I think, upon our 23rd of January. They were celebrated in

Jerusalem, on Mount Zion in a house often used for such feasts. The seven virgins who were to leave the Temple with Mary, had already departed. They were recalled to accompany Mary on Her festal journey to Nazareth, where Anne had already prepared Her little home. The marriage feast lasted seven or eight days. The women and the virgins, companions of Mary in the Temple were present, also many relatives of Joachim and Anne. Many lambs were slaughtered and offered in sacrifice.

(by Filas—*Joseph Most Just,* from p. 67)

Because the disorder of concupiscence is a sequel of original sin, and Mary was conceived without original sin, She never inherited the power and propensity which inclined to disordered movements. But Joseph was not conceived without original sin. Therefore, such a *propensity* did exist in him.

Although the restraining of concupiscence would be a most unusual gift freely bestowed by God, in granting it, God would foresee the perfect manner in which Joseph would cooperate with the grace. The saint failed in no way at any time in his life.

The purity of Mary was so great, Her humility so deep, Her modesty so pronounced, that far from provoking any sinful thought, She must have inflamed hearts with the love of God. Contact, too, with Jesus would not tend to incite selfish reactions; the very opposite would be true.

(by Filas—*Joseph and Jesus*, from pp. 28, 36 & 38)

Joseph and Mary would not have received the title of spouse to each other unless that title had been based on a stable, genuine marriage.

St. Augustine bases his proof for the genuinity of the union of Joseph and Mary on the angel's words, "Do not be afraid, Joseph, son of David, to take to thee Mary thy Wife." Scripture says, on the authority of an angel, that he was Her husband.

(by Filas—*Joseph, The Man Closest*, from pp. 114 & 251)

The question existed whether or not it was a true marriage between Joseph and Mary, since it was never consummated. St. Thomas Aquinas said: "Marriage or wedlock is said to be true by reason of its attaining its perfection. Now, perfection of anything is twofold; first and second. The first perfection of a thing consists in its very form, by which it receives its species; while the second perfection of a thing consists in its operation, by which in some way a thing attains its end.

"Now, the form of matrimony consists in a certain inseparable union of souls by which husband and wife are pledged to each other with a bond of mutual affection that cannot be sundered. And the end of matrimony is the begetting and upbringing of children; the first of which is attained by conjugal intercourse; the second, by the other duties of husband and wife by which they help each other in rearing their offspring.

"Thus we must say, as to the first perfection, that the marriage of the Virgin Mother of God and Joseph was absolutely true; because both consented to the nuptial bond, but not expressly to the bond of the flesh, save on the condition that it was pleasing to God. The marriage had its second perfection in the upbringing of the Child."

St. Francis de Sales, Bishop of Geneva and Doctor of the Church, pictures our Lord as the fruit of the virginal marriage. The marriage protects the honor of our Lord and of our Lady, and by reason of it, Joseph can be called an intimate cooperator in the circumstances of the Incarnation. In God's plan, he was necessary in order that Jesus might be born of the Virgin Mary within the bonds of a true marriage.

(by Filas—*St. Joseph, After,* from p. 61)

He begins as an obscure Palestinian youth, when, through the providence of God, he meets Mary (while probably in his mid-teens), and realizes that he and She are to be husband and Wife.

(by Fox—*St. Joseph, His Life*, from p. 2)

The American Catholic bishops, in their Marian Pastoral, *"Behold Your Mother, Woman of Faith,"* had this to say about the age of Joseph. "According to the custom of his time and people, Mary was probably no more than 14 when Her parents arranged Her marriage, and Joseph probably about 18."

(by Gasnier—*Joseph the Silent*, from pp. 54, 60, 70 & 75)

Among those who took part in this ceremony was a young man, very rich, very noble, named Agabus. His disappointment was so great that having broken his staff—Raphael has left us a famous painting, "The Espousals," of this scene— he fled into the desert for life.

It is generally believed that Mary's parents had died, and She had been placed in the care of the priest, Zachary.

St. Epiphanius stated that Joseph had passed his eightieth year at his betrothal to the Blessed Virgin.

Ordinary common sense demands that Joseph be in the flower of his age in order that on one side the fatherhood of the Child Jesus might be attributed to him, and that on the other, he would be able to fulfill the duties of protector and foster father, which God was to confide to him.

Custom in Israel required that young men be married at 18 or shortly after. Nothing obliges us to think that Joseph was older than others. Some documentary iconographs picture him as a beardless young man.

From the time of betrothal, they belonged irrevocably to each other, for in the Hebrew Law the betrothal was not a simple promise of marriage in the future, but, with binding force, was equivalent to it. In Deuteronomy, as in the Gospel, the betrothed was called "wife" because she was indeed that. Accused of infidelity, she would be obliged to suffer the punishment for adultery, and she would be stoned to death. Did her betrothed die, she would be looked upon as a widow. Nor could she be rejected except through the same process of divorce as the Law required for a married woman.

Cohabitation, however, was generally postponed for some months, perhaps a year. The rabbis held the bride should be given the time to prepare her trousseau; the groom, to fulfill the promises of the contract and prepare the home.

Actually, the betrothed could have marital relations, and if the bride conceived a child by her groom, no fault would be found. In fact, congratulations would have been in order, since fecundity was esteemed the joy and glory of the conjugal union.

Did he suspect Mary of sin? Certain Fathers of the Church—outstanding ones, too—St. Justin, St. John Chrysostom, St. Ambrose, St. Augustine— think he did. The others—it is the opinion we adopt—find it impossible to think that for one

instant St. Joseph ever attributed to Mary anything unworthy of Her. St. Jerome's magnificent
sentence covers the case: "Joseph knew Mary's
holiness hid in silence a mystery he did not
understand."

How could he have doubted Her innocence?
Think Her capable of weakness? He repelled such
a thought as criminal. He could more easily have
believed someone who told him the Jordon had
returned to its source, or the mountains of
Hermon had vanished!

There was then only one thing for him to do,
one risk to take. He would put Her aside, not
because he believed Her guilty, but because he
reverenced in Her a mystery. He must return Her
ring, take back the wedding gifts, and go away
no one would know where. He would be blamed
for cowardly behavior, for unfaithfulness—but no
blame would fall on Her.

"Do not be afraid...to take to thee Mary thy
Wife." If Joseph was getting ready to leave Mary,
it was not because he doubted Her, but because
he feared that in staying with Her, a fatherhood
which he dared not assume would be attributed
to him, a fatherhood in whose mystery he dared
not intrude, lest in doing so he offend his Lord.

(by Griffin—*Saint Joseph & Third*, from pp. 89, 101,
162, 273, 291 & 341)

John Paul II states: "The Son of Mary is also
Joseph's Son by virtue of the marriage bond
that unites them. By reason of their faithful
marriage, both of them deserve to be called

Christ's parents, not only His Mother, but also His father, who was a parent in the same way that he was the Mother's spouse—in mind, not in flesh. In this marriage none of the requirements of marriage were lacking. In Christ's parents all the goods of marriage were realized—offspring, fidelity, the sacrament: the *offspring* being the Lord Jesus Himself; *fidelity* since there was no adultery; the *sacrament* since there was no divorce."

Gerson believed that St. Joseph was about 36 (as this is the age which Aristotle identifies as the prime of life) when he married Mary, who was probably only 13 or 14.

It is important to note that the marriage between Joseph and Mary was genuine to the highest degree.

Jean Guitton establishes a striking parallel between the virginal love in the home of Nazareth and that of Adam and Eve before the Fall. Here was an improbable and peaceful moment which recalled that first love during the first days of the world between Adam and Eve, pure before their sin.

Bishop Fulton Sheen has called the union of Mary and Joseph "the world's happiest marriage, for they brought to their espousal not only their vows of virginity, but also two hearts with greater torrents of love than had ever before coursed through human breasts. No husband and wife ever loved one another so much as did Joseph and Mary." In the beautiful language of Pope Leo XIII: "The consummation of their love was in Jesus."

Art and popular imagination have usually portrayed Joseph as an old man, which is probably a false notion. Bishop Sheen points out that the assumption seems to have been that senility was a better protection of virginity than adolescence. This, however, casts a suspicious eye upon Joseph.

Actually, the rabbis at the time of Christ commonly taught that men should marry between the ages of 13 and 19. Joseph as a "just (that is, law-abiding) man" would likely have conformed to this practice. Hence, the companionship of the two, closer in age, was all the more compatible. Surely, too, it would have required a man of vim and vigor to travel to Bethlehem and to engineer the flight into Egypt and back to Nazareth.

Blessed José Maria Escriva said: "I don't agree with the traditional picture of St. Joseph as an old man, even though it may have been prompted by a desire to emphasize the perpetual virginity of Mary. I see him as a strong young man, perhaps a few years older than our Lady, but in the prime of his life and work.

"You don't have to wait to be old or lifeless to practice the virtue of chastity. Purity comes from love; and the strength and gaiety of youth are no obstacle for noble love. Joseph had a young heart and a young body when he married Mary, when he learned of the mystery of Her Divine Motherhood, when he lived in Her company, respecting the integrity God wished to give the world as one more sign that He had come to share the life of His creatures. Anyone who cannot understand a love like that knows very little of true love, and is a complete stranger to the Christian meaning of chastity."

(by Griffin—*Saint Joseph, Theo.*, from p. 7)

It is interesting to note that the earliest known paintings or pieces of sculpture in the catacombs show Joseph as a young man, probably no more than 25 years old. This trend continued until the fourth century.

In the fourth century, the perpetual virginity of Mary was under attack, and by way of implication, it was asserted that Joseph was the natural father of Christ. Hence, the artists of the times were convinced that it was not advisable to depict Joseph as a young man, for fear that the faithful would imagine him to be the natural father of Christ.

The Gospel assures us that the contemporaries of the Holy Family thought that Joseph was the natural father of Jesus. Is it likely that people would have come to such a conclusion had Joseph already been a very old man?

In addition, how could such an old man have worked as a carpenter to support his Wife and Child? Could he have taken the long journeys related in the Gospel? How could he have protected his family on such trips? It is not necessary to portray Joseph as a decrepit old man in order to affirm his virginity, for virginity comes from virtue and the grace of God, and not from debilitating old-age.

Is it possible to be more specific about his age at the time of his marriage? Yes...scholars of oriental history assure us that most Jewish men married when they were 16 years old; they rarely deferred marriage beyond 24. Thus, in all likelihood, Joseph was married when he was in his late teens.

(by Healy Thompson—*Life And*, from pp. 3, 103, 121, 126, 131 & 138)

In order to conceal this mystery of love from the world until the appointed time had come, and to safeguard at the same time the reputation of the Virgin Mother and the honor of the Divine Son, God willed that Mary, by a marriage altogether Heavenly, should be espoused to the humblest, the purest, and the holiest of the royal race of David, one therefore expressly predestined for this end; a virgin spouse for the Virgin Mother, who at the same time should be in the place of a father to the Divine Son.

In the Divine mind, Joseph was the one chosen from amongst all others. Joseph held the first place. Joseph was predestined to this office. True, from the tribe of Juda, from the family of David, great patriarchs were to arise, famous leaders of the people, most noble kings; but God did not choose any of these. He chose Joseph alone. Joseph was the beloved one. Joseph was especially preordained to become one day the happy spouse of Mary and the foster-father of Jesus. "As Mary," says Echius, the famous opponent of Luther, "was from eternity predestined to be the Mother of the Son of God; so also was Joseph elected to be the guardian and protector of Jesus and of Mary."

Thus Joseph was, after Mary, comprehended in the very decree of the Incarnation, and, after Mary, was called to have an integral part, as it were, in this ineffable mystery. It is easy to perceive how much honor then redounds to Joseph; for if, next to the mystery of the

Most Holy Trinity, the mystery of the Divine Incarnation is the essential foundation of the Christian faith, who can fail to see that to be included in the eternal decree of so admirable a mystery, into which the angels themselves "desire to look," it is an incomparable glory to this great saint?

We must always, therefore, bear well in mind this singular destination of Joseph, because this is truly the ground of all his greatness. This is the basis upon which all his glories are raised. Whoever thoroughly realizes the fact of this preordination will no longer marvel at God's predilection for Joseph, and at seeing him so highly privileged and exalted to be the guardian and patron of the Universal Church.

Several writers of high authority are of the opinion that Joseph went to practice in Jerusalem the trade which he had learned, in order to have constant access to the Temple and take part in its sacrifices.

Joseph was Mary's nearest of kin, being, as seems most probable, nephew to Her mother and nearly related to Her also through Joachim, Her father. From humility and the love of poverty, more than from any absolute necessity, he, the lineal descendant of kings, had subjected himself to the daily toil of a mechanic, which, although it in no way degraded him in the eyes of true Hebrews, placed him in a position of some social inferiority.

Our Lady said to St. Bridget, "Regard it as most certain that, before being espoused to him, Joseph knew by the inspiration of the Holy Spirit that I had made a vow of virginity." St. Thomas, also, enquiring how it was that Mary consented to be espoused to Joseph when She had made a vow of virginity, thus replies to his own question: "The Blessed Virgin, before contracting marriage with Joseph, was certified by God that he had formed a similar resolve, and, therefore, that She exposed Herself to no risk in espousing him."

She knew, in short, that in taking a husband She was taking a superior, a confidant of Her thoughts, a depositary of Her secrets, a witness of Her actions. He must, therefore, be eminently prudent, faithful, and chaste; in a word, he must be eminently holy.

Between the betrothal and the marriage of Mary and Joseph, a certain period, according to the custom of the Hebrew people, intervened. It is supposed in their case to have been two months, their mutual promises being interchanged in November, and the marriage itself probably taking place on the 23 of January, when the Church celebrates the feast of the Espousals of the Blessed Virgin.

In the absence of all direct evidence, it would seem that those who have given the subject the fullest consideration, and weighed and compared probabilities, consider that at the time of his marriage with Mary, he was, most likely, approaching his 40th year, and, therefore, of an age which can be considered neither young nor old, but in the prime of his strength, whether of mind or body.

If we accept the testimony of St. Justin Martyr—followed or corroborated, perhaps from additional sources, by Gerson and other doctors—that in beauty and in bodily appearance, he was most like to our Lord. We may gather that, next to Jesus and Mary, Joseph was the fairest of the children of men.

The ancient Joseph, who was the type of our saint and who even, prophetically, bore his significant name, is described as of "a beautiful countenance and comely to behold." Can his prototype have been less personally favored, destined as he was for incomparably higher honor? Sister Emmerich likewise describes St. Joseph as having in his whole person an expression of extreme benignity and readiness to be of service to others. She says that he had fair hair.

That of the Blessed Virgin, she tells us, was more abundant, and of a rich auburn; Her eyebrows dark and arched; Her eyes, which had long black lashes, were large, but habitually cast down; Her features exquisitely modeled; while in height She was about the middle stature, and She bore Her attire, which for the Espousals was rich and becoming—the Sister describes it in elaborate detail—with much grace and dignity.

St. Epiphanius, quoted by Nicephorus, has left us a very similar portrait of the holy Virgin, of whose admirable beauty so many other early Fathers speak. The saying of St. Denis, the Areopagite, who saw Her, is well known: that Her beauty was so dazzling that he should have adored Her as a goddess if he had not known that there is but one God.

From the motive of humility, our Blessed Lady would never again wear the robe in which, according to Hebrew custom, She was clad upon that day. The robe was preserved as a precious treasure in Palestine, whereafter it was sent to Constantinople about the year 461. The gown was of the color of nankeen with flowers blue, white, violet, and gold. It is now the sacred relic of Chartres, having been given by Charles the Bald to the Church there in 877. Many miracles have been attributed to it. The nuptial ring of the Blessed Virgin is still preserved at Perugia in the Cathedral Church of San Lorenzo.

(by Joseph—*Joseph, Son of David*, from p. 53)

Fulton J. Sheen says in *The World's First Love*—
Joseph was probably a *young* man, strong, virile,
athletic, handsome, chaste, and disciplined; the
kind of man one sees sometimes shepherding
sheep, or piloting a plane, or working at a
carpenter's bench. Instead of being a man
incapable of loving, he must have been on fire
with love. Just as we would give very little credit
to the Blessed Mother if She had taken Her vow
of virginity after having been an old maid for
fifty years, so neither could we give much credit
to a Joseph who became Her spouse because he
was advanced in years.

Young girls in those days, like Mary, took
vows of love to God uniquely, and so did young
men, of whom Joseph was one so pre-eminent as
to be called the "just." Instead, then, of being
dried fruit to be served on the table of the King,
he was rather a blossom filled with promise and
power. He was not in the evening of life but in
its morning, bubbling over with energy, strength,
and controlled passion.

Mary with Joseph brought to their espousals,
not only their vows of virginity, but also two
hearts with greater torrents of love than had
ever before coursed through human breasts. No
husband and wife ever loved one another so
much as Joseph and Mary... Love usually makes
husband and wife one. In the case of Mary and
Joseph, it was not their combined loves but Jesus
Who made them one. No deeper love ever beat
under the roof of the world since the beginning,
nor will it ever beat, even unto the end. They did

not go to God through love of one another; rather, because they went first to God, they had a deep and pure love, One for the other...

How much more beautiful Mary and Joseph become when we see in their loves what might be called the first Divine Romance!... In both Mary and Joseph, there was youth, beauty, and promise. God loves cascading cataracts and billowing waterfalls, but He loves them better, not when they overflow and drown His flowers, but when they are harnessed and bridled to light a city and to slake the thirst of a child. In Joseph and Mary, we do not find one controlled waterfall and one dried-up lake, but rather two youths who, before they knew the beauty of the One and the handsome strength of the other, willed to surrender theses things for Jesus.

(by Levy—*Joseph, the Just Man*, from p. 25)

The common practice in the days of Mary was for Jewish girls to marry quite young. Consequently, when She attained Her 14th year, at which age consecrated virgins left the Temple for their future homes, the High Priest desired Mary to marry, particularly since She was now an orphan; but She reminded him of Her vow of virginity. In his embarrassment, the High Priest consulted the Lord; after which he summoned all the young men of the family of David, promising Mary in marriage to the one "whose rod should bloom."

Now an ancient tradition tells us that the lot fell to the holy, just, humble Joseph, and that his rod did actually bloom.

(by Llamera—*Saint Joseph*, from pp. 30, 35, 47, 107, 113, & 169)

St. Matthew writes: "When Mary had been betrothed...before they came together, She was found..." It is to be supposed that Mary was living in Her parents' home and had not yet gone to live in the house of Joseph. This is the interpretation of the text, which eliminated the possibility of any conjugal relations. The idea of a natural generation is excluded by a negative argument: the future spouses were not living together when the Conception took place; and also by a positive explanation: this Conception was the effect of the power of God. Therefore, the phrase "before they came together" is not to be interpreted, as formerly, to mean before marital union, because in the judgment of modern exegetes, this is contrary to the intention of the sacred writer (Matt. 1:25; Luke 1:34).

Betrothed signifies the same as bound by matrimony, because the betrothals of the Hebrews implied not only the promise of matrimony, as with us, but it constituted true matrimony with all its rights and obligations. For this reason the punishment for infidelity in a betrothed woman was the same as for an adulteress (Deut. 22:23). A year after the espousal, the solemn nuptials were celebrated and the bride went to live with her husband.

This, then, is the substance of the Gospel narration. Joseph and Mary, blood relatives, both of the family of David in the full bloom of youth and interiorly directed by the Holy Spirit, were united in true matrimony, according to the customs of the Jews. Once the mystery of the Incarnation was effected and explained to Joseph, the solemn nuptials were celebrated and they lived together under the same roof, but without ever having any marital contact.

It was a true marriage. For the Angelic Doctor and for his entire school, it is certain (*certum est*) that this was a true marriage as to its essence, i.e., the mutual consent of the spouses in the inseparable union of spirit. The marriage of Joseph and Mary was not only true, but most perfect.

The Gospel frequently calls Mary Spouse, for the celebration of nuptials does not signify the loss of virginity, but the ratification of matrimony. Mary was married, but She conceived from quite another source.

Mary's virginity was a married virginity (virginitas uxoratae), because it required and presupposed a like virginity in Her husband.

Mary's virginity is, therefore, ordained to a most exalted end, the human generation of the Son of God. There is nothing more beautiful, more noble or more divine! But the Virgin had to be at the same time a married woman. Now, the virginity of a wife depends necessarily upon the consent of her husband, for without such consent, her virginity is not legitimate. Consequently, if Mary, according to the divine decree, was to become a Mother while remaining a Virgin in the married state, She could not be a Mother without Her husband's consent, because upon him depends Her virginity.

It was determined from all eternity that the Son would become a Man, born in a miraculous manner of Mary, who was a Virgin, and at the same time united in true matrimony to the just man Joseph.

St. Bernardine said: "The marriage between Mary and Joseph was a real marriage, entered into under divine inspiration; and marriage involves so close a union of souls that bridegroom and bride are said to be one person: "They shall be two in one flesh" (Gen. 2:24). Can any discerning person, then, imagine that the Holy Spirit would join in that union the soul of such a Maiden to one who was not like Her in virtue? Therefore, do I believe that this man, the holy Joseph, was graced with perfect virginity, with the deepest humility, with the most ardent love for God, the loftiest contemplation, and the utmost solicitude toward the Virgin who was his Wife. She knew that he was given to Her by the Holy Spirit to be Her husband and the faithful protector of Her virginity; She knew that he was given, moreover, to share Her devoted love and tender care for the Divine Son of God. Therefore, do I believe that She loved St. Joseph fondly and with heartfelt affection.

(by Molinari—*Vocation and Mission*, from p. 13)

Joseph had that disposition of heart which enabled Mary to respond to him and to be at ease with him. There was a correspondence, a mutuality between them which was the basis for their betrothal.

83.

(by Neuzil—*Our Lady of America*, from p. 29)

The color of Joseph's hair, as also his rather small and slightly forked beard, seemed a very dark brown. His eyes resembled in color the hair and beard. He was clothed in a white robe that reached to his ankles. Over this, he wore a sort of cloak, which did not come together at the throat, but covering the shoulders and draped gracefully over each arm, reached to the hem of the robe. The cloak at times had, or seemed to have, the appearance of a brown, sometimes a purple, hue, or perhaps a slight blending of the two. The belt about his waist was of a gold color, as were his sandals.

His appearance, though quite youthful, gave at the same time the impression of rare maturity combined with great strength. He seemed a bit taller than medium height. The lines of his face appeared strong and purposeful, softened somewhat by a gentle serenity. I also saw his most pure heart at this time. Moreover, I saw the Holy Spirit in the form of a dove hovering over his head.

(by Poranganel—*St. Joseph—Envoy*, from p. 32)

The Father prepared Joseph from the beginning of time to be a fit person in all respects to be the spouse of His most well-beloved Daughter, Mary, and to be the foster father of His Eternal Son Jesus, in His Own stead. Since the bond of marriage is so deeply intimate and because of the sanctity of their love, there is no doubt that more than any other person, he approached that super-eminent dignity by which the Mother of God is raised far above all created natures.

(by Sabat-Rivers—*Saint Joseph's Day*, from p. 15)

But not only did Joseph's staff blossom, a dove also hovered above his head.

(by Sparks—*Dominicans*, from pp. 19 & 155)

The Gospel text: *But since Joseph was a just man and was unwilling to "traduce" (traducere) Her, he wished to dismiss Her quietly* and is explained in three ways.

First, "to traduce," that is "to *transfer* Her to his own house." For according to some, he had not yet introduced Her into his house, but She was still in Her parents' house.

Second, "to traduce," that is, "*to go through with* the marriage solemnities." For Joseph had already brought Mary into his own home, as was the custom then for men with regard to their espoused. And this, for St. Thomas, is the better explanation. For conceiving in Joseph's house rather than in the house of Her parents, She could be less suspected of adultery since he would be very zealous for Her virtue. Besides he would be a better witness of Her chastity.

Third, "to traduce," that is, *to put to open shame*.

And what the angel said: *"Do not be afraid to take unto yourself Mary your Wife"* is to be understood as to keep Her whom you have already received into your house.

As to Joseph's age, it is more likely that he was neither an old man nor a youth, but somewhere between: he was of a mature and serious age. The marriage of Mary and Joseph had to appear normal to their contemporaries, to protect Mary's honor. I cannot persuade myself that he was an old man, one without strength. Rather I think of him as a man in the prime of life, and full of energy.

Joseph, before his marriage to the Blessed Virgin, was not a widower, but was celibate and a virgin. The marriage between Joseph and Mary should be so perfect that no other was more so. The marriage of Mary and Joseph was more perfect that it might, more perfectly than the marriage of Adam and Eve, represent the spiritual marriage of Christ with the Church. Hence it had to be the marriage of a Virgin with a virgin, of One with one only, as the Virgin Christ espoused to Himself the virgin Church and never another spouse.

(by Stein—*The Tapestry*, from pp. 18 & 29)

The Talmud recommends 18 up to the age of 20 for marriage, and thus the early paintings in the catacombs show St. Joseph young and beardless, not elderly.

St. Jerome gives the first reason for the marriage of Mary and Joseph through the genealogy of Joseph thus Mary's origin might be known. For with the Jews, genealogy was always reckoned through the father instead of the mother, since father and mother had to be of the same tribe and family.

(by Stramare—*Saint Joseph*, from p. 105)

Since the essence of marriage consists in the indivisible union of souls, the validity of the marriage of Mary and Joseph is assured. Because of the distinction between the two perfections of marriage, one regarding its nature and the other its exercise, there is removed the error of those who confuse conjugal union with conjugal intercourse, as if both were identical.

Against Julian the Pelagian, who denied the validity of a marriage that is not consummated, the Bishop of Hippo defended the marriage of Mary and Joseph by establishing its essence in the *union of souls*.

Just as in the case of fatherhood, he attaches the greatest importance to the affection of charity, so also in marriage he assigns the first place to the union of souls. Joseph is the husband of Mary, his Partner in continence, not by carnal embrace but by affection; not by union of bodies, but—what matters more—by the communion of souls. Not without cause is Mary called the Wife of Joseph, both by reason of Her sex and by reason of the union of souls, although he was not joined to Her by carnal union. Just as Mary was virginally the Wife, so was Joseph virginally the husband.

The conjugal bond is by no means dissolved by the mutual decision to abstain permanently from the use of marriage. On the contrary, the bond will be all the more stable the more their mutual agreement was made not on the basis of pleasurable ties of their bodies, but by the voluntary affections of their souls. For it was not by any error that the angel said to Joseph: "Do not be afraid to take Mary as your Wife" (Mt 1:20). She is called Wife already from the first moment of Her matrimonial consent, She who had not had, nor in the future would have, sexual union.

The title of husband was not lost, nor did it remain a fiction, by the fact that there neither was nor would be carnal union. Indeed, that virgin was undoubtedly more holily and admirably pleasing to Her husband since, even though She was fruitful without a husband and different by reason of Her offspring, She was equal to him by reason of Her consent.

The reason for this apparent paradox is always to be sought in the conviction that "what makes a spouse is not passion but conjugal love... The more passion is dominated, the more does conjugal love gain in strength and solidity... Therefore, one must not deny that they are husband and wife who, though not joined together in the flesh, bind themselves to each other with their hearts."

Joseph was united with Mary in their genealogy in order that the faithful might not consider the union of bodies of such importance in marriage, as not to consider themselves married without it; but rather, that Christian couples might understand that they would be more intimately united to the members of Christ the more they imitated the parents of Christ.

(by Suarez—*Joseph of Nazareth*, from p. 34)

St. Bernardine of Laredo makes Joseph some forty years old, since "one concludes that a male begins his prime of life at the age of 35, and remains in it until he is almost 50."

(*The Glories of Saint Joseph*, from p. 48)

Such was this son of David's purity of heart that Mary, while She was totally his, could still belong totally to God. They were united in a true marriage, so that each might be closer to God, with, one might say, the help of the other. Concupiscence was extinguished in Joseph, and his soul shone with brilliant purity when he came into the presence of the Blessed Virgin. It could not be that She should be loved by someone who was not perfectly chaste.

We see in St. Joseph a totally purified soul, a soul in which sin has lost its power. St. Augustine, while asserting that no one is ever free from sin in this life and that even the saints must pray "Forgive us our sins," recognized that God could, if He so desired, by way of exception and special privilege, "completely take away the corruption which causes a man to sin, and array him with incorruptibility in this life so that he might see God everywhere present, just as the saints in Heaven see Him, but without a veil."

Surely this marvelous privilege was granted to Saint Joseph who was called to virginity in marriage, and who had the Son of God always before his eyes. Was he not, as Saint Augustine says, completely taken up with unceasing contemplation of his God? How could he sin? In the holy house of Nazareth, there was no place for sin.

O Joseph, we catch a glimpse of your holiness in its dazzling mystery—Mary can be yours, but no less God's for all that. Furthermore, being yours, She belongs to God even more than before, and it is when She became yours that the great mystery for which She was created was accomplished in Her.

How admirable God's arrangement! How it brought to light St. Joseph's extraordinary purity of soul, he who did not keep the love of the creature for himself, but returned everything to God!

What a lesson you teach us, O great saint! You wanted nothing which is not of God. In Mary, you experienced only God, as Mary experienced only God in you. Obtain for us, great saint, the grace to be able to imitate such purity of heart (Dom Bernard Maréchaux).

(by Toschi—*Joseph in the New*, from pp. 2 & 24)

The Infancy Story of Thomas recounts numerous bizarre miracles worked by the Child Jesus. The resulting composite story had Joseph as a carpenter who makes plows, yokes, other wooden tools for cultivation, and also wooden beds. At the age of 40, he marries Melcha or Escha, and during their 49 years of marriage, he has four sons and two daughters, whose names are given. It is after he has been widowed for a year that the episode occurs with his staff blossoming and the dove flying out of it, thus indicating that he is divinely chosen for the 12-year-old Mary. The Annunciation takes place two years later. At Bethlehem, Joseph is out searching for a midwife when the baby is born miraculously without Mary losing Her virginity.

There is no evidence whatsoever in the Gospel to support the image of an old widowed Joseph presented in the Apocrypha, which merit no claim to historicity. The most likely presumption on reading that Mary and Joseph are "betrothed" (Mt 1:18) is that they are two youths of ordinary marriageable age.

(by Valtorta—*Poem, Vol. 1*, from p. 61)

I see a rich hall with a beautiful floor, curtains, carpets, and inlaid furniture. It must be still part of the Temple: there are priests in it, including Zacharias, and many men of every age, from 20 to 50 approximately.

They are all talking in low but animated voices. They seem to be anxious about something I do not know. They are dressed in their best clothes, which seem to be new or just recently washed, and they are obviously dressed for some special feast. Many have removed the piece of cloth covering their heads, others still wear it, particularly the elder ones, whereas the young people show their bare heads. Their hair is mostly short, but some wear it long down to their shoulders.

They do not all know one another, because they observe one another inquisitively. But they seem to be akin somehow, because it is clear that they are all concerned with the same matter.

In a corner, I can see Joseph. He is talking to a hale and hearty elderly man. Joseph is about 30 years old. He is a handsome man with short and rather curly hair, dark brown like his beard and his moustache, which cover a well-shaped chin and rise toward his rosy-brown cheeks, which are not olive-colored, as is normal in most people with a brown complexion. His eyes are dark, kindly and deep, very serious, and perhaps somewhat sad. But when he smiles, as he does now, they become gay and young looking. He is dressed in light brown, very simple but very tidy.

A group of young Levites comes in and they take up position between the door and a long narrow table, which is against the same wall as the door, which is left wide open. A single curtain, hanging down to about 20 centimeters from the floor, is drawn to cover the empty space.

The curiosity of the group increases. It grows more so when a hand pulls the curtain to one side to admit a Levite, who is carrying in his arms a bundle of dry branches on which one in blossom is gently laid; it looks like a light foam of white petals, with a vague pinkish hue that spreads softer and softer from the center to the top of the light petals. The Levite lays the bundle of branches on the table very gently to avoid detracting from the miracle of the branch full of flowers among so many dry ones.

Whispering spreads in the hall. They all stretch their necks and sharpen their eyes to see. Zacharias, who is near the table with the other priests, also endeavors to see. But he can see nothing. Joseph, in his corner, gives a quick glance to the bundle of branches and when the man he was speaking to says something to him, he shakes his head in denial, as if to say: "Impossible" and smiles.

A trumpet is heard beyond the curtain. They all become quiet and turn in an orderly way towards the door, which is now completely clear as the curtain has been pulled to one side. The High Priest enters surrounded by elders. They all make a deep bow. The Pontiff goes to the table and begins to speak, standing up.

"Men of the race of David, gathered here at my request, please listen. The Lord has spoken, glory be to Him! From His Glory a ray has descended and, like the sun in springtime, it has given life to a dry branch which has blossomed miraculously, whereas no other branch on earth is in bloom today, the last day of the Feast of Dedication, and the snow that fell on the mountains in Judah has not yet melted and everything is white between Zion and Bethany.

"God has spoken and has made Himself the Father and the Guardian of the Virgin of David,

Who has Him alone as Her protection. A holy Girl, the glory of the Temple, She deserved the word of God to learn the name of a husband agreeable to the Eternal One.

"And he must be very just to be chosen by the Lord as the protector of the Virgin so dear to Him! For this reason our sorrow in losing Her is alleviated and all worries about Her destiny as a Wife cease. And to the man appointed by God, we entrust with full confidence the Virgin blessed by God and by ourselves. The name of the husband is Joseph of Jacob of Bethlehem, of the tribe of David, a carpenter in Nazareth in Galilee. Joseph: come forward. It is an order of the High Priest."

There is a lot of whispering. Heads move around, eyes cast inquisitive glances, hands make signs; there are expressions of disappointment and relief. Someone, particularly amongst the older people, must be happy that it was not his fate. Joseph, blushing and embarrassed moves forward. He is now near the table, in front of the Pontiff, whom he has greeted reverently.

"Everyone must come here to see the name engraved on the branch, and everyone must take his own branch to make sure that there is no deception." The men obey. They look at the branch gently held by the High Priest and then each takes his own; some break it, some keep it. They all look at Joseph. Some look and are silent, others look and congratulate him. The elderly man to whom Joseph was speaking before exclaims: "I told you, Joseph. Who feels less certain, is the one who wins the game!" They have all now passed before the Pontiff.

The High Priest gives Joseph his branch in bloom; he lays his hand on his shoulder and says to him: "The Spouse, the Lord has presented you with, is not rich, as you know. But all virtues are in Her. Be more and more worthy of Her. There is no flower in Israel as beautiful, as pure, as She is. Please, all go out now. You Joseph, stay here. And you, Zacharias, since you are Her relative, please bring in the Bride." They all go out, except the High Priest and Joseph. The curtain is drawn once again over the door. Joseph is standing in a very humble attitude, near the Priest. There is silence; then the Priest says to Joseph: "Mary wishes to inform you of a vow She made. Please help Her shyness. Be good to Her, Who is so good."

Mary enters with Zacharias and Anna of Phanuel. "Come Mary," says the Pontiff. "Here is the spouse that God has destined for You. He is Joseph of Nazareth. You will therefore go back to Your Own town. I will leave You now. May God give You His blessing. May the Lord protect You and bless You, may He show His Face to You and have mercy on You. May He turn His Face to You and give You peace."

Zacharias goes out escorting the Pontiff. Anna congratulates Joseph and then she goes out, too. The betrothed are now facing each other.

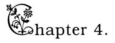

hapter 4.

The Vow of Chastity

(by Agreda—*City of God (Conception)*, from pp. 340,
567 & 578; *(Transfixion)*, from p. 164)

At the age of three, having just entered the
Temple, Mary was raised body and soul to the
Empyrean Heaven, where She was received by
the Holy Trinity, and She saw, intuitively and
face to face, the Divinity Itself. The Most High
gave Her to understand that He would admit
Her to suffering and labor for His love in the
course of Her life, without revealing to Her the
manner.

She asked His Majesty to be allowed to make
four vows in His presence: of chastity, of poverty,
of obedience, and of perpetual enclosure
in the Temple. Our Lord answered and said:
"Thou dost not yet know what is to happen
to Thee in the course of Thy life, and why it
is impossible to fulfill Thy fervent desires
altogether in the manner in which Thou now
dost imagine. The vow of chastity I permit
and I desire that Thou make it; I wish that
from this moment Thou renounce earthly riches.
It is also My will that as far as possible, Thou

observe whatever pertains to the other vows, just as if Thou hadst made them all." The most holy Child, in the presence of the Lord, made the vow of chastity and renounced affection for terrestrial and created things.

As distant as Heaven is from earth, were the thoughts of most holy Mary from the plans which the Most High now made known to Her, by commanding Her to accept a husband for Her protection and company; for as far as depended upon Her will, She had desired and resolved during all Her life not to have a husband, and She had often repeated and renewed the vow of chastity, which She had taken at such a premature age.

For the confirmation and increase of Saint Joseph's good qualities, was then added the intercession of the Blessed Lady; for as soon as She was informed that the Lord wished Her to enter the married state with him, She earnestly besought the Lord to sanctify Saint Joseph and inspire him with most chaste thoughts and desires in conformity with Her own.

The Lord listened to Her prayer, and permitted Her to see what great effects His Right Hand wrought in the mind and spirit of the patriarch St. Joseph. They were so copious, that they cannot be described in human words. He infused into Joseph's soul the most perfect habits of all the virtues and gifts. He balanced anew all his faculties and filled him with grace, confirming it in an admirable manner.

In the virtue and perfection of chastity, the holy spouse was elevated higher than the Seraphim; for the purity, which they possessed without a body, Saint Joseph possessed in his earthly body and in mortal flesh; never did an image of the impurities of the animal and sensible nature engage, even for one moment, any of his faculties.

This freedom from all such imaginations and his angelic simplicity fitted him for the companionship and presence of the most Pure among all creatures, and without this excellence, he would not have been worthy of so great a dignity and rare excellence.

Having arrived at their home in Nazareth, where the Princess of Heaven had inherited the possessions and estates of Her blessed parents, they were welcomed and visited by their friends and relatives with the joyful congratulations customary on such occasions. After they had, in a most holy manner, complied with the natural duties of friendship and politeness, and satisfied the worldly obligations connected with the conversation and intercourse of their fellowmen, the two most holy spouses, Joseph and Mary, were left at leisure and to their own counsel in their house.

Custom had introduced the practice among the Hebrews, that for the first few days of their married state, the husband and wife should enter upon a sort of study or trial of each other's habits and temperament, in order that afterwards they might be able to make reciprocal allowance in their conduct, one toward the other.

During this time, Saint Joseph said to his spouse Mary: "My Spouse and Lady, I give thanks to the Lord Most High God for the favor of having designed me as Your husband without my merits, though I judged myself unworthy even of Thy company; but His Majesty, Who can raise up the lowly whenever He wishes, showed this mercy to me, and I desire and hope, relying on

Thy discretion and virtue, that Thou help me to make a proper return in serving Him with an upright heart. Hold me, therefore, as Thy servant, and by the true love which I have for Thee, I beg of Thee to supply my deficiencies in the fulfillment of the domestic duties and other things, which as a worthy husband, I should know how to perform; tell me, Lady, what is Thy pleasure, in order that I may fulfill it?"

The Heavenly Spouse heard these words with an humble heart, and yet also with a serene earnestness, and She answered the saint: "My master, I am fortunate that the Most High, in order to place Me in this state of life, has chosen thee for My husband, and that He has given Me such evident manifestation of His will, that I serve thee; but if thou givest Me leave, I will manifest to thee for this purpose."

The Most High forestalled the sincere and upright heart of Saint Joseph with His grace, and inflamed it anew with Divine Love through the word of the most holy Mary, and he answered Her saying, "Speak, Lady, Thy servant hears."

Mary spoke to Her spouse Saint Joseph, and said to him: "My lord and spouse, it is just that we give praise and glory with all reverence to our God and Creator, who is infinite in goodness and incomprehensible in His judgments. To us, who are so needy, He has manifested His greatness and mercy in choosing us for His service. I acknowledge Myself among all creatures as more beholden and indebted to Him than all others, and more than all of them together; for, meriting less, I have received from His liberal Hand more than they.

"At a tender age, being compelled thereto by the force of this truth, which, with the knowledge of the deceitfulness of visible things, His divine light made known to Me, I consecrated Myself to God by a perpetual vow of chastity in body and soul; His I am, and Him I acknowledge as My Spouse and Lord, with fixed resolve to preserve for Him My chastity. I beseech thee, My master, to help Me in fulfilling this vow, while in all other things I will be thy servant, willing to work for the comfort of thy life as long as Mine shall last. Yield, My spouse, to this resolve, and make a like resolve, in order that, offering ourselves as an acceptable sacrifice to our eternal God, He may receive us in the odor of sweetness and bestow on us the eternal goods for which we hope."

The most chaste spouse, Joseph, full of interior joy at the words of his Heavenly Spouse, answered Her: "My Mistress, in making known to me Thy chaste and welcome sentiments, Thou hast penetrated and dilated my heart. I have not opened my thoughts to Thee before knowing Thy own. I also acknowledge myself under greater obligation to the Lord of Creation than other men; for very early He has called me by His true enlightenment to love Him with an upright heart; and I desire Thee to know, Lady, that at the age of twelve years, I also made a promise to serve the Most High in perpetual chastity.

"On this account I now gladly ratify this vow in order not to impede Thy own; in the presence of His Majesty, I promise to aid Thee, as far as in me lies, in serving Him and loving Him according to Thy full desires. I will be, with the divine grace, Thy most faithful servant and companion, and I pray Thee accept my chaste love and hold me as Thy brother, without ever entertaining any other kind of love, outside the one which Thou owest to God, and after God to me."

In this conversation, the Most High confirmed anew the virtue of chastity in the heart of Saint Joseph, and the pure and holy love due to his most holy Spouse Mary. This love the saint already had in an eminent degree, and the Lady Herself augmented it sweetly, dilating his heart by Her most prudent discourse.

By divine operation, the two most holy and chaste spouses felt an incomparable joy and consolation. The Heavenly Princess, as One Who is the Mistress of all virtues, and Who in all things pursued the highest perfection of all virtues, lovingly corresponded to the desires of Saint Joseph. The Most High also gave Saint Joseph new purity and complete command over his natural inclinations, so that without hinderance of any trace of sensual desires, but with admirable and new grace, he might serve his Spouse Mary, and in Her, execute His will and pleasure.

(by Baij—*Life of*, from pp. 4, 19, 21, 34 & 59)

Even at these earliest stages of his earthly existence, Joseph could not bear to have anyone approach him and bestow caresses so customarily given to little ones. He demonstrated, even at this tender age, how he was to preserve undiminished later on the luster of his purity and innocence. Only his parents were permitted some demonstration of their heartfelt love; but even they were inclined to be very reserved in this regard, since they observed how the infant tended to avoid caresses.

At a most tender age, Joseph had the use of reason. The angel often exhorted him to offer to God the distress he experienced while in the diaper stage. Whenever his mother came to change his diapers, Joseph's eyes closed and his face would flush, thus giving evidence of his distress at being thus exposed.

Joseph, now seven years of age, continued on in this way, and preserved undiminished the luster of his innocence, so much so, that he never caused the slightest displeasure to his parents. All his actions were exceedingly pleasing to God. He had a special love for holy purity, for God had in a wonderful manner, infused into his soul the love for this virtue. His angel recommended it to him, telling him how extremely precious it was to God, so that he was all the more drawn to it, and was determined to preserve it all his life.

In order that he might be better able to accomplish this, he implored God for the necessary graces, and resolved to shun all dangerous occasions, so that the resplendence of this virtue would not be diminished. The success he achieved was largely due to the fact that he made every conceivable effort to maintain a strict guard over his senses, especially his eyes, which he generally kept cast down, except when directed upwards towards Heaven.

One night as Joseph was sleeping, the angel appeared and told him that God was most pleased over the resolution he made to lead a life of perpetual celibacy, and that He promised him His special help and blessing. Then the angel showed him a cincture of incomparable value and beauty and said to him: "God wishes to present to you this cincture as a token of His approval of your decision. As an indication of the grace which He is granting you for the purpose of preserving untarnished the luster of your purity, He has commissioned me to clothe you with it." Thereupon, the angel approached Joseph and girded his loins with the cincture, admonishing him to thank God for the favor and grace granted to him.

As Joseph awoke, he arose immediately, knelt down, and thanked God fervently for this blessing. It developed that Joseph was never to be harassed by temptations against chastity. Although the devil attacked him with various other temptations, he never was able to lay snares for him in this domain, because God did not permit it. Almighty God maintained him in this remarkable state of purity, so that he would be worthy of becoming the guardian of the Queen of Virgins.

He guarded his senses most carefully, especially his eyes, remembering how David and many others had fallen through curious looks which ought to have been avoided. The more that he mortified his senses in order to remain faithful to God, the more grace did he receive from God, and the more intense did his love become for this one and only object of all his love and desires.

When he felt impelled to gaze at something which would delight the eye, but which became an occasion for remorse, considering the likelihood of being drawn into sin, he would quickly raise his eyes towards Heaven and seek contentment in contemplating with the eyes of the spirit the uncreated beauties of God. By means of contemplation of Heavenly things, he gradually lost all enjoyment in creatures; inflamed ever more with the love of God, he experienced all that joy which is to be found in occupying oneself solely with God and seeking one's delight in Him alone.

The demon then devised another scheme for tormenting Joseph. Indeed, this temptation proved to be more painful than the others. The devil implanted into the hearts of various individuals the desire of arranging a marriage for Joseph, all under the guise of affection and concern of his welfare. Certainly, they declared, he would no longer have to suffer living all by himself in his shop and shunned by everyone! He would also be able to live more comfortably!

They persuaded several other individuals of good zeal to enlist in this project of convincing Joseph that he should marry. Since he was such a diligent and industrious person, they said, he ought to have no difficulty in finding a spouse. The saint rebelled at these suggestions, inasmuch, as he had dedicated his virginal life to God by a vow, and with flushed countenance he told them to stop speaking to him of marriage, since he was exceedingly well-satisfied with his present state.

Nevertheless, they did not stop harassing him and even tried to persuade him to marry by flattering him and making him various promises. Joseph was disturbed by this and he prayed that God would help and defend him against these importunate men who, under the pretext of seeking his well-being, wanted to make him lose the precious virtue of virginity. "You know that I have vowed my virginity to You, my God," he said. "Do not permit them to torment me thus." God heard the prayers of His faithful servant, but delayed in giving His help so as to increase Joseph's merit.

These people selected a young woman whom they wished to present to him as a marriage prospect. Seeing, however, that he expressed more and more firmly his opposition, they were at a loss as to how they could get him to succumb to their artful persuasion. One day they agreed upon a plan whereby Joseph would be induced to come with them, under the pretext of having him take measurements for a prospective piece of work; they hoped to use this opportunity to arrange a meeting with the maiden they had picked out for him.

Joseph came to the home to which they brought him. After he had taken the necessary measurements for the item to be constructed, he was preparing to leave when the others drew him aside and pointed out to him the maiden whom they considered as a suitable consort, saying: "Observe, Joseph, this is the young woman we have been trying to offer to you as a bride. Surely, you cannot refuse, for she is adorned with both virtue and graciousness."

At these words, Joseph felt a sharp jab of pain and departed hastily. His reaction not only surprised them, but confounded them as well, and they never disturbed him again. The saint hurried to the Temple, and there amid tears, he implored God to deliver him from this grave tribulation, which seemed to him to be unbearable. God reassured him with the promise that he would no longer be afflicted in this regard. Fully comforted, Joseph wiped away his tears, and gave thanks to Almighty God.

The following night, the angel appeared again to Joseph and confirmed God's promise to him. He also assured him that Almighty God was most pleased with his constancy and firmness in respect to the virginity which he had so solemnly promised Him. Joseph was very much consoled.

(by Binet—*Divine Favors*, from pp. 9 & 94)

There can be no doubt that this great saint was a virgin. Cardinal St. Peter Damian affirms it so positively, that he seems to make it an article of faith. Some learned authors even hold that by a special inspiration of God, he made the vow of virginity. Such is the belief of the great chancellor Gerson, of St. Bernardine of Siena, of Suarez, and of several others. In any case we cannot doubt that he had lived a pure angelical life when he united himself by chaste bonds to the Virgin Mary, his one and only Spouse.

A secret inspiration from Heaven caused both Mary and Joseph to contract this alliance, while adoring in their hearts the impenetrable counsel of the great God.

When the first Joseph (of the Old Testament) drove out of the palace of Pharaoh in a royal chariot, Scripture tells us that the people pressed around as he passed, to contemplate the magnificence of his person, and the beauty of his countenance. Indeed, Joseph appeared to be more like an angel than like a man. Now Saint Bernard establishes a parallel between the two Josephs, which is entirely to the advantage of the second; and this cannot surprise us, because the latter, being appointed to an office infinitely more honorable than that of the former, must consequently possess far superior qualities and virtues.

What virginal modesty appeared in his venerable countenance!...what sweetness in his eyes!...what gravity in his words!...what wisdom and discernment in the manner he governed God's family, composed of only two persons, but whose value outweighed that of all creation!

When it pleases the King of kings to call a man to authority, He imprints on his brow a character of majesty which commands respect and obedience.

To this portrait we shall only add one word, which Mary could not say, but which St. Bernardine has said for Her. Joseph was the living image of his Virgin Spouse; they resembled each other like two pearls. Tell me what was the beauty of Mary, and I shall tell you what was that of Joseph. But we would do great injustice to our glorious Patriarch were we to imagine that his resemblance to his most chaste Spouse were merely outward. "All the glory of the King's Daughter is within." This may also be said of St. Joseph.

That the soul of St. Joseph was adorned with all virtues, is a truth that we would loudly proclaim, even had it not been expressly affirmed by Saint Bernardine of Siena. "I believe," says that great light of the Seraphic Order,[] "that the spouse of Mary, and foster father of Jesus, was endowed with virginity most pure, humility most profound, charity most ardent, contemplation most sublime, and most ardent zeal for the salvation of men, after the example of the most holy Virgin, to Whom the Holy Spirit would not have given him as spouse, had he not been Her faithful likeness."

What renders St. Joseph still more dear to me, is that, as Gerson relates, the Face of Jesus and his face resembled each other perfectly; for grace, which often is pleased to imitate nature, had given the Infant Jesus features which made Him appear the real son of Joseph. But oh!..my God, how much closer was the resemblance between his heart and the Heart of Jesus, since in the one as in the Other was to be found the union of all virtues! Only in Heaven, great saint, shall we see your merits in all their splendor; for as long as you were on earth, your extreme humility kept all your treasures hidden in your heart.

(by Bl. Eymard—*Month of St. Joseph*, from pp. 10 & 64)

Thoughts from Bossuet.—Saint Augustine saw in the marriage of Saint Joseph the sacred contract by which he and Mary gave themselves to each other. In the reality of that marriage, we must admire the triumph of purity. Mary belonged to Joseph, and Joseph to Mary, so much so that their marriage was very real, since they gave themselves to each other. But how could they do this? Behold the triumph of purity. They reciprocally gave their virginity, and over this virginity they gave each other a mutual right. What right? To safeguard the other's virtue.

Yes, Mary and Joseph were the protectors of each other's virginity. Neither could dispose of it, and the entire fidelity of their marriage consisted in guarding their virginity. Behold the promises that unite them, the contract that binds them! By desires of mutual chastity, they preserve their treasure eternally. And it seems to me that I see these two stars coming together, but only by the blending of their rays. Such was that marriage bond. As Saint Augustine says: "It was stronger by reason of the inviolable promises made, and more inviolable because it was more holy."

Thoughts from St. Francis de Sales.—To what degree do you think Joseph possessed virginity, the virtue which makes us like the angels? To have been sent by the Eternal Father as guardian of Mary's virginity, or rather I should say as Her companion, since She needed no one but Herself to guard Her virginity, he must have been remarkable in this virtue.

They had both taken the vow of perpetual virginity, yet God wanted them united in holy marriage. Was it that they might retract their vow or repent of having made it? No, it was that they might strengthen and support each other to perseverance in their holy resolve: that is why they renewed it again for the rest of their lives.

Joseph is nothing else than a mighty rampart about the Blessed Virgin to help Her purity preserve its marvelous integrity in the protecting shadow of holy marriage. He is the incorruptible wood with which the door of the great King must be reinforced, as the Holy Spirit says in the Canticle. In a word, God gave him to Mary as companion of Her purity. For that reason he had to surpass all the saints, and even the angels and the cherubim, in this beautiful virtue of virginity.

(by Chorpenning—*Just Man*, from pp. 204 & 206)

Abdias of Babylon, who was a contemporary of the apostles, writes, in his life of Saints Simon and Jude, that Saint Joseph was a virgin who made a vow of chastity.

One author says that not only was St. Joseph a virgin, but that he was more chaste than the angels in Heaven. This statement seems an exaggeration; however, if closely examined, it is true. If the angels are unable to sin against chastity by thought, word, or deed, so, too, was St. Joseph. Since their nature is incorporeal, the angels are not able to sin against chastity. But the thoughts, words, and deeds of Joseph, who had a mortal body, never even had the whiff of impropriety, and thus he merits the most excellent crown of virginity and chastity. Joseph was chaste by grace; the angels, by nature. Since grace is superior to nature, Joseph's chastity surpasses that of the angels.

(by Griffin—*Saint Joseph & Third*, from pp. 17 & 279)

Although Joseph and Mary were truly married and formed a family together, Joseph "knew Her not until She had borne a Son" (Mt. 1:25).

If one considers the divine plan in all its entirety, without leaving aside the circumstances which are bound up with the mystery of the Incarnation as concretely willed by God, Mary must fulfill at least two conditions to become the Mother of God: She must be a Wife, and She must be a Virgin Wife. The Incarnation of the Word could not be realized without these two dispositions.

Now Saint Joseph had a role to fulfill in the accomplishment of each of these two conditions: he had to consent to become the husband of Mary, and equally, he had to agree to protect and preserve virginity in their marriage. That is why it can be said that Saint Joseph truly cooperated in his own way and in his own position in the coming of the Savior on earth. Indeed, without him, there could be no fulfillment, for according to God's providential design, his consent to the marriage and his willingness to remain virginal with Mary were required for the birth of Jesus.

(by Healy Thompson—*Life*, from pp. 93, 164 & 173)

How, then, it may be asked, did Joseph derive this love of virginity, a state not encouraged by the ancient Law? It can hardly have had other source than a divine impression, produced in his soul by grace, of the excellence of this virtue, joined to a profound humility. For let us consider that St. Joseph must have conceived this design at the time when, the scepter having departed from Juda, his nation had entered into new conditions by being formally placed under the dominion of a foreign king; at a period, therefore, when the promises made by God to his house might be deemed near their accomplishment, and when, possibly, he himself, as being of the house and family of David, might be chosen by God to bear a part in the looked-for redemption of Israel.

Thus, we may perceive how solidly Joseph's virtue must have been based upon humility for him to esteem himself quite unworthy of having any share in an honor which for generations had been so coveted by his people. He resolved to remain chaste in the midst of the world, and thus excluded himself from the road to all human greatness and glory.

111.

Mary and Joseph, in their humility, would hide from profane eyes this Heavenly virtue under the veil of marriage. Nevertheless, they must have known that they would thus incur, in the eyes of the vulgar, the opprobrium of sterility. But what of that? So great was their love and devotion to virginity, that they made no account of the disgrace, as it was thought, of infecundity, and cared not for the reproach it would bring upon them.

Others hastened to contract marriage, at the sacrifice of their virginity, with the hope of having the Messias born of their race, while these two holy spouses, on the contrary, had made a vow of perpetual virginity, reputing themselves unworthy of that honor; and lo! It was they to whom the Messias would be given without loss of their angelic purity. They had hidden it, heedless of what men would think on beholding them childless. But God delivered the humble from the contempt of the proud, and to these virgin spouses divinely conceded a Son, the fairest and the most exalted among the children of men.

"How shall this be done, because I know not man?" These words of Mary are a manifest testimony to Her Own virginity and that of Joseph. St. Augustine draws from them an indisputable argument to prove that both She and Joseph had bound themselves thereto by a perpetual vow.

(by John Paul II—*Guardian*, from p. 24)

According to Jewish custom, marriage took place in two stages: first, the legal, or true marriage was celebrated, and then, only after a certain period of time, the husband brought the wife into his own house. Thus, before he lived with Mary, Joseph was already Her "husband." Mary, however preserved Her deep desire to give Herself exclusively to God. One may well ask how this desire of Mary's could be reconciled with a "wedding." The answer can only come from the saving events as they unfold, from the special action of God Himself.

From the moment of the Annunciation, Mary knew that She was to fulfill Her virginal desire to give Herself exclusively and fully to God, precisely by becoming the Mother of God's Son. Becoming a Mother by the power of the Holy Spirit was the form taken by Her gift of Self: a form which God Himself expected of the Virgin Mary, who was "betrothed" to Joseph. Mary uttered Her fiat. The fact that Mary was "betrothed" to Joseph was part of the very plan of God. This is pointed out by Luke, and especially by Matthew.

The words spoken to Joseph are very significant: "Do not fear to take Mary your Wife, for that which has been conceived in Her is of the Holy Spirit" (Mt 1:20). These words explain the mystery of Joseph's Wife: in Her Motherhood, Mary is a Virgin. In Her, "the Son of the Most High" assumed a human body and became "the Son of Man."

Addressing Joseph through the words of the angel, God speaks to him as the husband of the Virgin of Nazareth. What took place in Her through the power of the Holy Spirit also confirmed in a special way the marriage bond which already existed between Joseph and Mary. God's messenger was clear in what he said to Joseph: "Do not fear to take Mary your Wife into your home." Hence, what had taken place earlier, namely, Joseph's marriage to Mary, happened in accord with God's will and was meant to endure. In Her Divine Motherhood, Mary had to continue to live as "a Virgin, the Wife of Her husband" (cf. Lk 1:27).

In the words of the "annunciation" by night, Joseph not only heard the divine truth concerning his Wife's indescribable vocation, he also heard once again the truth about his own vocation. This "just" man, who, in the spirit of the noblest traditions of the Chosen People, loved the Virgin of Nazareth and was bound to Her by a husband's love, was once again called by God to this love.

"Joseph did as the angel of the Lord commanded him; he took his Wife into his home" (Mt 1:24); what was conceived in Mary was "of the Holy Spirit." From expressions such as these, are we not to suppose that his love as a man was also given new birth by the Holy Spirit? Are we not to think that the love of God, which has been poured forth into the human heart through the Holy Spirit (cf. Rm 5:5), molds every human love to perfection? This love of God also molds—in a completely unique way—the love of husband and wife, deepening with it everything of human worth and beauty, everything that bespeaks an exclusive gift of self, a covenant between persons, and an authentic communion according to the model of the Blessed Trinity.

Joseph...took his Wife; but he knew Her not, until She had borne a Son" (Mt 1:24-25). These words indicate another kind of closeness in marriage. The deep spiritual closeness arising from marital union, and the interpersonal contact between man and woman, have their definitive origin in the Spirit, the Giver of Life (cf. Jn 6:63). Joseph, in obedience to the Spirit, found in the Spirit the source of love, the conjugal love which he experienced as a man. And this love proved to be greater than this "just man" could ever have expected within the limits of his human heart.

In the Liturgy, Mary is celebrated as "united to Joseph, the just man, by a bond of marital and virginal love." There are really two kinds of love here, both of which together represent the mystery of the Church—virgin and spouse—as symbolized in the marriage of Mary and Joseph. "Virginity or celibacy for the sake of the Kingdom of God not only does not contradict the dignity of marriage, but presupposes and confirms it. Marriage and virginity are two ways of expressing and living the one mystery of the Covenant of God with His people," the Covenant which is a communion of love between God and human beings.

Through his complete self-sacrifice, Joseph expressed his generous love for the Mother of God, and gave Her a husband's "gift of self." Even though he decided to draw back, so as not to interfere in the plan of God which was coming to pass in Mary, Joseph obeyed the explicit command of the angel and took Mary into his home, while respecting the fact that She belonged exclusively to God.

On the other hand, it was from his marriage to Mary that Joseph derived his singular dignity and his rights in regard to Jesus. "It is certain that the dignity of the Mother of God is so exalted that nothing could be more sublime; yet, because Mary was united to Joseph by the bond of Marriage, there can be no doubt but that Joseph approached, as no other person ever could, that eminent dignity whereby the Mother of God towers above all creatures.

Since marriage is the highest degree of association and friendship, involving by its very nature a communion of goods, it follows that God, by giving Joseph to the Virgin, did not give him to Her only as a companion for life, a witness of Her virginity and protector of Her honor: He also gave Joseph to Mary in order that he might share, through the marriage pact, in Her own sublime greatness."

(by O'Carroll—*Joseph, Son of David*, from p. 64)

Modern Catholic scholars generally agree that the relationship between the "brothers" and Our Lord was one of cousins. According to Semitic usage, cousins were spoken of as brothers. There is no need to reproduce here the attempts made, on the available evidence, to attribute the "brothers" as children to Alpheus and Cleophas, husbands of the Mary who is mentioned in St. John's Gospel. This Mary was possibly a stepsister of our Lady from Her father's earlier marriage. She first married Alpheus, and after his death Cleophas, brother of Saint Joseph. Cleophas' sons, James and Joseph, were double first-cousins of our Lord.

It is now generally held that the intention and will to live as virgins does not invalidate a marriage. The two are one flesh in their very intention to renounce mutually and voluntarily the exercise of their marriage rights. They enter a heroic way, to which few are called, but they do not thereby cease to be truly married. If ill-health renders exercise of marriage rights altogether impossible, the reality of the marriage persists.

(by O'Carroll—*The King*, from pp. 13, 26, 30 & 37)

A point of resemblance of the two Josephs is the flight into Egypt. The shining virtue of each was chastity. It was exemplified in the first Joseph by his resistance to insidious temptation in the house of Putiphar; it was the singular ornament of the second, for he was espoused and wed to the Queen of Virgins.

The ideal of love was realized between Mary and Joseph through their total acceptance of the primacy of spirit. Their hopes for the future were the same. Conflicts or tension between Mary and Joseph on any fundamental problem of life was impossible.

The first and crucial test of that harmony of spirit was Mary's vow of virginity. We know from Her word to the Archangel Gabriel that Joseph's love had passed the test; for though espoused to him, She still could say, "How shall this be done since I know not man?" The praise of Joseph implicit in these words is high. He had taken Mary, but he had taken Her in God, and God Who had accepted Her vow spoke to Joseph the message that would ensure Mary's protection.

Who can doubt that his resolve to love Mary gave him a communion with Her spirit and that he, like Her, had through the spirit triumphed over the flesh? Spirit answered spirit and as

117.

they mounted high above mere physical need, their flight became completely one.

Their physical nature they had consecrated, and thus their bodily appetites elevated by chastity became, as it were, sacramentals. The tenderness which accompanies love on the physical plane was not a prelude to physical union. It was for them the symbol, the external sign of spirit and of grace. In the expression of this symbolic language, there was peace. They had serenity, for they were established in an order which was guaranteed by God.

Mary was blessed amongst women, for as a Woman, She had the partnership of the most perfect man. The deep satisfaction of soul and body which came from that partnership braced Her for the heroism of the Annunciation.

Since Mary and Joseph undertook to live a virginal life, it has seemed to some that they did not contract a true marriage. Yet we may assert with an eminent theologian, "This marriage is really the most beautiful, the noblest, the holiest and, let us add, in a certain sense the most fruitful, of all the matrimonial unions which have ever existed."

(by O'Rafferty—*Discourses*, from pp. 36 & 45)

If Mary was the first among women to make a vow of virginity, contrary to the custom of Jewish women, who deplored this condition, it is reasonable to believe that Joseph was the first among men to make such a vow. Though many men among the Hebrews—Elias, Eliseus,

Jeremias, and Daniel among them—knew the value of virginity and lived that life, yet they did not bind themselves to it by formal and perpetual vow, as we believe St. Joseph did.

The Gospel calls St. Joseph "a just man," which means that he possessed all the virtues, and this would not be true if he lacked the virtue of chastity. Indeed, it is precisely because he possessed this virtue that he had all the other virtues, which are, as it were, the companions and servants of chastity. Humility, modesty, recollection, contempt of the world, voluntary poverty, abnegation, obedience, mortification, lively faith, firm hope, ardent charity, all wait upon chastity as their mistress. In proclaiming St. Joseph Patron of the Universal Church in 1870, Holy Church concludes Her decree by giving to the saint the beautiful title of: "The Most Chaste Joseph."

While St. Joseph's extraordinary chastity is due chiefly to God's singular grace, yet we must not fail to give credit to the saint for corresponding with this grace. His great chastity was the fruit of continual vigilance on his part, together with his invocation of God's help. St. Joseph continually watched over his mind, his heart, his senses; he was careful to avoid idleness, which is the root of all evil; to avoid worldly pleasures and amusements; to avoid bad company, bad conversations, everything that could be an occasion of sin. And knowing that chastity depends on prayer, he never ceased to implore God's help and God's grace.

(by Patrignani—*Manual*, from pp. 21, 47 & 72)

It is worthy of remark, that the virginity of St. Joseph was considered, at the period in which he lived, as an inconceivable and unheard-of circumstance, since he it was who first made it compatible with the state of marriage. From the union of these two virginal hearts, that super-angelic purity, which constituted the principal merit and glory of Mary and Joseph, received an additional degree of lustre.

Permit me to say it, O ye blessed spirits! Yes, forbid me not to say, that the purity of St. Joseph was far superior to yours. The vision of the angel Gabriel in human form, and the words of his salutation, made the Queen of Heaven fearful (says St. Ambrose). Never did the aspect of Her holy spouse produce this fear—this agitation; She lived and conversed with him in the most perfect confidence. I hesitate not, then, to say, with St. Francis de Sales, that St. Joseph surpassed in purity the most exalted order of spirits, during the 20 or 30 years that he spent in the society of the Mother of God. Could it be otherwise, when so intimately connected with this Virgin Mother, Who was purity itself?

As resemblance is said to produce love, is it, then, surprising that the angels should so highly venerate and esteem one who, though born of Earth, has, by a special privilege of grace, been raised to an equality with them in purity and holiness? Wherefore it was not without a mysterious signification that the angel, in his first apparition to St. Joseph, called upon him by name, "Joseph, Son of David." We see in Holy Writ, that is was not usual with the angels to act thus when announcing the decrees of Heaven to men. "Son of man, stand upon your feet," said the angel to Ezechiel; "Rise quickly," said he to

St. Peter; and to St. John the Evangelist, "Write what you see."

The angels seem to make no account, or else to be unacquainted with the names of these illustrious personages. But how differently do they act with regard to St. Joseph; they call him by his own name, and greet him as a Prince of the royal house of David: "Joseph, Son of David." This magnificent title belonged to him, and was given him by the angels as a mark of distinction justly due to one who, for sanctity alone, stands unrivaled among the children of men.

Again they were proud to claim him as a fellow citizen, even while he yet dwelt in this land of exile; and it might truly be said that St. Joseph, though dwelling corporally upon Earth, was in spirit an inhabitant of Heaven, and enjoyed a foretaste of its inconceivable bliss. This is the sentiment of our Holy Mother the Church, who thus apostrophizes St. Joseph: "Admirable destiny!—even in this life equal to the angels—you participate in their happiness— you enjoy the intimate Presence of God."

St. Francis de Sales assures us, that St. Joseph's purity surpassed that of the angels of the first hierarchy; for, as he says, if the material sun can perfect the dazzling whiteness of the lily in a few days, who can conceive the admirable degree of perfection to which St. Joseph's purity was raised, when it was exposed, not for a few days only, but for the space of 30 years, to the rays of the Sun of Justice and of the Mystical Moon, which derived from that Sun all Her splendor?

Among the panegyrists of St. Joseph, is Mary Herself, his Immaculate Spouse: She has been pleased to dictate Her praises of him to Her servant St. Bridget, who on this occasion, acts as secretary to the Mother of God. I shall here mention only a few of the most remarkable passages:

"Be assured," says She to this saint, "that, previous to our marriage, St. Joseph had been informed by the Holy Spirit of My having consecrated Myself to God by a vow of virginity, and of the angelic purity of My thoughts, affections, and actions; he, therefore, determined ever to consider himself My servant, and to look up to Me as to his Queen and Sovereign.

"By the light of the same Holy Spirit, I foresaw that My Virginity should ever remain pure and stainless, although, by a mysterious dispensation of Providence, I consented to take a spouse. Saint Joseph's astonishment is not to be described, when he saw that I was about to become a Mother; nevertheless, not the shade of any reflection, in the slightest degree derogatory to Me, crossed his mind for a moment; but on the contrary, remembering the prediction that the Son of God was to be born of a Virgin, he deemed himself unworthy to serve the Mother of such a Son. However, as he knew nothing certain as to the matter, and undecided as to what part he ought to take, he judged it might be expedient to leave Me secretly.

"But an angel of the Lord appeared to him in a dream, saying: 'Do not abandon this Virgin, who has been confided to your care; it is by virtue of the Holy Spirit that She has conceived, and She shall soon give birth to the Savior of the world.'

"From that time forward, St. Joseph rendered Me all the homage and respect due to a Queen; nevertheless, I always continued to serve him as his humble and devoted Handmaid. In the performance of the mutual services we rendered each other, I never knew a complaint or an impatient word to escape him. He endured the labors and privations attached to poverty with admirable resignation. In order to supply our necessities, he applied himself unsparingly to the hardest labor, and when reviled or ill-treated, the most angelic meekness was his only revenge.

"Toward Myself, he discharged all the duties of the most devoted spouse; he served Me with the utmost reverence and affection; he was the faithful guardian of My virginity, and the irrefutable witness of the wonders that God wrought in Me. Moreover, Saint Joseph was perfectly dead to the world and the flesh; all his aspirations were after Heavenly things.

"So great was his confidence in the Divine promises, that I frequently heard him exclaim: 'Ah! If anything could make me anxious to prolong my life, it would be my ardent desire to see the great designs of God accomplished!' His only aim was to accomplish this adorable will... and to the conformity of his will to the will of God, must be attributed the greatness of his glory in Heaven."

(by Petrisko—*St. Joseph and the Triumph*, from p. 189)

Fr. Michael O'Carroll (in his book *Joseph, Son of David*) writes that the modern era holds an exaggerated emphasis on sex which makes it difficult for us to understand a marriage in which the dominant element is a spiritual union through love. However, O'Carroll notes that this is a feature of marriage only in a perfect state.

Thus, says O'Carroll, when a man and a woman decide to live together as virgins, and with the grace of God succeed in doing so, they attain perfection in the state to which God called them. We certainly can understand this in looking at the Holy Family, and perhaps see it again to a degree in the early "virginal" marriage of Zelie and Louis Martin (parents of the Little Flower and her four sister nuns) which eventually produced so many spiritually rich blessings through their offspring.

(by Sabat-Rivers—*St. Joseph's Day*, from p. 16)

Joseph's virginal chastity is emphasized; in this respect he is so great that only Christ is worthy of being his Son.

Virginal and silent, he neither charms nor fecundates the wedding bed with offspring nor the air with sweet echoes. The nun refers to what she considers two important virtues in Joseph: virginity and silence.

(by St. Bridget—*Revelations*, from p. 23)

Know most certainly that before he married Me, Joseph knew in the Holy Ghost, that I had vowed My Virginity to My God, and was immaculate in thought, word, and deed, and that he espoused Me with the intention of serving Me, holding Me in the light of a Sovereign Mistress, not a Wife. And I knew most certainly in the Holy Ghost that My perpetual virginity would remain intact although, by a secret dispensation of God, I was married to a husband.

But when I had consented to the Annunciation of God, Joseph, seeing My womb increase by the operation of the Holy Ghost, feared vehemently: not suspecting anything amiss in Me, but remembering the sayings of the prophets, foretelling that the Son of God should be born of a Virgin, deeming himself unworthy to serve such a Mother, until the angel in a dream ordered him not to fear, but to minister unto Me in charity.

(by Valtorta—*Poem, Vol. 1*, from pp. 51, 63, 68, 71 81 & 93)

In the Temple, Mary is praying for the coming of the Messiah. Her hair is a very pale gold color, so light that it seems to be blended with silver. Her face is pensive and mature, although it is the face of a young girl, a beautiful and pure girl, all dressed in white.

She tells Anna of Phanuel: "The secular Law of Israel wants every girl to be a wife, and every wife to be a mother. But while obeying the

Law, I must obey the Voice that whispers to Me: 'I want You.' I am a Virgin and a Virgin I shall remain. How shall I succeed? This sweet invisible Presence that is with Me will help Me, because it is Its desire. I am not afraid. I have no longer My father and mother. Now I have but God. I therefore obey Him unquestioningly. When I think of them, I imagine them in the quiet expectation among the Patriarchs, and I hasten with My sacrifice the coming of the Messiah, to open for them the gates of Heaven.

When the time comes, I will reveal My secret to the spouse, and he will accept it. I shall have God with Me. God will enlighten the heart of the spouse...life will lose the incentives of the senses and become a pure flower with the fragrance of charity.

Later...Joseph is standing in a very humble attitude, near the Priest. There is silence; then the Priest says to Joseph: "Mary wishes to inform you of a vow She made. Please help Her shyness. Be good to Her, Who is so good." Mary enters with Zacharias and Anna of Phanuel. Zacharias goes out escorting the Priest. Anna congratulates Joseph and then she goes out, too. The betrothed are now facing each other. Mary, full of blushes, is standing with Her head bowed. Joseph, who is also red in the face, looks at Her and tries to find the first words to be said. He eventually finds them and a bright smile lights up his eyes.

Afterwards, he says: "As You know, Your house is still intact, but for over three years, the trees and the vines have never been pruned and the land is untilled and hard. But the trees that saw You when You were a little Girl are still there, and if You agree, I will at once take care of them.

"Look, this is the branch of the almond tree near Your house there at Nazareth. It is from Your garden. I was not expecting to be the chosen one, as I am a Nazirite (Hebrew who had taken special vows of abstinence, see Numbers 6), and I have obeyed because it is an order of the Priest, not because I wish to get married. When he says to Her, "I am a Nazirite," Her face becomes bright and She takes courage and says: "Also, I am all of the Lord, Joseph. I do not know whether the High Priest told you..."

"He only told me that You are good and pure, that You wish to inform me of a vow, and that I must be good to You. Speak Mary. Your Joseph wants You to be happy in all Your desires. I do not love You with my body. I love You with my soul, holy Girl given to me by God! Please see in me a father and a brother, in addition to a husband. And open Your heart to me as to a father and rely on me as a brother."

Mary responds, "Since My childhood, I have consecrated Myself to the Lord. I know this is not the custom in Israel. But I heard a Voice requesting My virginity as a sacrifice of love for the coming of the Messiah. Israel has been waiting for Him for such a long time! It is not too much to forgo the joy of being a mother for that!"

Joseph gazes at Her as if he wanted to read Her heart. Then he takes Her tiny hands, which are still holding the branch in blossom which he had given to Her, and says: "I will join my sacrifice to Yours and we shall love the Eternal Father *so much* with our chastity, that He will send His Savior to the world earlier, and will allow us to see His Light shining in the world.

"Come, Mary. Let us go before His House and take an oath that we shall love each other as the angels do. Then I will go to Nazareth to prepare everything, if You wish so. Now let us go and tell the Most High that we bless Him." In Her heart, Mary feels a sense of confidence.

Later, Anna of Phanuel asks Mary: "And what did Joseph say about Your vow? You haven't told me yet." Mary answers: "He made no objection. On the contrary, when I told him the reasons, he said: 'I will join my sacrifice to Yours.'" Anna of Phanuel responds: "He is a holy young man."

At the Annunciation by Angel Gabriel, our Lady asks: "How can this come about, since I do not know man?" Perhaps the Lord God will no longer accept the offer of His Maidservant and does not want Me a Virgin for His love? Saint Gabriel responded: "Not by deed of man You will be a Mother, Mary. You are the *Eternal Virgin*, the Holy Virgin of God. The Holy Spirit will come upon You and the power of the Most High will cover You with its shadow. So the Child born of You will be called Holy and the Son of God."

(Mary says:)

When I came back to the reality of earthly life after the ecstasy that had filled Me with inexpressible joy, My first thought was for Joseph: a thought as sharp as a rose thorn, that pierced My heart enraptured among the roses of Divine Love, Who had become My Spouse only a few moments before.

By this time, I loved My holy and provident guardian. Since the time when, by the will of God manifested to Me by the word of the Priest, I had become married to Joseph, I had the possibility of knowing and appreciating the holiness of that just man. When I became united to him, My dismay at being an orphan disappeared, and I no longer regretted the lost retreat of the Temple. He was as sweet as My deceased father. With him, I felt as safe as with the Priest. All perplexity had disappeared, nay it had been forgotten, so far it was from My Virginal heart. I had, in fact, understood that there was no reason whatsoever for hesitation or fear with regard to Joseph. My virginity entrusted to Joseph was safer than a child in his mother's arms.

(Jesus says:)

You have seen how Joseph, not by human culture, but by supernatural education can read in the Sealed Book of the Immaculate Virgin, and how he borders upon prophetic truths by his "seeing" a superhuman mystery, where others could only see a great virtue. Since he is imbued with this wisdom, which is a breath of the power of God and a definite emanation of the Almighty, he sails with a secure spirit the Sea of this Mystery of Grace, which is Mary.

He penetrates with Her spiritual contacts, in which, rather than the lips, the two spirits speak to each other in the sacred silence of their souls, where God only can hear voices and those who are well-liked by God, because they are His faithful servants and are full of Him.

The wisdom of the just man, which increases by his union and closeness to Mary, Full of Grace, prepares him to penetrate the deepest secrets of God and enables him to protect and defend them from the snares of man and demon. And in the meantime, it invigorates him. It makes the just man a saint, and the saint, the guardian of the Spouse and of the Son of God.

Without removing the Seal of God, he, a chaste man, now elevating his chastity to angelical heroism, can read the Word of Fire written by God on the Virginal Diamond, and he reads what his wisdom does not repeat, but is greater than what Moses read on the stone tablets. And to prevent profane eyes from prying into the mystery, he places himself, seal upon the Seal, as an archangel of fire on the threshold of Paradise, within which the Eternal Father takes His delight, "walking in the cool of the evening" and talking to Her, Who is His Love, Garden of Lilies in bloom, Air scented with perfumes, fresh morning Breeze, lovely Star, Delight of God.

The new Eve is there, in front of him, not bone from his bones, nor flesh from his flesh, but companion of his life, living Ark of God, Whom he receives in guardianship, and Whom he must return to God as pure as he received Her.

"Spouse to God" was written in the Immaculate pages of that Mystical Book. And when, in the hour of trial, suspicion hissed its torture, he suffered *as a man and as a servant of God*, as no man suffered, because of the suspected sacrilege. But this was to be the future trial. Now, in this time of grace, he sees and he puts himself at the most true service of God. Then the storm of the trial will come, as for all saints, to be tested and made coadjutors of God.

What do you read in Leviticus? "Tell Aaron, your brother, that he must not enter the Sanctuary beyond the Veil in front of the Throne of Mercy that is over the Ark whenever he chooses. He may die; for I appear in a cloud on the Throne of Mercy, unless he has done these things first: he will offer a young bull for a sacrifice for sin and a ram for holocaust; he is to wear a linen tunic, and cover his nakedness with a linen girdle."

And Joseph really enters the Sanctuary of God, when, and as far as God wants, beyond the veil that conceals the Ark on which the Spirit of God hovers, and he offers himself and will offer the Lamb, a Holocaust for the sin of the world, and in expiation of such sin. And he does that dressed in linen, and mortifying his virile limbs to abolish their faculty of sensation, which once, at the beginning of time, did triumph, impairing the rights of God on man and which will now be crushed in the Son, in the Mother, and in the putative father, to lead men back to Grace and restore the right of God on man. He does that with his perpetual chastity.

Was Joseph not on Golgatha? Do you think he is not amongst the co-redeemers? I tell you solemnly that he was the first, and, therefore, he is great in the eyes of God. Great for his sacrifice, his patience, his perseverance, his faith. Which faith is greater than this one that believed without seeing the miracles of the Messiah?

Praise be to My putative father, an example to you of what you lack most: purity, faithfulness, and perfect love. Praise be to the magnificent reader of the Sealed Book, imbued with Wisdom to be able to understand the mysteries of Grace and chosen to protect the Salvation of the World from the snares of all enemies.

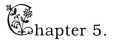

hapter 5.

The Birth of Jesus

(by Agreda—*City (Incarnation)*, from pp. 301, 327, 345, 354, 378, 382, 389, 407, 425, 450, 455, 467, 488 & 516)

The divine pregnancy of the Princess of Heaven had advanced to its fifth month when the most chaste Joseph, Her husband, commenced to notice the condition of the Virgin, for on account of the natural elegance and perfection of Her virginal body, any change could not long remain concealed and would so much the sooner be discovered.

Without doubt, if the saint had believed that his Spouse had any guilt in causing this condition, he would have died of sorrow. The strong and sure bond which truth, reason, and justice had woven about Her fidelity could not be broken. He found no suitable occasion for opening his mind to his Heavenly Spouse, nor did Her serene and Heavenly equanimity seem to invite him to such an explanation.

Later...Saint Joseph awoke, understanding all that Saint Gabriel had told him in the dream, with a full consciousness that his Spouse was the true Mother of God. Full of joy on account of his good fortune and of his inconceivable happiness, and at the same time deeply moved by sudden sorrow for what he had done, he prostrated himself to the earth and with many other humble, reverential, and joyful tokens of his feelings, he performed heroic acts of humiliation and of thanksgiving. He gave thanks to the Lord for having revealed to him this mystery and for having made him the husband of Her, whom God had chosen for His Mother, notwithstanding that he was not worthy to be even Her slave. The remembrance of his experiences was to him a lesson which lasted all his life.

Weeping, he began to show his reverence for his Heavenly Spouse, by setting the rooms in order, scrubbing the floors, which were to be touched by the sacred feet of the most holy Mary. He also performed other chores which he had been accustomed to leave to the Heavenly Lady before he knew Her dignity. He resolved to change entirely his relation toward Her, assume for himself the position of servant and leave to Her the dignity of Mistress. From that day on arose a wonderful contention between the two, which of them should be allowed to show most eagerness to serve and most humility.

A few times, in reward of his holiness and reverence, or for the increase of both, the Infant God manifested Himself to Joseph in a wonderful manner: he saw Him in the womb of His purest Mother, enclosed as it were in the clearest crystal. What blessings did He not shower upon Saint Joseph, to whom He entrusted the true ark and the Lawgiver Himself enshrined in Her!

Joseph said: "Is it possible that in Thy most chaste arms I shall see my God and Redeemer. Would that I possessed the richest palaces for

His entertainment and many treasures to offer Him." And the Sovereign Queen answered: "This great God and Lord does not wish to enter into the world in the pomp of ostentatious riches and royal majesty. He has need of none of these (Ps. 15:2), nor does He come from Heaven for such vanities. He comes to redeem the world and to guide men on the path of eternal life (John 10:10); and this is to be done by means of humility and poverty; in these He wishes to be born, live, and die, in order to destroy in the hearts of men the fetters of covetousness and pride, which keep them from blessedness. On this account He chose our poor and humble house, and desired us not to be rich in apparent, deceitful, and transitory goods, which are but vanity of vanities and affliction of spirit (Eccles 1:24) and which oppress and obscure the understanding."

...After much anxious inquiry, Saint Joseph found an unpretentious little beast. It was privileged not only to bear the Queen of all creation and the blessed Fruit of Her womb, the King of kings and the Lord of lords, but afterwards to be present at His birth (Isaias 1:3); it gave to its Creator the homage denied to Him by men. The journey to Bethlehem, would last five days.

They were accompanied by 10,000 angels. These Heavenly squadrons marched along as their retinue in human forms visible to the Heavenly Lady, more refulgent than so many suns. A few times when their travel extended beyond nightfall, the holy angels spread about such effulgence as not all the lights of heaven in their noontide splendor would have thrown forth in the clearest heavens. This light and vision of the angels also Saint Joseph enjoyed at those times; then all of them together would form celestial choirs, in which they and the two holy travelers alternated in singing wonderful hymns and canticles of praise.

On account of their poverty and timid retirement, they were treated very badly in the taverns and resting places...despised, persecuted, neglected, and cast out by the blind ignorance and pride of the world! In the midst of a cold rain and snow storm, they were obliged to take shelter in the stables of the animals. In many places, they were met with harsh words and insults. Having already applied at more than 50 different places, they found themselves rejected and sent away from them all.

They arrived in Bethlehem at four o'clock, and it was at nine o'clock when the faithful Joseph, full of bitter and heart-rending sorrow, returned to his most prudent Spouse, remembering that outside the city walls there was a cave which served as a shelter for shepherds and their animals. Our Lady said: "Let thy tears of sorrow be turned into tears of joy, and let us lovingly embrace poverty, which is the inestimable and precious treasure of My most Holy Son. Let us go gladly wherever the Lord shall guide us." The holy angels accompanied the Heavenly pair, brilliantly lighting up the way, and when they arrived at the city gate, they saw that the cave was forsaken and unoccupied. Full of Heavenly consolation, they thanked the Lord for this favor.

Our Lady said: "My Son sought destitution and poverty, not because He had any need of them for bringing the practice of virtues to the highest perfection, but in order to teach mortals the shortest and surest way for reaching the heights of divine love and union with God. Let no difficulty or hardship disturb thee, nor deter thee from any virtuous exercise, no matter how hard it may be. Work also for the salvation of souls."

The cave was held in such contempt, that though the town of Bethlehem was full of strangers in want of night-shelter, none would demean or degrade himself so far as to make use of it for a lodging.

Our Lady set about cleaning the cave with Her own hands. Joseph besought Her not to deprive him of this work, although the humble Queen continued to assist him. Then the holy angels, abashed at such eagerness for humiliation, speedily joined in the work, and in the shortest time possible, they had cleansed and set in order that cave, filling it with holy fragrance.

While praying, Joseph went into a blessed ecstasy, and did not return to consciousness until his Heavenly Spouse called him. The birth of Jesus did not cause Our Lady any pain or hardship, but filled Her with incomparable joy and delight. It took place at midnight, on a Sunday, in the year of the creation of the world 5199, which is the date given in the Roman Church, and which date has been manifested to me as the true and certain one.

When Joseph was called by Mary, the first sight of his eyes was the Divine Child in the arms of the Virgin Mother reclining against Her sacred countenance and breast. There Joseph adored Him in profoundest humility and in tears of joy. He would have died of joy, if God had not sustained him.

An ox from the neighboring fields ran up in great haste and, entering the cave, joined the beast of burden brought by the Queen. The animals prostrated themselves before the Child, warming Him with their breath and rendering Him the service refused by men.

His desire to hold the Infant God and his reverential fear of Him, caused in Saint Joseph heroic acts of love, of faith, of humility, and profoundest reverence. Trembling with discreet fear, he fell on his knees to receive Him from the hands of His most holy Mother, while sweetest tears of joy and delight copiously flowed from his eyes at a happiness so extraordinary. The Divine Infant looked at him caressingly and at the same time renewed his inmost soul with such divine efficacy as no words will suffice to explain.

He replaced Him into the arms of His fortunate Mother, both of them being on their knees in receiving and giving Him. Similar reverence the most prudent Mother observed every time She took Him up or relinquished Him, in which also Saint Joseph imitated Her.

The priest asked the parents what name they wished to give to the Child in Circumcision; the great Lady, always attentive to honor Her spouse asked Saint Joseph to mention the name. Saint Joseph turned toward Her in like reverence and gave Her to understand that he thought it proper this sweet name should first flow from Her mouth. Therefore, by divine interference, both Mary and Joseph said, at the same time: "Jesus is His name."

After the Circumcision, the holy spouse suggested to the Mistress of Heaven that they leave their poor and forsaken habitation on account of the insufficient shelter which it afforded the Divine Infant and to Her; for it would now be possible to find a lodging in Bethlehem, where they could remain until after presenting the Child in the Temple of Jerusalem.

While they were thus conferring, the Lord Himself informed them through the two archangels Michael and Gabriel, saying: "Divine Providence has ordained that three kings of the earth, coming from the Orient in search of the King of Heaven, should adore the Divine Word in this very place (Ps. 71:6). From Bethlehem to Jerusalem, there was only a distance of two hours.

The three Magi Kings, who came to find the Divine Infant after His birth, were natives of Persia, Arabia, and Sabba (Ps. 71:10), countries to the east of Palestine. After receiving Heavenly revelations in their sleep, the three Kings awoke at the same hour of the night, and prostrating themselves on the ground and humiliating themselves to the dust, they adored in spirit the immutable being of God.

As the three of them set out and followed the guidance of this miraculous star, they soon met, rejoicing and more inflamed with devotion and with the pious desire of adoring the newborn God. Upon seeing Mary, the light of Heaven shone in Her countenance, and still more visible was this light in the Child, shedding through the cavern effulgent splendor, which made it like a Heaven. They also perceived the multitude of angelic spirits.

After the Magi left, the Holy Family resided in a home of a pious woman, who lived near the cave, till the 40 days of the purification of Mary and the presentation of the Child would be accomplished in Jerusalem, according to the requirements of the law.

When the most holy Mary and glorious Saint Joseph returned from the presentation of the Infant Jesus in the temple, they concluded to stay in Jerusalem for nine days in order to be able, each day, to visit the temple and repeat the offering of the Sacred Victim, their Divine Son, thus rendering fitting thanks for the immense blessing for which they had been singled out from among all men.

On the fifth day of the novena, God, in a vision, said to Our Lady: "Thou canst not finish the nine day's devotion, which Thou hast begun, for I have in store for Thee other exercises of Thy love. In order to save the life of Thy Son and raise Him up, Thou must leave Thy home and Thy country, fly with Him and Thy spouse Joseph into Egypt, where Thou are to remain until I shall ordain otherwise; for Herod is seeking the life of the Child. The journey is long, most laborious, and most fatiguing; do Thou suffer it all for My sake; for I am, and always will be, with Thee.

That same night, while Saint Joseph was asleep, the angel of the Lord appeared to him, and spoke to him as recorded by Saint Matthew, to flee into Egypt.

(by Baij—*Life of Saint Joseph*, from pp. 108, 120, 132, 142, 148, 158, 165 & 183)

On his way to Elizabeth's home to bring Mary back to Nazareth, on one of those traveling days, Joseph was carried off into ecstacy, and it was revealed to him that the Messiah would not only come to live among men, but also that He would be greatly humiliated, and would live among the ordinary, simple, and poor people. Filled with consolation, Joseph murmured: "That means that if He comes in our day, He will not be ashamed to associate with us! How fortunate shall we be to merit such a blessing!" Hopeful now that the Messiah would not disdain to associate with him, Joseph not only sought His coming with greater ardor, but also had greater peace of heart.

Every morning Joseph stationed himself at Mary's door, and there he waited with anticipation to ascertain whether these indications, that She was with Child, were becoming more pronounced. When this proved to be the case, he became so anxious that he actually began to waste away, as if stricken by a disease.

The distressed Joseph finally decided to ask his Spouse the reason of this condition within Her. But he was not able to carry this out, even though he decided to do so many times. Whenever he intended to put the question to Mary, he would be filled with shame, together with a most reverential fear. His tribulation was only increased.

The saint went out to Mary, but he cast his eyes to the ground so that he would not see Her. He wanted only to hear Her speak to him, and She did so with such affection and such graciousness that the afflicted Joseph felt comforted, and his mind was relieved. As soon as he inadvertently raised his eyes and perceived Her evident condition, he was again afflicted with pain.

Joseph eventually decided to present a more stern demeanor towards his Spouse, and at the same time to avoid Her as much as possible. However, he was unable to accomplish this, for whenever he heard Her voice, he felt overpowered by Her love, and consequently, was unable to react otherwise than most cordially. He made many similar resolves, only to find himself incapable of putting them into execution. Though he would feel impelled by passion to take these various courses of action, the divine grace abiding in his soul never allowed him to act towards Her in anything but a befitting manner. Joseph deemed himself to be forsaken by God.

Amid bitter tears, Joseph got up and gathered together what he needed for traveling and made himself a little bundle. He went to bed to take a little rest and to wait for the coming of daybreak. He had already decided to leave in the early morning, when his Spouse would not see him, and also to prevent his neighbors, or anyone else, from noticing his departure. Mary was making ardent supplications to God, asking Him to comfort Her sorrowful Joseph. She, too, was beset with an intense sadness.

In the dream where the angel informed Joseph that Jesus was truly conceived in Mary by the Holy Spirit, the angel also said: "May you appreciate the eminent favor that God has bestowed upon you in thus permitting that the promised Messiah be born of Mary. Consider the worthiness and holiness of your Spouse! Yet you declare you want to leave Her, whereas God has chosen Her to be the Mother of the Incarnate Word!"

The saint could not stay alone for long, and would come full of ardor to the most holy Mother, kneel down before Her and adore his God. On some occasions, the presence of the Incarnate Word within the womb of Mary was clearly manifested to him, whereupon he adored Him and offered himself to Him. The Divine Infant, in turn, would then gaze lovingly upon Joseph. He already sympathized deeply with the suffering Savior, even though He had not even seen the light of day; in this way, he earned for himself the merit of suffering with the Savior, even though he himself was not destined to be alive at the time of the Savior's Passion.

Joseph considered making a cradle for the Infant, and proceeded to apply all his knowledge and skill to making a suitable and comfortable little bed. In the process of doing so, many times he shed tears of joy, moved by the consideration that it was destined to serve the Incarnate God.

Mary Herself was fully aware that Her Divine
Son wished to be born in direst poverty, and to
be deprived of every comfort, even of things that
were necessary. She did not reveal any of this
to Joseph, because the Heavenly Father did not
want Her to do so.

Joseph and Mary decided that She should
come with him to Bethlehem. During the night,
Joseph's angel again appeared to him and told
him that what he had decided upon with his
Spouse was in accordance with the divine will,
and that he should proceed to carry it out. This
message of the angel made Joseph feel completely
satisfied.

In Bethlehem, in the face of the continual
refusals that followed, Joseph eventually began to
realize that they might be totally rejected, and
his heart was rent with anguish. Then God
provided a new initiative for the disconsolate
Joseph by recalling to his mind that there had
been a cave very close to Bethlehem which
served as a shelter for animals.

Joseph promptly decided to go there, in
preference to being forced to remain in the open
streets. Upon entering it, they experienced a
tremendous consolation, just as if they were
entering a sumptuous mansion, and the afflicted
Joseph saw quite clearly that it was God's will
for them to find their shelter here. Joseph went
into a dream-ecstacy, and as Joseph's dream
ended it was midnight, and just then his angel
appeared to him and said: "Joseph, arise quickly
and adore the Savior of the World, Who has just
been born."

Sometimes the Divine Infant would look
smilingly upon Joseph and would permit His
Divine Voice to be perceived within Joseph's
heart, saying to him: "Oh My Joseph, how much

do I love you! How pleased I am to accept your service and your love! After My beloved Mother, I love you most of all." This would cause Joseph to be overcome with love and gratitude, and he would express his own ardent and heartfelt affection.

The one, who was eventually contracted to perform the circumcision, was amazed at the poverty in which he found these holy personages. He was even more astounded at the beauty, majesty, and charm of the Divine Infant and at the rare beauty and reserve of His Mother. Joseph displayed the greatest humility and resignation, even in the midst of this grave poverty.

Joseph was asked what name should be given to the Child. In his humility, Joseph did not wish to make this declaration himself, and so he waited for the Mother of God to make the announcement first. By divine dispensation, it so happened that they pronounced the name of "Jesus" together.

Joseph's angel presently came to reveal to him that three kings from the East were coming to the cave to adore the newly-born Savior and to bring Him precious gifts. Through these monarchs, the whole pagan world would be represented as coming to acknowledge and adore the true God.

Upon leaving Jerusalem after complying with the laws of the Purification of Mary and the Presentation of the Christ Child, Mary and Joseph decided to go back once more to the cave at Bethlehem, to venerate the place of the Savior's birth. They derived much consolation from being there, and experienced manifold effects within their hearts. From there, they then resumed their journey to Nazareth. Shortly after arriving there, the angel spoke to Joseph again commanding him to take the Child and His Mother into Egypt.

It was the thought of what the Divine Infant and Mary would have to suffer that made Joseph feel so distressed. Wherefore, he said to Mary: "Oh my Spouse, who would have thought that after having barely arrived at our home, we should again be forced to endure so great a trial as to find it necessary to set forth anew on another journey, and what is more, at such an inclement season and into a strange land?

Joseph hastily gathered their essential things and made a small bundle. Mary took along diapers for Her Baby Jesus, and some other items that She considered necessary. Being real fugitives, they stole away at night; they increased their pace for Joseph still was very fearful. Joseph did not know exactly what course to take in order to get to Egypt, so he abandoned himself entirely to Divine Providence.

(by Binet—*Divine Favors*, from p. 79)

Origen, St. Bernard, and several other Fathers, are overcome in contemplating the humility of this holy Patriarch. They believe that when he proposed to separate himself from Our Lady, it was because he considered himself unworthy to dwell under the same roof with the Mother of God and Queen of Angels. "Depart from me," said Peter to Jesus Christ, "for I am a sinful man." In the same way, Joseph, penetrated by a sense of his lowliness, said to himself: "How unworthy I am to converse with this chosen Virgin, Whom the Holy Spirit has filled with grace, and adorned with so many virtues!"

Afterwards, when he saw the Infant God submit Himself in all things to his direction and orders, he felt that he could not descend low enough into the abyss of humility, and said to himself the words written later by St. Bernard: "How shall a man not be humble in the presence of a humble God?"

Our Lady revealed to St. Bridget, that Her chaste spouse had constantly in his mouth these words: "Heaven grant that I may live so as to accomplish the Will of my God." He adored the judgments of God in profound silence submitting his will, without any reserve, to the orders of Divine Majesty. When he sought in vain, among the inns of Bethlehem, for a place wherein to shelter his Spouse and the Child She was about to bring into the world, not one complaint issued from his lips, and he felt content in the poor stable.

(*Birgitta of Sweden*, from p. 202)

When I was at the manger of the Lord in Bethlehem, I saw a Virgin, pregnant and most very beautiful. She removed the veil from Her head and Her most beautiful hair—as if of gold—spread out upon Her shoulder blades. With Her there was a very dignified old man—Joseph. He lighted a candle and fixed it in the wall and went outside in order not to be personally present at the birth.

145.

(by Burkey—*Brindisi*, from pp. 129, 266 & 286)

In another sermon, St. Lawrence simply tells us that Mary was living with Joseph already at the time of the Incarnation. Christ willed to be conceived in Galilee but born in Judea, to be conceived in Nazareth but born in Bethlehem, to be conceived in the house of Joseph but born in a stable, to be conceived in the womb of the Virgin and laid in a manger.

Luke mentions six main characters besides Christ and His Precursor, namely Zachary, Elizabeth, Simeon, Anna, Mary, and Joseph, and he indicates that the first four were up in age. When he comes to Mary and Joseph, however, he is silent. Luke's silence is a good indication that he considered Mary and Joseph's age as normal.

While Joseph was not Christ's natural father but rather His putative father with regard to generation, he was much more than a putative father, much more than an adoptive father, and much more than a foster father. He was Christ's father in every way except by generation. He was His true father by affection, by care and solicitude, by education, by authority, by right of marriage, by right of naming Him, and by appointment as such by God Himself. And Joseph was loved, honored, and obeyed by Jesus Christ as His true father.

As one further argument for Joseph's great holiness, Lawrence points out, in his unpublished sermon, that since God gave Joseph the most precious thing He had—His Own Son—why would He not give him also the fullness of His grace? He had given him the greater, why wouldn't He give him the less?

(by Chorpenning—*Just Man*, from pp. 84 & 214)

A just man, such as Joseph, understanding that his Wife was blameless and had not consented to adultery, did not want to vilify Her nor hand Her over to justice, blaming himself instead for having neglected the safekeeping of that innocent dove, ewe, and precious jewel that was entrusted to him, and he wanted to punish himself with the most severe penalty possible, which was to separate himself from his Spouse's sweet, gentle, and holy company. He would feel this separation more acutely than if his soul had been torn from his body. And filled with remorse for this negligence and carelessness, he wanted to go to a desert to live out his days with tears and by doing penance.

In a revelation by our Lady to St. Bridget of Sweden, the Blessed Mother said: "From the moment I gave My consent to God's messenger, then Joseph, seeing that, having conceived by the power of the Holy Spirit, I was pregnant and that I was growing, wondered greatly. Because he would not suspect evil but remembered the words of the prophet who foretold that the Son of God would be born of a Virgin, he reputed himself unworthy to serve such a Mother, until the angel in a dream commanded him not to fear but to minister to Me with charity."

St. John Chrysostom puts it this way: "O inestimable tribute to Mary! Joseph believed in Her chastity more than in Her womb, in grace more than in nature! He plainly saw the conception, and he was incapable of suspecting fornication. He believed that it was more possible for a virgin to conceive and remain a virgin than for Mary to be able to sin."

Mary and Joseph stayed in Zechariah's house for nearly three months.

(by Cirrincione—*St. Joseph, Fatima,* from pp. 10 & 16)

The term "Father" in general means "source of life." In the first of several instructions sent to St. Joseph by God through an angel, we note that he is treated as the real father, for it is he who shall give the Child His name, Jesus. These instructions from Heaven, by which Joseph is guided thereafter, indicate the second of two titles by which Joseph could truly claim to be the "father of Jesus."

The first is that, as the husband of Mary, by Jewish law, after their marriage, whatever belonged to the wife belonged also to the husband. Since Jesus was Mary's Son, therefore, He was also the Son of Joseph.

But the second title is even more convincing, that of Father, because, namely, God willed to share His Own Fatherhood of Jesus with St. Joseph—that St. Joseph was to be His vicar, His representative, the person in whom Jesus was to see reflected in an earthly manner His Heavenly Father. As God united Mary to Himself in a unique and very intimate manner through Her conception of the Child Jesus by the power of the Holy Spirit, so He willed to unite St. Joseph in a unique and very intimate manner in the exercise of his fatherhood of Jesus. If I may say this without disrespect, these relayed messages from God the Father seem in one respect to make God and St. Joseph "Co-Fathers" of Jesus.

The fact that St. Joseph did not beget Jesus by carnal relations with his Wife implies no defect in his fatherhood, any more than Mary's conception of Jesus without carnal relations implies a defect in Her Motherhood. Both Mary and Joseph cooperated with God in attaining the motherhood and fatherhood which God desired of them.

(by Cristiani—*The Father of Jesus*, from pp. 23 & 32)

Because he was "just," Joseph experienced anxiety. To a Jew, the word "just" means one who is a careful observer of the Law. He was anxious to obey the Law.

If the Gospel speaks of the "first-born son," it is because it was the special title used for the first child, even though no other children followed. The word "first-born" stressed the dignity and rights of that child.

A recently uncovered inscription dating from the time of Christ speaks of a mother who "died while bringing her first-born child into the world." This proves the expression was used as we said, and that it by no means contradicts the dogma of Mary's perpetual virginity.

In biblical times, the child's father or, in his absence, the mother, performed the rite of circumcision. At the time of Jesus, however, there was an official agent called the *Mohel* who performed the rite free of charge. The newborn child was given his name as soon as this age-old rite, fixed for the eighth day after birth, was performed.

On the day of the circumcision, it was the father, with the mother's assent, who bestowed the name. Hence, it can be said of Joseph that he fully assumed his role as father. He would be not only a "legal" father, but a father of the heart, a father by the deepest love this word can express.

Usually the mother went alone to the Temple for her ritual "purification" in order to redeem her first-born son, but Joseph accompanied Mary. There was no legal compulsion for him to accompany Her. The ritual for Mary's purification, 40 days after the birth of Jesus, was also called the "Presentation of Jesus in the Temple."

(Dairy of Blessed Sister M. Faustina, from p. 332)

December 25, 1936. (Notebook II, #846) Midnight Mass.—During Mass, God's presence pierced me through and through. A moment before the Elevation, I saw the Mother of God and the Infant Jesus, and the good old man, St. Joseph.

(by De Domenico—*True Devotion*, from pp. 12 & 18)

It should be clear to everyone that one who begets a child has a certain responsibility for him, whereas animals act by instinct and have no moral responsibility. Thus, a moral bond exists between parent and child and this moral bond, which results from our likeness to God, is by its nature far more excellent that the physical bond. Thus, Joseph is the father of Jesus by a moral bond because of his marriage to the Mother of Jesus.

(by Deiss—*Joseph, Mary, Jesus*, from pp. 29 & 99)

The donkey, in Palestine, was part of all journeys. Nowhere in the Gospels is there any word about Joseph's she-donkey. However, it was there throughout his days, his labors, his comings and goings.

We speak of a she-donkey of jenny, rather than simply a donkey. People preferred female donkeys to males because, on the one hand, they gave excellent milk, and on the other, they were more tractable and less stubborn. In the enumeration of Job's riches, only she-donkeys are mentioned (1:3; 42:12).

In Palestine, the jenny was the preferred mount. Its sure-footed negotiating of the rocky paths in the Palestinian hills and its endurance made it the indispensable companion of the Holy Family in all its travels. How else could Mary, then at the end of Her pregnancy, have managed to journey from Nazareth to Bethlehem? As the crow flies, the distance is some 62 miles and travelers must almost double that figure when they use the trails connecting the villages. And how can we imagine the flight into Egypt without the help of a donkey, when close to 200 miles separate Bethlehem from the Egyptian frontier?

151.

(by de la Potterie—*Mary in the Mystery*, from pp. 53 & 64)

From the Greek translation of Holy Scripture, the parallelism jumps out before our eyes. Clearly, Joseph *knew* what had happened to Mary, and that the Child in Her womb came from the Holy Spirit. On a particular aspect of Greek syntax, which has not been made known until this century, the translation is: "Joseph, son of David, do not fear to take Mary, your Spouse, to your home; *for, certainly*, that which has been begotten in Her comes from the Holy Spirit..."

In most translations, quite contrary to ours, the announcement of the angel has precisely as object to *reveal* the virginal conception to Joseph, who then is understood *to have known nothing about it*; thus, for example, in the Jerusalem Bible: "Joseph, son of David, do not be afraid to take Mary home as your wife, *because* She has conceived what is in Her by the Holy Spirit." This is totally different, and we believe less accurate. It results in two different theological views.

The angel said to Joseph: "Do not fear to take Mary home as your Wife..." Why use these words "do not fear" in speaking of two married persons living together? This is the "holy fear" that one experiences before a revelation of God's presence, in a vision or another form of divine intervention (the Transfiguration, the Easter appearances).

For example, in Acts 10:22, the centurion Cornelius is called "a *just* and God fearing man." The just person is one who draws back respectfully before the intervention of God. And by "fear," for the actions of God with regard to his Spouse, Joseph is ready to withdraw with respect, secretly. The "just" Joseph wished to separate himself secretly from Mary, because he knows that God is at work in Her.

St. Bernard said:

"Why did Joseph wish to leave Mary? Listen now, no longer to my opinion, but to that of the Fathers. The reason why Joseph wished to leave Mary is the same for which Peter distances himself from the Lord by saying: '*Depart from me, Lord, for I am a sinner.*' This is also the reason why the centurion left his home while saying: 'Lord, I am not worthy that You should come under my roof.'

"And so, Joseph, considering himself unworthy and a sinner, said to himself that such a great Person, whose marvelous and superior dignity he admired, could not deign to live together with him. He saw, with sacred astonishment, that She bore a special quality of the Divine Presence, and while not being able to understand this mystery, he wished to leave Her.

"Peter dreaded the greatness of the power; the centurion feared the majesty of the presence; Joseph, also, being human, feared the novelty of so great a marvel, the profundity of the mystery; that is why he wished to leave Her secretly. You are astonished that Joseph considers himself unworthy of the company of that holy pregnant Virgin, and you notice that Saint Elizabeth could remain in Her presence only by maintaining a respectful fear. She indeed says: 'Whence is it that God should deem me worthy of this favor that the Mother of my God should come to me?' There is the reason Joseph wanted to leave Her."

(by Emmerich—*Life of Blessed*, from pp. 150, 167, 179, 187, 201 & 205)

Elizabeth only knew the Blessed Virgin by hearsay. Mary saw her from far off and recognized her at once. The neighbors, moved by Mary's marvelous beauty and struck by a supernatural dignity in Her whole being, withdrew shyly as She and Elizabeth met. They greeted each other warmly with outstretched hands, and at that moment I saw a shining brightness in the Blessed Virgin and, as it were, a ray of light passing from Her to Elizabeth, filling the latter with wonderful joy.

Joseph intended to journey with Mary to the Temple in Jerusalem after the days of Her purification, and then to go to Bethlehem and settle there. I do not know for certain what were his reasons, but Joseph did not like being in Nazareth. In an earlier trip to Bethlehem, he therefore looked about him and made inquiries about stones and timber, for he planned to build a house there.

I saw the Holy Family going on their way to Bethlehem and climbing Mount Gilboa. They did not pass though any town; they followed a young she-ass, which always took lonely by-ways. Relations or acquaintances of Joseph's still lived in Bethlehem, but they treated him as a stranger and as a person whom they did not want to know.

I was told much that had happened in the Cave of the Nativity at Shepherd's Valley, of symbolical and prophetical significance in Old Testament times, but can only remember that Seth, the child of promise, was here conceived and born by Eve after a seven-years' penance. Seth was hidden and suckled by his mother in this cave and in nearby Maratha's cave, for his brothers were hostile to him, just as Jacob's sons were to Joseph.

Abraham's nurse, Maratha, took him twice to the cave there to save his life, and it had also been a place of devotion since Abraham's time, particularly for mothers and their babies.

At the hour when the Child Jesus was born, the kings each saw a wonderful vision. The third king, who lived farther away, saw the same picture in his own home in the same hour. The kings were filled with inexpressible joy at this vision, and immediately gathered together their treasures and presents and began their journey. It was only after several days that all three met.

Christ was born when the year of the world 3997 was not yet quite completed. Afterwards, people forgot the period of three years and a portion of a year which intervened between His birth and the year 4000, and then reckoned our new era as beginning four years later, so that Christ was born seven years and a portion of a year earlier than according to our reckoning. Herod died about the time of Christ's sixth year. The flight into Egypt took place when Christ was nine months old, and the Massacre of the Innocents was in His second year.

(by Emmerich—*Life of Jesus*, from pp. 200, 209, 218, 272 & 287)

Joseph and Zachary came out and ate something. Joseph wanted to return at once, but they persuaded him to stay eight days. The Blessed Virgin remained with Elizabeth three months, until after the birth of John, but She returned to her home in Nazareth before his circumcision.

In Nazareth, the angel told Joseph to take Mary with him to Bethlehem, and that, besides the ass upon which Mary was to ride, he was to take with him a little she-ass of one year which had not yet foaled. This little animal they were to let run at large, and then follow the road it would take; when not needed, she did not make her appearance. Most of the roads were very narrow and ran over the mountains.

Near Bethlehem, they went to a large building to register, which was once the paternal home of Joseph, and ages before, it had been the family mansion of David. It was at this period used as the custom house of the Roman taxes.

Joseph still had in the city a brother, who was an innkeeper. He was not his own brother, but a stepbrother. Joseph did not go near him. Joseph had had five brothers, three own-brothers and two stepbrothers. Joseph was 45. He was 30 years older than Mary. He was thin, had a fair complexion, prominent cheekbones tinged with red, a high, open forehead, and a brownish beard.

At different places, he left Mary and the ass standing while he went up and down in search of an inn. Mary often had to wait long before Joseph, anxious and troubled, returned. After a long time, he was shedding tears because he had failed to find an inn. But suddenly he thought of a cave outside Bethlehem used as a storing place by shepherds when they brought their cattle to the city.

As Joseph and Mary entered the cave, the she-ass ran to meet them. She had left them near Joseph's paternal house, and had run around the city to this cave. She frolicked around and leaped gaily about them, so that Mary said: "Behold! It is surely God's will that we should be here."

When Mary told Joseph that Her time was drawing near and that he should now pray, he left Her to enter his little recess, but looking back once toward the part of the cave where Mary knelt upon Her couch in prayer, Her back to him, Her face toward the east, he saw the cave filled with the light that streamed from Mary, for She was entirely enveloped as if by flames. At His birth, the Infant was so bright He dazzled with a glittering and flashing of light. Even inanimate nature seemed stirred, for the stones of the rocky floor and the walls of the cave were glimmering and sparkling, as if instinct with life.

After the birth of the Child, I saw angels around the Mother and Child in human form prostrate on their faces. It may, perhaps, have been an hour after the birth when Mary called Saint Joseph, who still lay prostrate in prayer. When he approached, he fell on his knees, his face to the ground, in a transport of joy, devotion, and humility.

The hair of the Infant Jesus, which was yellow and crisp, ended in very fine rays of light which glistened and sparkled through one another.

Warned in their dreams, when the three kings left Bethlehem, I saw an angel by them pointing the way they should take. The caravan was now much smaller, and the beasts but lightly burdened. Each King rode at about a quarter of an hour's distance from the others. They seemed to have vanished all of a sudden. They met again in a little city, and then rode forward less rapidly than they had done on leaving Bethlehem. I always saw the angel going on before them, and sometimes speaking with them.

There were other caves in the hill under that of the crib, and there Joseph carefully concealed the gifts from the Magi. After the departure of the Kings, the Holy Family went over into the other cave, and I saw the Crib Cave quite empty, the ass alone still standing there.

After the Purification and Presentation in the Temple, I saw the Holy Family returning to Nazareth by a much more direct route than that by which they had gone to Bethlehem. On their first journey, they had shunned the inhabited districts and seldom put up at an inn, but now they took the straight route, which was much shorter.

(by Filas—*Joseph and Jesus*, from pp. 6 & 18)

The group of Apocrypha that center around the birth and Childhood of Christ:

The Protoevangelium of St. James the Less;
The Gospel of Pseudo-St. Matthew;
The Gospel of St. Thomas;
The History of Joseph the Carpenter;
The Gospel of the Nativity of Mary; and
The Arabic Gospel of the Infancy;
(found in Ante-Nicene texts).

From these legends have stemmed the fables of Joseph's life as widower and father of many children; the story of his great age; miracles. The Apocrypha powerfully influenced the concept of St. Joseph in certain centuries and localities. Nonetheless, we assume their unhistoric character as a proved fact.

The Gospels make it clear that Jesus was considered the legitimate Son of Mary and

Joseph. Therefore, one would be prone to conclude that Jesus had been conceived in Mary at a time when genuine marriage rights were considered by the public to belong to His virginal parents.

(by Filas—*Joseph, The Man Closest*, from p. 307)

The Incarnation also required a virginal marriage between St. Joseph and our Lady, and this by a necessity flowing from a twofold source:

a) First, *by the special law of God*, God wished Jesus to be born of a married Virgin for many reasons. Our Lord was not to have a human natural father; His reputation was to be protected as well as the reputation of His Mother; and He was to be received, reared, guarded, and loved within a true family circle specially chosen and fitted for the task.

b) Second, *according to the ordinary law* which God promulgated in nature at the time of creation, all children were to be conceived and born within marriage. It was the divine will that Jesus, too, should be received within the marriage that was to rear Him. He did not exempt Himself from the universal law.

(by Filas—*St. Joseph, After*, from pp. 48, 63, 78 & 82)

We should never let ourselves forget Joseph's conduct when he is in such a quandry about

Mary's pregnancy. Here is the one area where, despite all the relative silence in early Christian centuries, the Fathers of the Church spoke of Joseph in eloquent and resounding superlatives as they described his decision. Joseph withholds hasty judgment of Mary, and conceals in silence the mystery which he cannot fathom.

It is a nobility of character which appears again when Joseph takes Mary into his home as soon as God lets Joseph become a partaker in the secret of the Incarnation. Joseph is now head of the household, going with Mary to Bethlehem and welcoming Jesus at the moment when the couple see their Son, miraculously given to them both, adoring their Son as their Messiah, and at some time or other, beginning to realize that He is more than their Messiah; He is even their God.

In Joseph's case, his acceptance of the Incarnation lay implicitly in his acceptance of the divine will, and of his acceptance of Mary in their marriage with all this acceptance implied. We do not know how explicitly God enlightened Joseph with regard to his role. His subsequent prompt acquiescence to the angel's message (Mt. 1:20-23) indicated what his abiding will had been.

The supposition suggests a darkness of faith whereby God led Joseph from step to step and from action to action without enlightening him about future details. Joseph's holiness then developed from his complete acquiescence in the will of God insofar as he saw it unfold before him. His holiness would stem from a general acceptance of the will of God before he first encountered Mary in his life, and then in merging his own ideals with Hers; his holiness would grow by daily contact with One who was already the holiest of all human creatures.

It would increase by virtue of the trial God sent Joseph, whereby his Wife was miraculously pregnant without his knowledge; yet in his charity he withheld any rash judgment when God tested him in such a way that Joseph could only proceed on blind faith according to the scanty evidence he possessed. His holiness would continue to grow in acts of devotion to Mary, and then to the Divine Child born at Bethlehem.

We surmise that Mary Herself was not fully informed of God's plans (witness the prophecy of the sword of sorrow, as a vague intimation not explained in every detail), so was Joseph kept in ignorance of the exact plan of God. Our supposition is confirmed by the hesitating conduct of Joseph and Mary when the Child was lost in the Temple.

These are all indications of the holiness of Joseph just as they are, in a much higher degree, indications of the holiness of Mary. Joseph's holiness would stem first of all from his closeness to the Mother of God, and later from his closeness to the Son of God, Jesus Christ. We can be sure that for such a role so closely linked with the Divine Savior, God would not have chosen an unworthy character to have been the consort of One as worthy as Mary and divine as Jesus. Joseph had before his eyes the examples of Mary and Jesus.

Further, we must not overlook their grateful prayers for Joseph as husband and father. Jesus, the very source of grace, would see this man with whom He lived every day, wearing himself out in the service of the Lord in an act of self-devotion whose parallel can be found in no other human being, since no other human being was chosen by the providence of God to be the husband of Mary and the father of Jesus.

These are the basic reasons that emphasize Joseph's fatherhood as something existing for no other member of the human race, at the same time demonstrating its full agreement with a true fatherhood by means of spiritual ties. To put the same thought in different words, the tie between child and parent which normally occurs when a father generates his son or daughter, took place miraculously in this special instance of Joseph and Jesus. The tie is there because Jesus belongs to Joseph's family. Jesus was accepted as such from the moment that Joseph first learned of the miraculous conception in Mary and took Mary unto himself in solemnizing the marriage, which had already been a valid espoused marriage.

This was, however, Joseph's explicit acceptance. He had been given his fatherly relationship over Jesus at the moment when Mary pronounced Her fiat. We can discern a parallel to this situation in the case of natural fatherhood. The natural father explicitly accepts his son at the moment he learns of his wife's pregnancy, yet he actually becomes the father at the moment his wife becomes pregnant, a fact of which he is necessarily ignorant, just as she is ignorant of the moment when she becomes a mother and her explicit acceptance must come later with her knowledge.

This fatherhood of Joseph over Jesus has its own surpassing dignity because the Son in question is God Himself. It would be erroneous to think that the dignity of Joseph's fatherhood was less because the fatherhood of Joseph was not physical in the strict sense of the word. The dignity of the relationship (Joseph-father and Jesus-Son) is what particularly ennobles it. It is a true fatherhood because it is a relationship between a human being and the son that had been given to him within the bond of that man's marriage from that man's wife.

In normal parenthood, God bestows a son on the father who brings about the conditions whereby God, in His providence and through His laws of nature, must decide whether or not a son be generated. The fact that God gives Joseph a Son by miraculous conception in Mary does not in any way weaken, soften, or deny the genuinity of the fatherly relationship, on the score of its having been a unique and miraculous occurrence. Otherwise, we would be forced to deny the genuinity of Mary's Motherhood, because it, too, was miraculous—an idea acutely noted by St. Augustine centuries ago.

Granted the analogous nature of this fatherhood, in that it is not natural and physical, would this lessen its dignity? An answer can be given from the case of another analogous fatherhood, God's adoptive fatherhood of the just in the supernatural order. This is not a fatherhood by generation, such as the Fatherhood of God the Father over God the Son, but in dignity the Fatherhood of God respecting the souls of the just surpasses in dignity all other fatherhoods, including that fatherhood of Joseph over Jesus, because now the Father is God Himself. Next in dignity, however, is the fatherhood of Joseph over Jesus.

The patronage of Joseph in the order of grace must have begun with the consent which he gave in faith when he first learned from God's Heavenly messenger of the mystery that had occurred in Mary, and when, as Matthew tells us (1:24), Joseph, rising up from sleep did as the angel commanded and took Her unto himself. Yet, we must always return to Joseph's first dedication to God's will, to carry out whatever God wished of him. This primary consecration of Joseph to the good pleasure of His Creator, to do whatever God wished, whether or not Joseph knew what that office was to be, was the essence of the fiat of Joseph to God.

(by Fitzmyer—*Saint Joseph's Day,* from p. 16)

Joseph took Mary as his wife, "and he knew Her not until She had borne a Son; and he named Him Jesus" (1:25). So Matthew explains that Joseph had no intercourse with Mary in the conception of the Child, Whom he eventually called "Jesus," i.e., he had no sexual relations with Mary before She gave birth to Jesus. That is the sense of the strange way that Matthew has formulated the last verse of this episode: "he knew Her not until She had borne a Son."

In English, when something is denied or negated *until* a certain time, it usually means that after that time it did occur. However, it has been shown many times over that not only in Greek, but also in ancient Aramaic and Hebrew, such a negation has no implication; it says nothing about what happened after the time-limit indicated by "until" was reached. Consequently, the last verse of this episode is merely emphasizing the virginal conception of Jesus. In that Joseph was not involved, even if he did take Mary's Son to himself, legally name Him, and act as a foster-father and guardian to Him.

(by Gasnier—*Joseph the Silent,* from pp. 87 & 133)

Five days would have been needed to cover the distance—about 100 miles—from Nazareth to Bethlehem.

Joseph had no share in the natural conception of Jesus, but with that one exception, his fatherhood embraced all the privileges, all the duties, all the rights of an ordinary father in his home, so that the title that best fits him is that of virgin father of Jesus.

Joseph, reverencing Mary's virginity, prepared the way as it were for the Holy Spirit to make possible Her miraculous fecundity. He respected that virginity, deemed essential by God. Both, by common consent, had offered it to Heaven as an acceptable gift. And both in return had received in equal measure a Son, the fruit as it were, of their virginal union.

To call Jesus "his Son," and to consider Him so, was Joseph's right.

(by Gill—*Saint Joseph, A,* from pp. 51, 64, 71 & 80)

Joseph as a just man, in the first place, could not treat as guilty, One whom he firmly believed to be innocent, but it was equally incumbent on him as a just man to refuse to acknowledge as his, a Child of another.

Joseph undertakes the journey to Bethlehem, and it is he who takes Mary with him, since both affection and duty made it impossible for him to be separated from Her, who had been entrusted to his care and protection. We have to rely on tradition for many details concerning this journey. No doubt, Joseph took with him his carpenter's tools, for it would be necessary for him to find work in order to provide for the needs of Mary and himself, and for the Child about to be born. Their home would have been locked up and put under the charge of some relative.

Tradition, which is supported by evidence, tells us that Our Lady was provided with an ass, and that an ox was also taken with them. This animal, no doubt, was also employed in carrying Joseph's tools and other articles, such as the mats or thin mattresses for sleep, and what would be required for the newly-born Infant.

The journey would occupy about 4 days, so that the nights would be passed at various inns or lodgings. We are accustomed to pictures of Mary seated on the ass, which was led by Joseph. There would be nothing in their outward appearance to suggest that this simple group contained the greatest of God's treasures, and were the most beloved and privileged of the human race.

Our Lady, as other Jewish women, was clothed with a blue dress and red cloak, or red dress and blue cloak, with a large white veil covering the whole body, with shoes or sandals. Joseph wore the long robe of dark color, which served also as covering by night, for one slept in one's clothes, wrapped in the cloak on the mat or mattress referred to above.

In the cave, the solitude and remoteness of such a place was preferable to the crowded khan. Such a shelter may be compared to a court surrounded by cloisters, or separate partitions open towards the center, in one of which a family might be accommodated. The center portion was occupied by the asses and other animals brought by the travellers; no food was provided, but there was a supply of water.

The place must have been crowded by all sorts of people who, no doubt, would have spent the greater part of the night in coming and going, and was a meeting-place for relatives and friends who would have passed the night in loud talk and the usual noisy greetings. It is clear that in such a place, conditions would have been even more distressing than in a grotto. In the stable, there was a least peace and quietness, and a manger for the newly-born Child.

It was, therefore, with a sense of relief that Mary found Herself in this grotto. Joseph would easily have procured plenty of hay or straw, both for the simple couch to which Mary was accustomed, as well as for the animals, which they may have brought with them. There was nothing abnormal in the presence of the ass and ox. In the descriptions of the dwellings of poor people, we read that there was a raised platform on which the family slept on their mats, while the lower portion of the chamber was occupied by the animals.

It is probable that, soon after the birth of Jesus, Joseph succeeded in obtaining a better lodging for Mary and Her Child. The crowds would have dispersed, and there would now "be room for them." In support of this view, is the statement of St. Matthew that when the Magi came to present their gifts, they found Mary with the Child in a "house." It was here that Mary passed the 40 days which were to intervene before She came with Joseph to present and redeem Jesus in the Temple.

The first-born boy of all Jews was at first destined for the sanctuary, but later on, this dignity was reserved exclusively to the tribe of Levi. The first-born sons of other tribes had to be redeemed by a payment which went to the Temple treasury. Jesus, Who belonged to the tribe of Juda, had, therefore, to be redeemed.

Another law prescribed that for the space of 40 days after the birth of a son, the mother was obliged to live in retirement. At the end of that period, the mothers were to present themselves at the Temple or a synagogue to be purified from the legal "impurities" they had contracted by childbirth.

It is probable that this law, like others concerning "uncleanness," had its origin in hygienic reasons, but among the Jews, they had assumed a religious character. It was usual to combine the observation of the redemption of the child with the ceremony of the purification of the mother, and, if possible, in the Temple of Jerusalem itself.

The proximity of Bethlehem, and the desire of Joseph and Mary to carry out the law in all its exactness, naturally induced them to do so at the first opportunity. It is pointed out by the Fathers and theologians that neither Mary nor Jesus could be said to come under this law. Nevertheless, apart from their personal devotion, it is evident that Jesus being "as was supposed" the son of Joseph as well as of Mary, could not, in the eyes of men, be exempt from a minute amount of the external observances so rigidly adhered to by all Jews.

Therefore, Jesus, as belonging to the tribe of Juda, must needs be redeemed, and Mary, His Mother, take part of the ceremony of purification. Thus, "after the days of Her purification according to the Law of Moses were accomplished, they carried Him to Jerusalem to present Him to the Lord."

(by Griffin—*Saint Joseph & Third*, from pp. 20, 52,
70, 73, 86, 91, 299 & 303)

Mary and Joseph had a house in Bethlehem, at least by the time the Magi arrived. Matthew does not say when they occupied the house at Bethlehem, nor how soon after Birth the visit of the Magi occurred, nor even if the house was theirs.

That the *dramatis personae* in the story did not have a knowledge of the divine origin of Mary's Child is the whole point of the angelic revelation to Joseph. The decision to divorce stems from Joseph's ignorance of the paternity; he is not the father, and he can think only that another is. When the angel says to him, "Do not fear to take Mary your Wife to your home, for the Child conceived in Her is of the Holy Spirit," the angel is not telling Joseph something he already knows, but something he needs to know.

To establish paternity, it is not sufficient to ask the wife, because she might lie about the father in order to avoid being accused of adultery. Rather, the husband should give testimony, since most men are reluctant to acknowledge a child unless it is their own. The Mishna Baba Bathra (8:6), written some 200 years after Jesus' birth, is lucidly clear: "If a man says, 'This is my son,' he is to be believed."

If Elizabeth said of the Redeemer's Mother, "Blessed is She who believed," in a certain sense this blessedness can be referred to Joseph as well, since he responded positively to the word of God when it was communicated to him at the decisive moment.

Saint Joseph was called by God to serve the Person and mission of Jesus directly through the exercise of his fatherhood...in having turned his human vocation to domestic love into a superhuman oblation of self, an oblation of his heart and all his abilities into love placed at the service of the Messiah growing up in his house.

In conferring the name, Joseph declares his own legal fatherhood over Jesus, and in speaking the name, he proclaims the Child's mission as Savior.

St. Joseph is much more than an "adoptive" father of Jesus. An adoptive father receives a child born outside of the marriage covenant. Jesus' conception and birth were within the marriage covenant. Thus Joseph was the father of Jesus in every way, except biological.

The profound oneness created by the covenant of marriage includes the complete and total sharing of goods. For marriage is the most intimate of all unions, which from its essence imparts a community of gifts between those that by it are joined together. St. Joseph shared with the Blessed Virgin both Her unique graces and the Supreme Good given to their marriage, namely the Christ Child.

Joseph had the heart of a father bestowed on him by the Eternal Father in the sharing of their common name...Father.

(by Griffin—*Saint Joseph, Theo.*, from p. 11, 15 & 31)

Naming the child was considered, according to the Jewish mentality, as a special prerogative of the father: it was an exercise of paternal authority. And so eight days after His birth, on the occasion of the circumcision, we find Joseph presiding over the ceremony (though in all likelihood he did not perform the circumcision), and as he directed, the Child was called Jesus.

This rite made Christ a member of the chosen people, heir to all the promises that had been foretold by the prophets. At the same time, He also received His legal ancestry, becoming a member of the Davidic dynasty. True, both Mary and Joseph were descendants of the house of David, but it is through Joseph that Christ received the title, Son of David, according to which the Messiah was to be recognized.

We have already seen that Mary and Joseph were married, though not living together, at the time that Christ was conceived. In all probability, Mary did not feel She had a right to inform Joseph of the mysterious event. Yet She was anxious for him to be informed, and knew he would be profoundly disturbed if he learned of Her pregnancy and did not know of its miraculous origin.

This is exactly what came to pass. Joseph learned that his Wife was with Child, and knowing that he himself was not the natural father of the Child, his mind was in a state of agonizing confusion.

Now that Joseph knew of the pregnancy of his Wife, how did he account for this fact? Did he, as a few of the Fathers of the Church held, think that Mary had been raped or that She had committed adultery? Or are we to surmise that Joseph came to the conclusion that Mary had miraculously conceived a Child by the power of God? Some have suggested a third possibility, namely, that Saint Joseph knew this could have happened, and that at first he simply did not know what to do.

The first opinion, that Joseph thought She had been unfaithful, is not acceptable to modern scholars. It is extremely unlikely that Joseph entertained such an opinion. He knew Mary to be the holiest Person he had ever met and he was aware that his young Wife was a Woman of profound spiritual insight and totally committed to the faithful fulfillment of the will of God. Never for an instant could we imagine him questioning Her innocence.

He would, under the circumstances, be much more likely to be sympathetic to the second opinion: that She had miraculously conceived a Child by the power of God. Rather than harbor any suspicion against his Wife, he would have been prepared to accept this possibility on blind faith. Nevertheless, it is not likely that he came to this conclusion. A miraculous virginal conception was unheard of. Such an event would never have entered the mind of man without the aid of a divine revelation.

Thus, by a process of elimination, we come to the third possibility: Saint Joseph was baffled; he just did not know what to think. He was dumfounded.

Since Joseph was convinced of Mary's innocence, he naturally did not believe that he had an obligation of accusing Mary to the authorities, who, in turn, would be obliged to have Her stoned as an adulteress. All his feelings told him that Mary was more truly and fully good than any other person he had ever known. More than anything else, he did not want to be separated from Her.

The heart has its reasons, said Pascal; it has reasons that cannot always be formulated in concepts, as we know from the teachings of the great mystics. And if ever that were true, it was true of the sentiments that Joseph experienced in wanting to take Mary to be his Wife.

The great mystical writers have described the condition of the soul that "feels" that it has been abandoned by God, though it knows full well "by the obscure light of faith" that such is not the case.

In the case of Saint Joseph, it may well have been a mystical struggle that he was experiencing in which his deepest feelings and sentiments told him that he must never give Mary up, whereas reason (in the absence of any clear revelation from on high) made him suspect that he was obliged in conscience (a judgment of the practical intellect that is not *infallible* without a special revelation) to do the thing that he dreaded most— namely, to be forever divorced from Mary.

Surely he prayed for light. And waited. And God responded to his faith: "Behold, an angel of the Lord appeared to him in a dream, saying: 'Do not be afraid, Joseph, son of David, to take to thee Mary thy Wife, for that which is begotten in Her is of the Holy Spirit'" (Mt. 1:20).

We can easily imagine the joy that filled his heart. He determined to celebrate the solemnization of the marriage as soon as possible. As he reflected on the words of the angel, there seemed to be more and more reason for happiness and joy, since the angel's words meant that Mary would be forever his, and it also meant that, in a way that was difficult to put into words, the Child was not completely a Stranger to him, but that It was somehow his Son.

In this account of Matthew we would say, in current English, that there had arisen a first-class misunderstanding between Joseph and Mary,

between husband and Wife. And it is admirable
what manliness Joseph exhibits in striving to
overcome the misunderstanding according to the
light of reason and of faith. Torn between his
conscience, he was prepared to follow the only
light on God's will that he had. He, like Abraham
before him, was prepared to sacrifice what was
dearest to him in all the world...but at the
appropriate time, God intervened (as always) to help
the weakness of His servant.

As Abraham was prepared to sacrifice Isaac,
who was most dear to him, because of the
signified (clearly indicated) will of God, so
Joseph was similarly concerned with responding
to the will of God as he understood that will
during the time of his doubt. This was not a
theoretical question, but a real existential spiritual
trial that Joseph, the "just man," underwent.

Recalling that Joseph was probably only a
teenager at the time, sheds a great deal of light
on the Scriptural mention of his justice. Not only
was he trying to do what was just or fair, but this
effort was prompted by his inner goodness, by
his life-long generous fidelity to the will of God.
Only a man open to the holiness of God would
have struggled with the problem, as did Joseph.
Only such a man could have been tempted to
make the mistake he did, namely, of selling
himself short because he was convinced that it
was the very thing God was demanding of him, an
ordinary teenager—or for that matter, an ordinary
man—would have been tempted to sell God short
rather than himself.

The love that Abraham nourished towards his
God was proven by his willingness to sacrifice
Isaac; and God rewarded him by making him the
"father of many." Abraham's descendent, Joseph,
was rewarded even more amply for the selflessness
and purity of his love. Through the words of the

Angel, he was told that he was to take Mary to be his Wife, and that he would be at least somehow the father of the Redeemer and, thereby, the spiritual father, in a much more profound sense than Abraham, of the people of God here on earth.

Saint Augustine states, "the Holy Spirit gave a Divine Child to both of them."

(by Healy Thompson—*Life and,* from pp. 5, 10, 165, 198, 205, 229, 263, 287 & 296)

By the Hypostatic Union is meant that the Eternal Son of God, in His incarnation, assumed human nature, and united it to Himself in Personal unity; in other words, that in the one Divine Person of Jesus Christ, the two Natures, the Divine Nature and the Human Nature, ever distinct in themselves, become inseparably and eternally united.

Now, Joseph by divine predestination was placed in this sovereign order of the Hypostatic Union. Three only composed it—Jesus, Mary, Joseph. That Joseph should be comprised in this supreme order is not a mere devout opinion or the fruit of pious meditation; it is a sure decision of the soundest theology.

Suarez, that eminent theologian, after having spoken of the order of the Apostles, upon which he said the greatest grace was conferred, goes on to say; "There are other ministries appertaining to the order of the Hypostatic Union, which in its kind is more perfect, as we affirmed of the dignity of the Mother of God, and in this order is constituted the ministry of St. Joseph;

and although it be in the lowest grade of it, nevertheless, in this respect, it surpasses all others, because it exists in a superior order."

To be comprised in the order of the Hypostatic Union implies being, after Jesus and Mary, superior to all the other saints, both of the Old and the New Testament. St. Francis de Sales said, "We may say that the Holy Family was a Trinity on Earth, which in a certain way represented the Heavenly Trinity Itself."

Finally, it follows that Joseph, in that he was comprised in that sublime order, superior to that of all the other saints, must as a natural consequence have been predestined to receive greater gifts and graces than all the other saints, that he might be made worthy to be so near to Jesus and Mary, and fitted to discharge most faithfully those high ministries to which he was elected.

Let us rejoice, then, with our most loving Patriarch that he has been exalted to so sublime an order and has obtained such grace, power, and dignity as none other, after Jesus and Mary, has ever received to the glory of God Who made him so great, and for our profit and that of the whole Church.

The Law of Moses did not leave to a man the choice either of retaining his wife, if guilty of adultery, or even of concealing her crime, if it became known to him. If Joseph, then, did not denounce Mary, and was desirous that no suspicion should be directed to Her, it is manifest that he did not himself suspect Her of infidelity; otherwise how could Joseph, in concealing the sin of his wife be called *just*? The angel did not bid Joseph to discard his suspicions, for Joseph had none, but to abide without fear with the divine Mother as his wife, and assume the legitimate rights and position of a father.

St. Bridget tells us in her *Revelations* how the Blessed Virgin assured her that, when Joseph beheld Her with Child by the operation of the Holy Ghost, he feared exceedingly, suspecting no evil of Her, but, remembering those words of the prophet which foretold how the Son of God would be born of a Virgin, reputed himself unworthy to serve such a Mother, until the angel in sleep bade him not to fear, but to minister to Her with charity. And our Lady added: "From that moment, Joseph never ceased to serve Me as his Sovereign, and I humbled Myself to the lowest offices to show him My submission."

The Imperial decree must have deeply concerned Joseph, not for himself, for nothing which only personally affected him could either grieve or disturb him, but rather through his solicitude for Mary, and the pain he felt at Her having to make this journey of 90 miles in Her present state, and in the depth of winter. We may be certain that the five days they are believed to have spent on the way to Bethlehem were days of privation, fatigue, and discomfort of every kind.

Some have seen in St. Luke's employment of the phrase "entering into the house" a proof that the Holy Family had moved from the cave of the Nativity into a house in the city, but no such inference can be drawn from the use of the word which in Scripture we find indiscriminately applies to all the habitations of living beings. St. Jerome, the surest witness of the sacred traditions, said that we may confidently rest on the Church's tradition that on the sixth of January, this is, 12 days after the birth of the Divine Infant, the Magi adored Him in the stable of Bethlehem where He was born.

It is most probable that Joseph, after the Purification, returned to Bethlehem, and with the purpose of settling there, believing that all the signs which had accompanied the Nativity of the Divine Infant marked it as the place befitting Him and agreeable to the will of God signified thereby. We find later, on the return of the Holy Family from their exile in Egypt, that Joseph was, apparently, not intending to go back to Nazareth, but that, when he arrived on the confines of Judea, and heard that "Archelaus reigned in Judea in the place of Herod, his father, he was afraid to go there." It was to Bethlehem, then, that he had probably contemplated taking Mary and Jesus. If he had been on his road to Galilee, this news would not have alarmed him, neither would he have needed the angel's warning, which caused him to "retire into the quarters of Galilee."

Happy sons, if so indeed it was, to be numbered among the Holy Innocents, instead of growing up to tread, perhaps, in the steps of their father! What was the number of these slaughtered babes we know not. The Greeks and Abyssinians in their liturgy have retained the number of 14,000, but the Holy Roman Church simply says that Herod, enraged, slew many children.

(by Joseph—*Joseph, Son of David,* from p. 1)

The Holy Family did not remain long in the stable at Bethlehem... Within a very short time after the birth of Jesus, St. Joseph found Him a more becoming place to dwell. In this new dwelling occurred, after the passage of eight days, the circumcision of the Child.

(by Keyes—*St. Anne*, from p. 88)

St. Anne was only eight years old when her sister, Hismarian, married, and that Hismarian's baby, Elizabeth, was born shortly thereafter, whereas Anne had been married twenty years before the birth of Mary; and though Elizabeth, after her marriage to Zacharias, lived at Ain Karim, only a few miles from Jerusalem, the fact that Mary was brought up in the Temple would have precluded much visiting on Her part. Probably She did not care to do any, especially as these kinfolk would have been free to visit Her, since Zacharias was a priest "of the course of Abia."

Mary's life was full and complete, and when She left the Temple for Nazareth, She had the companionship of other cousins near Her own age, Joseph among them. But now She was aware of a new kinship with Elizabeth; they were both expecting children under circumstances which were miraculous: Elizabeth because of her great age, Mary because of the Incarnation. They would have much to say to each other, much to learn from each other, because of these great mysteries, which they could share with no one else so well.

(by Levy—*Joseph, the Just Man*, from p. 33)

Why was Jesus conceived of an espoused Virgin, rather than of one that was free? First, that by the genealogy of Joseph, the lineage of Mary might be shown. Secondly, lest She should be stoned by the Jews as an adulteress. Thirdly, that She might have a comforter when fleeing into Egypt. The Martyr Ignatius even added a forth reason why He should have been conceived of an espoused Virgin: that His birth, he says, might be concealed from the devil, since he would suppose that He had been born, not of a Virgin, but of a married Woman.

(by Llamera—*Saint Joseph*, from pp. 53, 86, & 111)

Paternity would not be worthy of esteem, except for the excellence of the moral bond, of which it is the natural principle, just as it is of the physical bond. If the physical bond could exist of itself separate from the moral bond, human paternity would not be above that of the brute animal. On the other hand, if the moral bond could exist without the physical, it alone would suffice for true paternity, because it is more beautiful, more perfect, and more sublime.

The purity of Mary is not only the trust, but also the property of Her virginal spouse. She belongs to him by marriage...O fruitful virginity! If you are the property of Mary, you are also the property of Joseph. Mary has vowed virginity; Joseph guards it; and the two spouses present it to the Eternal Father as a treasure preserved by their common solicitude. If Joseph has so great a share in the saintly virginity of Mary, he also partakes of the fruit which She bears; and this is why Jesus is *his* Son.

It is evident that God put into the breast of St. Joseph a truly fatherly heart, so that he experienced the same love which a natural father has for his son. It was, in fact, a more perfect love.

Father Faber has written: "His love for Jesus was so intense and holy that, shared among all the parents in the world, it would give them more happiness than they themselves could imagine. It is the strongest and holiest paternal love that has ever existed; and even if it could be shared by every father on earth, it would still not be exhausted.

If Mary's marriage with Joseph was a necessary condition, according to the divine decree, for the Incarnation of the Word; if this condition was dependent on the free will of Joseph, and he freely complied, it cannot be denied, nor even doubted, that he has, by this moral cooperation, influenced the realization of the mystery in which the Son of God received human life, and therefore he is truly the father of this Son.

(by Meinardus—*The Holy Family in Egypt,* from p. 6)

If we add the three and a half years residence of the Holy Family in Egypt (according to Coptic tradition) to the date of the death of King Herod (4 B.C.), we arrive at the date of 7 B.C. for the birth of Christ. We discover that the date of the first census was in 7 B.C., the year of the birth of Christ. With regard to the star, W. Keller writes in *The Bible as History*, that according to the calculation of Kepler and Schnabel, this particular phenomenon occurred in the year 7 B.C.

(by O'Carroll—*Joseph, Son of David*, from pp. 54, & 59)

Mary went in haste to a city of Juda. After a journey of about five days, She came to the dwelling of Her cousin. The city of Juda had been identified as Ain Karim, a town between four and a half and five miles southwest of Jerusalem; the strongest tradition marks it as the birthplace of John the Baptist. It fits the description, for the district round about was known as mountain land. There are two churches today deriving from two separate traditions, the Church of the Nativity of St. John, and the Church of the Visitation.

It was believed that Elizabeth had retired from Zachary's home in the town of Ain Karim to a country home or villa in the valley west of the town. This was the scene of the visitation commemorated in the church of that name. Some time after the arrival of Mary, the pair would have returned to Zachary's home, where the Baptist was born.

Mary and Joseph were married two weeks after Her return from Ain Karim. Our Lord was born five months later.

(by O'Carroll—*The King Uncrowned*, from pp. 32, 46 & 58)

When those three months were passed, Mary returned to Nazareth. Some time after came the great crisis in the love of Joseph. He learned that Mary was a Mother. This discovery caused him total bewilderment and perplexity.

What did Joseph think during the period of waiting? We can reject the view put forward by Fouard and others that suspicions wounded his loyalty to his Beloved. We can reject it on psychological grounds of great solidity. If Joseph had wounded thus the delicate plant of their love, he would have shown himself unworthy of Her. It would stamp him as a man of inferior quality. He would appear devoid of the intuition which is nature's sure vehicle from heart to heart. No; this kind of man cannot misunderstand this kind of woman.

Did he think Her the victim of an outrage. That solution, too, is unacceptable, for Mary's first impulse would have been to inform him of such a calamity. Her attitude of silence left him completely without an explanation, although he felt that She was guarding a sacred secret that placed Her in this difficult and unexpected situation.

It would have been an act of grave injustice to God and to the family of which he was the custodian to acknowledge as his Heir One Whom he believed to be the Son of an unknown father. Thus, no matter how much he loved Mary or was convinced of Mary's innocence, he could not as a man of honor acknowledge Her Child as his own.

Bound in deepest union with Her was Her beloved husband. He alone with Her had witnessed all the happenings of these months.

He, too, kept all things, pondering them in his heart.

Jesus Christ was not a stranger for St. Joseph, for He was born of his lawful Wife Whom no other man had rendered fruitful; for this reason the Savior inherited the property of St. Joseph not as an adoptive Son, but by natural law.

Joseph had given his heart to this Woman. Here before him was the Image of Her in masculine form. The attraction which Her immaculate flesh and Her physical integrity has exercised on him, came upon him again in this Child of Her womb, Who as Her's was also the Child of Her lawful husband.

Jesus was His name, and the choice had not lain with His parents. They followed the manifest will of God. The word meant "God helps." Both Mary and Joseph had heard the explanation. To the Mother, Gabriel had said: "And Thou shalt call His name Jesus. He shall be great and shall be called the Son of the Most High. And the Lord God shall give unto Him the Throne of David, His father; and He shall reign in the house of Jacob forever. And of His Kingdom, there shall be no end."

To Joseph the angel had spoken these words: "and thou shalt call His name Jesus; for He shall save His people from their sins."

It is suggested sometimes that Joseph was not present when the visit of the Magi was made to the Infant King. His name is not mentioned. But we have a serious reason for thinking that he was with the Mother and Child. The account of the incident is given by St. Matthew. Now Matthew, it would appear, got the facts for his narrative from a friend of St. Joseph. The omission then would be a characteristic act of modesty on St. Joseph's part.

The symbolism of the gifts of the Magi has been interpreted for us by tradition. It is excellently summarized by a recent writer. "Melchior is the first to present his offering. He brings gold, a heavy ingot of virgin gold, the weight of which is a strain on his aged hands. Gold!...the precious metal for which men slave and die. But Melchior offers gold, not only as a gift valuable in itself, but as a symbol of the royalty of the Holy Child, the King of the Jews. Eastern princes paid tribute to their sovereign in gold. Melchior's gold represents the sovereignty of Christ the King of the human race. Like a prince before a King, Melchior lays his gold before the feet of Jesus.

Casper comes next, the bronze-skinned youth, the son of Shem, the representative of the colored races, and he has a casket of frankincense. Frankincense!...the most costly and sweet-smelling perfume of the aromatic East, a bitter and brittle resin which gives off a fragrance surpassing the scent of the roses of Sharon and the lilies of Carmel. Frankincense was deemed too precious for human use and was reserved for the temples of the gods. Casper offers frankincense to Jesus as God.

Last comes Balthasar, the black. He represents the Negro races which have been enslaved so often by the others. Balthasar is a grave man of middle age. His vase of myrrh is like the story of his people—gorgeous but sad. Myrrh!...the resinous gum used in embalming the bodies of the royal dead! Balthasar acknowledges the humanity of Jesus, that one day He will die. The gifts of the Magi were princely; worthy of the rank and wealth of the donors, and worthy of acceptance by the King of the Jews."

(by O'Rafferty—*Discourses*, from pp. 73 & 86)

Whatever Joseph's sentiments in those circumstances were—whether feelings of suspicion of infidelity, or of humility at being the husband of the Mother of God and the reputed father of the Son of God—we learn from the Gospel that Joseph being a just man, and not wishing to expose Her publicly, was minded to put Mary away privately (Matt. 1:19). In either case, great, indeed, must have been the grief of Joseph's heart in deciding on this extreme measure of Mary's dismissal! To lose Mary forever; never to see Her again in this life; to leave Her secretly without being able to say a word of explanation to Her; this was, indeed, enough to make him die of a broken heart. Joseph would have preferred to die at Mary's feet than to separate himself from Her in this manner. Thus, we see how terrible were the tribulations with which God visited Joseph to try his virtue!

Mary, too, must have undergone great sufferings on that occasion. She must have been aware of Joseph's anxiety, and She must have longed to relieve him by making the secret known to him. But, since the Archangel had not given Her permission to do so, She remained silent, and Her silence only served to aggravate the suffering of both of them. Here we have the two most holy souls that ever lived on earth, tried by God with the most bitter trials.

It is true that Joseph was about to arrive at a drastic decision, but this was due solely to his desire to conform with God's holy will, and to show his absolute trust in God.

We have seen that Joseph and Mary left their home in Nazareth to betake themselves to Bethlehem, a 4 or 5 days' journey on foot.

(by O'Shea—*Mary and,* from pp. 40, 81, 99 & 359)

It can now be proved that Herod died in the year corresponding with 4 B.C. of the Christian era, and our Lord was certainly born before the death of Herod. Hence, at least four years, or probably six, must be added to the present date of the Christian era to determine more correctly the number of the years that have elapsed since the coming on earth of the Son of God.

Saurez says: "It is the common and more probable opinion that the Blessed Virgin, having spent eleven years in the Temple, was entrusted to St. Joseph on entering Her fourteenth year; four months afterwards, the Annunciation took place, and hence, in Her fifteenth year, She brought forth Her Son." This early age was not unusual, for the Jews of the period were warmly in favor of early marriage.

To the Jewish people, disparity in age between husband and wife was sternly reprobated. The rabbis went so far as to apply the prohibition in Lev. 19:29 to the father who gave his daughter in marriage to an old man.

A righteous Israelite was one punctilious in rendering his due to God and his neighbor. If Joseph really was an old man, he would not have dreamt of such a flagrant violation of law and custom as marriage with a young girl.

It was certainly the custom for men to marry at an early age. The age of 18 is recommended in the Talmud. The rabbis said that "up to the age of 20, the Holy One, blessed be He, watches for a man to marry, and curses him if he fails to do so by then." Hence, Isaiah, speaking of the coming of Christ, says, "For the young man shall dwell with the Virgin" (LXII 5), a prophecy applied by Lyra, and the ordinary gloss to this mystery.

The rabbis regarded marriage and the procreation of children as the natural duty of all Israelites, male and female. In fact, any Jew who remained single after he had passed the age of 20 could be compelled to marry by the court. The rabbis went so far as to declare, "He who is not married is, as it were, guilty of bloodshed and deserves death; he causes the Image of God to be diminished and the Divine Presence to withdraw from Israel.

Joseph did not know that Mary had been divinely chosen, but one thing he did know with absolute certainty, and that was that She had not sinned.

Joseph seems to have no doubt of Mary's innocence. Let it not be imagined that this is merely a pious explanation which owes its origin to an increasing veneration of the Mother of Jesus. It is Saint Jerome's own explanation, and none of the Fathers was so versed in the Scriptures as he. "How could Joseph be called just," he asks, "if he concealed his Wife's crime? The truth is that his silence is a witness of Mary's innocence; for Joseph, knowing Her chastity, and at the same time astonished at what had taken place, conceals by his silence the mystery which had not been made known to him.

(by Petrisko—*St. Joseph and*, from pp. 180 & 186)

The love of St. Joseph began to blossom like a flower, and he, in the tradition of his lineage, began to hunger interiorly for the coming of the Messiah. This hunger for the Messiah was given to him as another grace from God, to prepare him for his dual roles as husband of Mary and foster-father of Christ. He also began to long for the day that all souls would welcome, with love and open arms, the fulfillment of the messianic promise, and thus, his prayers became more focused on this longing of his heart.

One thing, however, has emerged to be understood about the man. His very constitution indicated that he would remain at all times loyal to truth. And the one truth that was most evident to him was the impeccable virtues of the Virgin Mary, his beloved Spouse. Thus, the crisis of the pregnancy, and how it came about, was never one of questioning the Virgin Mary's virtues. He knew, scholars say, "that sin was excluded."

(by Poranganel—*St. Joseph—Envoy*, from p. 20)

Mary gave Her consent for Her physical cooperation in giving Her flesh and blood to Christ, the Divine Person, to assume human nature. On the other hand, Joseph's contribution was not physical, but was only moral and legal, in that he gave his free consent to the Divine Person to assume human nature from his Spouse, Mary. Joseph's consent was, therefore, a condition precedent for Christ to assume human nature from Mary, since Her body became the property of Joseph after his marriage with Her. It was also ordained by God that the Hypostatic Union of Christ was to take place in the family unit of Mary and Joseph (Mt. 1:18).

According to Suarez, first Christ was in the Hypostatic order; Mary was second, and Joseph was third in descending order. Since Mary helped Jesus to assume human nature, She was second in rank, and Joseph was third, in that he gave his free consent to Mary, his Spouse, to be the Mother of God for Incarnation. And, he himself consented to nourish and cherish the Child as his own, with affection, care, and education, and thereby contributed his share in the work of Incarnation and Redemption with Jesus and Mary.

(by Sparks—*Dominicans*, from pp. 16, 129, 134 & 161)

Jesus wanted to have Joseph, holy spouse of His Mother, as His provider. Hence, he is correctly called the father of Christ, not from the effect of geniture, but from the task and care of providing.

"Behold the Magi came to Jerusalem from the East." That the Magi came immediately after Christ's birth is indicated by the word "Behold." It signifies that what is narrated took place immediately. The Magi came therefore before the purification of the Virgin Mother of God, for they found Christ in Bethlehem.

"*And entering the house*," that is a more commodious part of the place into which the Virgin Mother of God was received once the census had been completed and the crowd which had come for it had vacated the inn, the Magi "found the Child with Mary, His Mother."

Joseph and Mary did not remain there with the Child beyond the 40 days of purification required by the Mosaic Law. They went at once to Jerusalem "to offer Him to the Lord," and then, sometime afterward, returned to Galilee.

Basil of Seleucia says that God in a way communicated to Adam the glory of all the visible things of creation; though Adam could not be the author of their nature, he was the artificer of their names. Basil has God saying: "Adam, be the artificer of the names of things, even though you cannot be the author of their being. Let us share the glory of the forming of this creation. Let the things of creation acknowledge Me as Lord Who am the artificer of their nature; let them understand you as lord who will give them their names."

Why can we not by an equal right say that the Holy Spirit in a certain way communicated the glory of His work concerning Christ with St. Joseph? The Holy Spirit by His power formed the Body of Christ from the most pure blood of the Virgin Mary. He was the sole artificer of the Body assumed by the Son of God. But He conferred on St. Joseph the imposition of the name: "Let Him be formed by Me, let Him be named by you. Let us share the glory of the forming of this creation."

At the birth of Jesus, Joseph was present, but lost in ecstasy and wonder. He could not sufficiently understand why he was admitted to a hidden mystery of such dignity.

As to the place where the rite of circumcision occurred, Cardinal Gotti wishes to correct the error commonly portrayed by artist's license that Jesus was circumcised in the Temple. This ceremony was usually conducted in private homes, as in the case of John the Baptist. Jesus was only brought to the Temple 40 days after His birth. It is more commonly held that Jesus was circumcised in the same place were He was born, or at least in the inn close to the cave, and that His parents did not leave this place until the day of Purification.

(by St. Bridget—*Revelations*, from p. 23)

When I was at the crib in Bethlehem, I beheld a most beautiful Virgin with Child, in a white mantle and tunic, evidently soon about to be delivered. With Her was a most venerable old man, and they had an ox and an ass. When they entered the cave, the old man tied the ox and the ass to the crib; going out he brought the Virgin a lighted torch, and set it in the wall. Then he again withdrew so as not to be personally present at the birth.

Then the Virgin loosed Her shoes from off Her feet, and laid aside Her white mantle, and took off Her veil from Her head, and laid it beside Her, remaining in Her tunic, Her long hair, as beautiful as gold, falling down Her shoulders. Then She drew out two fine, clean linen cloths, and two of wool, which She had brought to wrap the newborn Child in, and two smaller linen ones to cover and tie His head. These She laid beside Her to use in due time.

When all these things were ready, then the Virgin, kneeling with great reverence, placed Herself in prayer, with Her back to the crib, Her face eastward, raised to Heaven. She stood with uplifted hands, and eyes fixed on Heaven, rapt as it were, in an ecstasy of contemplation, inebriated with the divine sweetness.

And while She thus stood in prayer, I beheld Her Child move in Her womb, and at once in a moment, and in the twinkling of an eye, She brought forth Her Son, from Whom such ineffable light and splendor radiated, that the sun could not be compared to it; nor did the torch which the old man had set, in any manner give light, because that divine splendor had totally annihilated the material splendor of the torch, and so sudden and momentary was that mode of bearing, that I could not perceive or discern how, or in what part She brought forth.

Nevertheless, I immediately beheld that glorious Babe lying naked and most pure on the ground, His flesh most clean from all filth or impurity... I then heard angelic chants of wonderful suavity and great sweetness... When the Virgin perceived that She had been delivered, She immediately bowed Her head, and joining Her hands, adored Her Son with great respect and reverence, saying. "Welcome, My God, and My Lord, and My Son."

Then the Child crying, and, as it were, shivering with cold on the hard floor where He lay, turned a little, and stretched out His limbs, seeking to find a mother's favor and caress. Then His Mother took Him in Her hands and clasped Him to Her Heart, and with Her cheek and breast, warmed Him with great joy and a mother's tender compassion. Then, sitting on the ground, She laid Her Son in Her lap... and began diligently to wrap Him up, at first in linen and then in woolen cloths, and drawing them tight on His little body, bound His legs and arms with fillets tied to the four corners of the outer woolen cloth. And then She wrapped, on Her Son's head, the two small linen cloths, which She had ready for the purpose.

When this was done, the old man entered and prostrating himself on his knees on the ground, he adored Him, weeping for joy. Nor did the Virgin on this occasion lose color or strength, as befalls other women who are delivered, except that Her size was diminished. Then She arose with the Child in Her arms, and both together, that is, She and Joseph, laid Him in the manger, and kneeling, adored Him with immense joy and gladness.

While the Blessed Virgin and Joseph were adoring the Infant in the crib, I beheld the shepherds, and those who tended the flocks, come to see and adore the Child. When they saw Him, they immediately adored Him with great reverence and joy; and afterwards returned, praising and glorifying God for all that they had heard and seen.

The Blessed Virgin Speaks

My daughter, know that I bore My Son as you have seen, praying alone on My knees in the stable. I bore Him with such joy and exultation of mind that I felt no pain or difficulty when He left My body. But I immediately wrapped Him up in clean swaddling clothes which I had previously prepared. When Joseph saw this, he wondered with great joy that I had been delivered without any aid; but as the great multitude of people in Bethlehem was busy with the census, the wonders of God could not be divulged among them. And therefore, know truly, that although men according to human ideas, would assert that My Son was born in the usual way, it is true beyond all

194.

doubt that He was born as I tell them, and thou hast seen.

Daughter, know that when the three royal Magi came into the stable to adore My Son, I knew of their coming by prescience. And when they entered and adored Him, then My Son exulted, and for joy wore a more cheerful countenance. I, too, rejoiced and exulted in wonderful joy of mind, observing their words and actions, retaining them and laying them up in My heart.

(by Stramare—*Saint Joseph,* from pp. 17, 78 & 114)

If Elizabeth said of the Redeemer's Mother, "blessed is She who believed," in a certain sense this blessedness can be referred to Joseph as well, since he responded positively to the word of God when it was communicated to him at the decisive moment.

The son of a woman who is legally his spouse belongs by right to him according to human law, as shown by genealogy; but he belongs to him also according to the divine will, which expressly calls Joseph to share with Him from Whom "all fatherhood in Heaven and on earth takes its name" (Eph 3:15) the title of "father." Such is the vocation of Joseph. No man can boast of a greater honor.

The angel tells both of them to give the name of the Infant, indicating the authority of His parents.

Obviously, Joseph's fatherhood toward Jesus belongs to him by virtue of his marriage to Mary.

Since the institution of marriage has as its juridical effect the legitimization of offspring born from it, there is, under this aspect, no difficulty in considering Jesus as the Son of Joseph, inasmuch as He is born of Joseph's lawful Spouse.

Joseph is called the father of Jesus in the same way that he is understood to be the husband of Mary, without carnal union, but by virtue of the conjugal bond; that is, he is much more intimately united to Him than if He had been adopted from outside the marriage. Joseph's title as father of Jesus cannot be denied him under the pretext that he had not begotten Jesus by physical union, since he would rightly be the father even of a son whom he had not begotten from his Wife, but adopted from outside the marriage.

Joseph's legal fatherhood, then, must not be equated to, or confused with, that of adoption; all the more since Jesus not only was born from his Wife—a circumstance that could hold true even in the case of an adulterous union—but *only* from his Wife, to the absolute exclusion of any infidelity (cf. Mt 1:18).

In developing the theme of offspring as a good of marriage, St. Thomas broadens the concept of fatherhood and extends it from generation to receiving and rearing.

It is thus more and more evident that the marriage of Mary and Joseph was decreed by God for the purpose of the "honorable and fitting" birth of Jesus, a birth that in the mind of God presides over the marriage itself by preordaining it and conditioning it. By reason of the Hypostatic Union, which always must be our point of departure, Jesus is said to be a good of marriage, not entirely as are other children, in so far as He was received in marriage, but not by means of it. The assumption of a human nature requires, nevertheless, the rearing of the child generated, the role of the mutual activity of the husband and wife inasmuch as they are united in marriage.

The reason for this demand is found in human nature. Nature intends in offspring not only being, but perfect being. In fact, nature intends not only the generation of offspring, but its development and its improvement up to the perfect state of man as man, which is the state of perfection. According to the Philosopher, we have, therefore, three things from parents: being, nourishment, and education.

No one can fail to see the perennial validity of these principles, the neglect of which results in the dissolution of the family, as can be easily shown today.

If the neglect on the part of both parents is fatal, no less serious is the damage resulting from the absence of the father figure, since it is acknowledged that the education of offspring devolves on the father. For St. Thomas, it is clear that the rearing of man requires not only the care of the mother, by whom he is nourished, but *even more* the care of the father, who must instruct, defend, and perfect him in both interior and exterior goods.

It is the duty of the father to attend to what regards the perfection of human life. Under Joseph's watchful eye, Jesus grew in size and strength, filled with wisdom (Lk 2:40; cf. 2:52). One must maintain that a father's presence and role are of such importance as to require in Joseph the moral and spiritual resources to match the docility of Jesus, expressed in those graphic words, "He was subject to them."

From the beginning, Joseph accepted, with the obedience of faith, his human fatherhood over Jesus. And thus, following the light of the Holy Spirit, Who gives Himself to human beings through faith, he certainly came to discover ever more fully the indescribable gift that was his fatherhood.

These reflections do not exhaust the theme of the fatherhood of St. Joseph, but they are nevertheless sufficient to make us understand how the intervention of the Holy Spirit in the conception of Jesus did not exclude the role of Joseph or empty him of his fatherhood.

One must instead hold that the fatherhood of St. Joseph, while not deriving from generation, is not an apparent or merely substitute fatherhood. Rather, it is one that fully shares in authentic human fatherhood and the mission of father in the family.

The title of father, which the Holy Spirit Himself attributes in Sacred Scripture to St. Joseph, launches its truth in directions that call for serious consideration, especially today when the foundation of generation is being threatened by genetic engineering. This truth clearly demonstrates how inadequate is a purely biological fatherhood to satisfy all the demands of perfection relating to a truly human fatherhood.

(by Suarez—*Joseph of*, from pp. 47, 90, 101 & 166)

The authors of the notes of the Jerusalem Bible pose the question in this way. "The justice of Joseph undoubtedly consists in his not wishing to conceal with his name, a Child whose father he did not know. But being convinced of Mary's virtue, neither does he refer to the rigorous process of the law (Deut 22:20 *et seq*) this mystery which he does not understand." For its part, Spadafora's Dictionary says: "As he was a just man, while not harboring the slightest suspicion against his Wife's integrity, he wished, in the face of the incomprehensible, to conceal the mystery and to eclipse himself personally."

The circumcision ceremony took place not in the synagogue but in the house where the child lived with his parents. The minister of circumcision was a practitioner or surgeon, skilled at his task, and responsible for performing it. He did so in the father's name. Witnesses and a sponsor were needed. It followed a specific rite in which the father was briefly involved. The minister of the circumcision would say: "Blessed is God our Lord, Who blessed us with His precepts and commanded this circumcision." The father of the child would then reply: "He blessed us with His precepts and commanded us to introduce the child to the covenant of Abraham, our father."

After the circumcision, the naming took place. As both ceremonies took place at home, relatives were usually present. It is unlikely that there was a big celebration in Jesus' case for, if they had relatives in Bethlehem, Mary would hardly have had to give birth in a stable. As there are no facts available, it is easy to understand that there is no agreement on whether the circumcision took place were Jesus was born, and where for the moment Mary and Joseph took refuge, or in another house in Bethlehem to which they may have moved. St. Epiphanus is inclined to favor the former.

At the imposition of the name, the father, as head of the family, had an important function. It was he who gave the name as he had authority in the family. He would say who, in his eyes, the new member of the chosen people was to be, for every name signified something. But in this case there is some doubt, for Saint Luke says that it was not Joseph, as head of the family, who gave the name of Jesus. Instead, "*they gave*" Him the name Jesus, the name the angel had given Him before His conception.

"**They** gave." Who did? The reference is necessarily to Joseph and Mary, for no other person had anything to do with it. In the revelation of God's plan for Our Lady at the Annunciation, the archangel had said "and You will give birth to a Son Whom You shall name Jesus. Both father and Mother then had been given the task of naming the Child. It was not to be a name they chose, nor any name tailored to their tastes and preferences, but precisely the one the angel had revealed. It was a name which revealed Who the Child really was and what all this would mean for the chosen people— *Jesus*, that is to say, *Savior*. He had to save men; He was to be the cause of their salvation.

According to general opinion, relatives and friends were not at the ceremony, as it took place a long distance away from Nazareth where they normally lived.

Later, Fr. Isadore Isolanis, in the first half of the 16th century, would write *The Greatest of the Gifts of Saint Joseph*. Commenting on the "gift of the imposition of the most holy name of Jesus," he reasons thus: as it was the custom for the father who had the authority to give his son a name, it follows that God the Father names His Son at His incarnation. This name was revealed to Mary by the archangel Gabriel, and by an angel to Joseph.

On presenting the name, Joseph "revealed a divine secret to the world, taking the place of the Heavenly Father."

St. Isadore ends by quoting a Commentary of St. Luke: "It was not fitting for such a glorious name to be first uttered by just any man, but by the most excellent being, so that no man would feel he was its author. For the same reason it was fitting that he who would impose the name would be more excellent than the rest." With this, one realizes how God sees the worth of Joseph.

Just as the Presentation concerned the Son, so did the Purification affect the Mother. When a woman gave birth to a son, she remained for the seven days following the birth in need of ritual purification under the Law. On the eighth day, the child was circumcised. "And after that she must wait for 33 days more...touching nothing that is hallowed, and never entering the sanctuary until the time is up" (Lev. 12:1 *et seq*). When this period was over, she had to be "purified" through the offering of "a lamb of one year old as a burnt sacrifice, and a young pigeon or a turtle dove by way of amends."

If the family were too poor and could not afford to offer a lamb, then another turtledove or pigeon could take its place. One of these was to be offered as a burnt sacrifice, and one by way of amends. Now at the priest's intercession, she would be "purified." The mother's presence at the ceremony was not indispensable; the husband, or even a third person, could offer the sacrifice.

When, as in the case of Mary and Joseph, the couple were living near Jerusalem (Bethlehem was some five miles or so distant), pious Jews would go up to the Holy Place in order to fulfill the Law.

Regarding the fatherhood of St. Joseph, when Mary and Joseph found Jesus in the Temple and His Mother asked Him: "Son, why have You treated us so?" and went on further to justify that question by speaking of the suffering His disappearance had caused them, She referred to Joseph as "father": "Behold, Your father and I have been looking for You anxiously" (Luke 2:48). St. Luke himself speaks of the time when Simeon "inspired by the Spirit, came into the temple... when the parents brought in the Child Jesus" (Luke 2:28); "and His father and Mother marvelled at what was said about Him" (Luke 2:33); "His parents went to Jerusalem every year at the feast of the Passover..." (Luke 2:41); when His parents saw Him there..." (Luke 2:48). Notice that he makes no attempt to give a precise definition of Joseph's relationship—no adjectives like "legal," "foster," "supposed," to draw the line. And really, once Mary's virginal conception by the work of the Holy Spirit has been clearly established, there is no need to go on pointing it out every time Joseph is mentioned in relation to Jesus.

But there is another reason. Joseph was, to all intents and purposes, Jesus' father. If the Register of Births had existed in those days, Joseph would have been listed as the father. The particular organization and customs of the Jews were such—and this was clearly more than the work of human minds—that the legal father was the one who passed on to his children all of their rights. Merely biological fatherhood, then, is not the only sort there is. Our Lady acknowledged this when She spoke to Jesus of "Your father and I."

(*The Glories of Saint Joseph*, from p. 89)

The reason Joseph wanted to separate from Mary is the one invoked by St. Peter himself to avoid the Lord: *"Depart from me, for I am a sinful man, O Lord"*; and by the centurion to keep Him from his house: *"Lord, I am not worthy that Thou shouldst enter under my roof."* So it was with St. Joseph, too. Feeling himself to be unworthy and sinful, he thought: "She is so perfect and so great that I do not deserve that She should share Her intimacy with me any longer; Her astonishing dignity surpasses me and frightens me."

He saw with sacred fear that She carried the clear marks of a Divine Presence. As he could not fathom the mystery, he preferred to leave Her. Fear struck Peter at the greatness of the Lord's power; fear seized the Centurion at the majesty of His Presence; fear seized St. Joseph quite naturally, as it would any man, at the uncanniness of the extraordinary miracle, at the depth of the mystery, and that is why he wanted to separate from Her privately.

In order not to be reduced to telling lies, or to laying an innocent one open to blame, it was quite right of St. Joseph, the just man, to separate from Our Lady in secret (St. Bernard).

(by Toschi—*Joseph in the New*, from pp. 74 & 77)

Circumcision and naming of a child took place on the eighth day after birth, as prescribed for the sign of the covenant made with Abraham. The purification of the mother took place on the 40th day after giving birth.

(by Valtorta—*Poem*, from pp. 93, 116, 125, 136, 168)

But, now, how could I tell him that I was a Mother? I endeavored to find suitable words to give him the news. A difficult task, as I did not want to boast of God's gift, and on the other hand, there was no way of justifying My maternity without saying: "The Lord had loved Me amongst all women and has made Me, His servant, His Bride." Neither did I wish to deceive him by concealing My condition from him.

And while I was praying, the Spirit of Whom I was full, said to Me: "Be silent. Entrust Me with the task of justifying You with Your spouse." When? How? I did not ask. I had always relied upon God, and I had always allowed Myself to be led by Him exactly as a flower is led away by running water. The Eternal Father had never abandoned Me without His help. His hand had always supported, protected, and guided Me so far. It would do so also now.

O my daughter, how beautiful and comforting is faith in our Eternal Good God! He holds us in His arms as in a cradle; like a boat He steers us into the bright harbor of Goodness; He warms our hearts, comforts and nourishes us; He bestows rest and happiness, light, and guidance on us. Reliance in God is everything, and God grants everything to those who trust in Him; He gives Himself.

At the circumcision of John the Baptist, Mary had made sure that everything is beautiful and in good order for the many guests. I see them bring back John, who is screaming at the top of his voice. Not even his mother's breast can calm him down. He is kicking like a little colt. Then Mary takes him, lulls him, and he becomes quiet, and lies down peacefully.

Zacharias, who is now enlightened privately, said to holy Virgin Mary: "You are blessed, because You obtained grace for the world and You are now bringing the Savior to it. Forgive Your servant if he did not see Your Majesty before."

Mary goes with them to the Temple for the Presentation of John. The stately ceremony is over, and the priests are now joyfully paying compliments to the mother and her child. The only one who is hardly noticed, nay, is avoided almost with disgust when they become aware of Her condition, is Mary. Joseph, who has been away from Mary for four months, comes to pick Her up to take Her back home.

Our Lady speaks: "Had Joseph not been so holy, he would have acted in a human way, denouncing Me as an adulteress so that I should be stoned, and the Son of My sin should perish with Me. If he had been less holy, God would not have granted him His light as guidance in his trial. But Joseph was holy. His pure spirit lived in God. His charity was ardent and strong. And out of charity, he saved your Savior for you, both when he refrained from accusing Me to the elders, and when he saved Jesus in Egypt, leaving everything with prompt obedience.

"The three days of Joseph's passion were short in number, but deep in intensity. And they were tremendous also for Me, those days of My first passion, because I was aware of his suffering which I could not alleviate. In fact I had to obey God's command, Who had said to Me: 'Be Silent.' If I had not been humble in the most perfect manner, I would not have deserved to conceive the Expected One, Who is coming to pay for the sin of pride that ruined man. And then, I obeyed. God had requested such obedience. I am the Handmaid of the Lord, and servants do not discuss the orders they receive. They fulfill them, even if they cause bitter tears.

Joseph said: "We shall have to make haste. I will come here... We will complete the wedding... Next week. Is that all right?"

Going to Bethlehem, Mary rides on a little grey donkey. Joseph is utterly disheartened finding no shelter for them. An old man shouts: "Down there, at the end, under those ruins, there is a den. Perhaps there is nobody in it yet." Inside, there was only a docile ox.

At the birth of the Child, a light is given off more and more intensely from Mary's body. It is now unbearable to the eye, and the Virgin disappears in so much light, as if She had been absorbed by an incandescent curtain... and the Mother emerges. The walls, the soil, everything looks like a crystal lit up by a white light. The holes are precious cups from which perfumes and scents are to arise.

Joseph, who was enraptured in prayer, is called by Mary to venerate, see, and hold the beautiful Babe. Mary says: "Come, let us offer Jesus to the Father."

Zacharias advises them to remain in Bethlehem. The Holy Family now reside in a small house in Bethlehem made available to them by a kind woman. It is here that the Magi pay their visit. Joseph is happy for the gifts, not for himself, but because he thinks that with them he will be able to make his Spouse's and the sweet Child's lives more comfortable. There is no greed in Joseph. He is a workman and will continue to work. But he is anxious that They, his two Loves, should be comfortable.

Neither he nor the Magi know that those gifts serve for a flight and a life in exile, when riches vanish like clouds scattered by winds, as well as for their return to their country, where they have lost everything, customers and household furnishings, and where only the walls of their house have been saved, which were protected by God, because there He was united to the Virgin and became Flesh.

Joseph is humble, in fact, although he is the guardian of God and of the Mother of God and Spouse of the Most High, he holds the stirrups of these Vassals of God. He is a poor carpenter, because sustained human pressures have deprived David's heirs of their royal wealth. But he is always the offspring of a king, and has the manners of a king. Also of him it must be said: "He was humble, because he was really great."

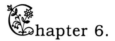hapter 6.

Flight Into Egypt

(Agreda, *City (Incarnation)*, from pp. 522, 529, 539, 542, 559, 575 & 601)

Gathering their poor clothing into the casket and loading it on the beast of burden which they had brought from Nazareth, they departed shortly after midnight, and hastened without delay on their journey to Egypt.

I will here add what I have been made to understand as to the concordance of the two Gospels of Saint Matthew and Saint Luke in regard to this event. For, since all of them wrote under guidance and light of the Holy Ghost, each of them knew what the other three had written, and what they had omitted to say in their Gospels. Hence it happened that according to divine predisposition, some of the happenings of the life of Christ and of the Gospel were described by all four of the Evangelists, while again some other things mentioned by one were omitted by the others.

Saint Matthew describes the adoration of the Kings and the flight into Egypt, while these events were not mentioned by Saint Luke. He again describes the Circumcision, Presentation, and Purification, which are omitted by Saint Matthew. Thus Saint Matthew, after referring to the departure of the Magi, immediately, without speaking of the Presentation, relates that the angel appeared to Saint Joseph commanding him to fly into Egypt; but it does not follow therefrom that the Child had not been presented before that time in the Temple, for it is certain that this was done after the departure of the Kings and before the flight into Egypt, as is narrated by Saint Luke.

This flight took place immediately after the Presentation, before most holy Mary and Joseph returned to Nazareth.

Neither must we wonder that God should consent to the death of the innocent children which Herod murdered; for it would not have been to their benefit to save them through a miracle, since by their death they were to gain eternal life, together with an abundant reward, which vastly recompensed them for the loss of their temporal life. If they had been allowed to escape the sword and die a natural death, all would eventually not have been saved.

The love that Mary and Joseph had for the Infant Jesus would naturally excite in them anxiety and suffering on an occasion like this. On passing the city gate, the Heavenly Mother longed to visit again the place of the Nativity, which was so nearby, but an angel discouraged Her saying: "Herod has commanded that You be sought after very carefully, and consequently a most diligent search is being made to find You. On this account the Most High has commanded You to fly at night and with so much haste." She therefore reverenced from afar the sacred place of the birth of Her Only-begotten.

During all this journey of 60 leagues through the desert, they had no other night-shelter than the sky and open air; moreover, it was in the time of winter, for this journey took place in the month of February, only six days after the Purification. In order to furnish them with some kind of shelter against the open air, however narrow and humble it might be, Saint Joseph formed a sort of tent for the Divine Word and most holy Mary by means of his cloak and some sticks.

On one of the first days of their journey, they partook of no sustenance until nine o'clock at night, not having any more even of the coarse and poor food which until then had sustained them in their hardships and labor. In order that the clamors of the sweetest Mother might proceed from yet greater tribulation, the Most High permitted the elements to afflict them more than at other times...and in addition to the sufferings caused by their fatigue, destitution, and hunger. For there arose a storm of wind and rain, which harassed and blinded them by its fury. This hardship grieved still more the tender-hearted and loving Mother on account of the delicate Child, which was not yet 50 days old.

Although She tried to cover and protect Him as much as possible, yet She could not prevent Him from feeling this inclemency of the weather, so that He shed tears and shivered from the cold in the same manner as other children are wont to do. Then the anxious Mother, making use of Her power as Queen and Mistress of creatures, commanded the elements not to afflict their Creator, but to afford Him shelter and refreshment, and wreak their vengeance upon Her alone.

The angels immediately constructed a resplendent and beautiful globe round about and over their incarnate God, His Mother, and Her spouse, and brought them delicious bread, well-seasoned fruits, and a most delicious drink.

When they lived in an inhabited area, they no longer were served with the miraculous assistance of the angels, and Saint Joseph begged for alms, upon which they sustained themselves during the first three days of their arrival in Heliopolis, the present Cairo in Egypt. In view of their great poverty, and of the great difficulty of sufficient employment as a carpenter, the great Lady resolved to assist Saint Joseph by the work of Her hands to earn a livelihood. As all that she attended to or busied Herself with was so perfect, the reputation of Her skill soon spread about, so that She never was in want of employment whereby to eke out the slender means of livelihood.

When the Holy Family could not be found by the soldiers, the command of Herod to kill the innocents was issued six months after the birth of the Savior.

The Child Jesus reached the end of His seventh year while in Egypt, whereafter the Holy Family returned to Nazareth.

(*Ante-Nicene*, from p. 389)

He retired into Egypt, and remained there the space of one whole year, until the hatred of Herod passed away.

211.

(by Baij—*Life of*, from pp. 176, 179, 183, 186
192 & 237)

Though all the prescribed activities in the Temple were now completed, Mary, Joseph, and their Son, nevertheless, stayed in Jerusalem for a short time. They made return visits to the Temple to pray in order to determine whether it was the divine will for them to return to Bethlehem, or instead to choose as their future abode their own homestead in Nazareth. They ascertained that they should betake themselves to Nazareth. This directive was also made quite clear to Joseph by his angel one night as he slept, so the holy couple once again made ready to depart.

Mary already knew that before long they would have to leave their home in Nazareth and flee into a strange land, and that in doing so, She and Her dear Joseph would have to suffer a great deal. Mary always tended to keep the divine secrets hidden, hence, the lack of a clearer explanation to Joseph. She waited for God Himself to reveal the facts to him, either through direct inspiration, or through the angel who spoke so often to him.

Then, during the night, the angel commanded Joseph to take the Child and His Mother into Egypt, there to remain until he received instructions to return. Mary reminded Joseph: "Our Savior has come into this world to suffer and not to rest. It is a great blessing to be permitted to partake of His sufferings, and we, therefore, should praise and thank Him for it."

The travelers suffered a great deal from hunger and thirst. They frequently had nothing to eat for days. Herbs were to be found only rarely on these plains. However, due to the operations of their loving God, those herbs that they did find seemed to be a most satisfactory food. Occasionally, they also would obtain water to drink in some ravine. The holy wanderers submitted to all this most generously—yes, even with a jubilant heart—because the mere thought that they had their Jesus with them made everything more easily acceptable.

It happened a number of times that they arrived at some villages during the evening hours. Ever since they crossed the border into Egypt, they decided to seek shelter in such instances, rather than spend the night out in the open. Joseph had much to endure on these occasions, due to the insolence and rudeness of those who had lodgings available for rental. The innkeepers would first regard with interest and admiration the beauty, the modesty, and the amiability of the Mother of God, and then they would turn upon Joseph and impute to him a total lack of consideration and common sense for taking his delicate Spouse through this territory at such an unseemly time of the year. They also reproached him with being a vagabond, and treated him with derision and rudeness. The saint simply remained silent, and made no excuses for himself. He suffered it all with great patience, offering it all up to God out of love.

The devil, who had been so determined to persecute Joseph and his Spouse, had planned to molest the holy pilgrims as they neared the city. He had already been gloating over the success that he expected from his attacks, only to find himself suddenly disconcerted and completely dismayed by the power which he felt being exerted over him, and as the idols toppled to the ground, he was compelled to take to flight. He gnashed his teeth in violent rage, and he was subsequently, able to stir up many persons against the Holy Family, but he did not succeed in doing Them a great deal of harm. The people simply could not believe that these poor, humble, and retiring individuals were to blame for the collapsing of their idols.

Joseph rejoiced at the falling of those idols when the Divine Infant entered into the city. It gave him hope that in time this unbelieving nation also would adore the true God. Mary judiciously confirmed him in this conviction when he mentioned it to Her, and they gave thanks to God together.

Unable to find a place to live, Joseph turned to God and implored Him for aid in his dire necessity. "Oh my God," he prayed, "it has happened that I found no shelter even among relatives and believers. What then can I expect from barbarians and unbelievers? I need Your assistance, oh Lord."

God heeded Joseph's petitions and ordained that a certain man should meet them who would be so touched by the tenderness and the rare beauty of the Mother of God, that in sympathy for Her, he would offer to find them a place to live. This man found a little house in an outlying section of the city where they could live more peacefully.

Since the whole city was still in an uproar over the destruction of the idols, the Holy Family remained in seclusion, and Joseph did not even venture to leave the house the first night in order to beg for some food. The next morning Joseph summoned up enough courage to go into the city begging for food. Though

he had to live in the midst of a pagan people,
Joseph found a charity which he had not
encountered among his own relatives...but still
they lived in extreme poverty here in this
strange land.

All in all, their sojourn in Egypt had lasted
six years—the seventh year had just about
begun. Joseph did everything with a satisfaction
and joy that found expression in his shining
eyes and his whole demeanor. They rejoiced
together over their departure and were of one
mind in giving praise to the Heavenly Father.
Joseph would glance over to Mary, and then
over to Jesus, and adjusted his pace to Theirs.
The atmosphere was pleasant and clear that
day, and it seemed as if all creation was, in its
own way, celebrating the occasion.

(by Binet—*Divine Favors*, from p. 82)

After the departure of the three kings, he is
to fly to a distant country where he knows no
one, where the demon is adored, where he will,
perhaps, have to remain for years. How many
objections would have presented themselves to a
less submissive spirit, but neither one of them
presented themselves to the mind of Joseph,
or he rejected them all; for the truly obedient
man has hands for the work, and feet for motion;
but he has no tongue wherewith to oppose the
decrees of God and of obedience.

215.

(by Emmerich—*Life of Blessed*, from pp. 295, 304, 313, 315, 320, 325, 342 & 345)

The day they started on the flight was what is now February 29. I saw the Holy Family in the Holy Land after they had crossed some of the ridges of the Mount of Olives, going in the direction of Hebron beyond Bethlehem. They went into a large cave, about a mile from the wood of Mambre, in a wild mountain gorge. I think that this was the sixth halting-place on their journey. I saw the Holy Family arriving here very exhausted and distressed. Everything they needed was lacking, and in their flight they kept to by-ways and avoided towns and public inns.

They had been ten days in the Jewish country and ten days in the Egyptian desert territory. In one place, by a large idol surrounded by a circle of stones like benches or tables, the people came there in crowds from the city to lay their offerings on them. Not far from this idol was a great tree under which the Holy Family sat down to rest. They rested there for only a short time, when there came an earthquake, and the large idol swayed and fell to the ground. There was an uproar among the people, and a crowd of canal-workers ran up from near at hand. Another quake uprooted the tree till nothing but its roots showed above ground. The gaping space where the idol had stood became full of dark and dirty water, in which the whole idol disappeared except for its horns. Some of the more evil among the raging mob were swallowed up into this dark pool. Meanwhile, the Holy Family hurriedly left the area and went quietly into the city.

The massacre took place a year later than the flight. The number killed was shown to me, but I have no clear recollection of it. I think that it was 717.

After staying in Heliopolis for a year and a half, until Jesus was about two years old, the Holy Family left the city because of lack of work and various persecutions. They moved southwards in the direction of Memphis and came to a place called Matarea. Joseph found much work here in strengthening the houses with wattles and building galleries on them. Here, too, when they arrived, an idol fell down in a small temple, and afterwards all the idols fell.

They had a very hard time in Matarea. There was great shortage of good water and wood. The inhabitants cooked with dry grass or reeds. The Holy Family generally had cold food to eat. Joseph was given a great deal of work in improving the huts, but the people there treated him just like a slave, giving him only what they liked. The Holy Family lived here for several years.

At last, I saw the Holy Family leaving Egypt. Though Herod had been dead for some time, they were not yet able to return, for there was still danger. Their sojourn in Egypt became increasingly difficult for Saint Joseph. The people there practiced an abominable idolatry, sacrificing deformed children, and even thinking it an act of special piety to offer healthy ones to be sacrificed. Besides this, they practiced obscene rites in secret. Even the Jews in their settlement had become infected by these horrors. Joseph, on the other hand, had arranged everything admirably in the school at Matarea, and others had accompanied him and had attached themselves to this Jewish community. The return from Egypt happened in September. Jesus was nearly eight years old.

217.

(by Emmerich—*Life of Jesus, Vol. 1*, from pp. 290, 292, 304 & 315)

When Herod saw that the Kings did not return, he thought they had failed to find Jesus, and the whole affair seemed to be dying out. But after Mary's return to Nazareth, Herod heard of Simeon's and Anna's prophecies at the Presentation of the Child in the Temple, and his fears were reawakened. I saw that he sent troops to various places around Jerusalem, from which the mothers were to be summoned to the Holy City. He caused their numbers to be everywhere ascertained. The soldiers remained about nine months in those places, and the murder of the little ones began when John was about two years old.

It was not yet midnight when the Holy Family left the house for Egypt. The Child Jesus was twelve weeks old. Of their ten days journey in Herod's Judean country before reaching Egypt, the Holy Family on their flight met only three rather unsafe inns at which to spend the night. At other times, they rested during their tiresome wanderings in valleys and caves and the most out-of-the-way places.

In Egypt, they learned of the slaughter of the innocents from an angel, and the Child Jesus, Who was now able to walk, being a year and a half old, shed tears the whole day.

They left Egypt when Jesus was seven years old. Mary was often very much distressed, because walking through the hot sand was so painful for the Boy Jesus. Joseph had made for Him, out of bark, shoes that reached above the ankle where they were firmly fastened. I saw the holy travelers frequently pausing while Mary shook the sand out of the Child's shoes. She Herself wore only sandals.

(by Bl. Eymard—*Month of St. Joseph*, from p. 66)

Although Saint Joseph did not make the vow of obedience as he did that of chastity, he is nevertheless an accomplished model of this virtue. His position in the Holy Family obliged him to command, but besides being the foster-father of Jesus, he was also Jesus' disciple. For thirty years he watched the God-Man display a simple and prompt obedience, and he grew to love and practice it very perfectly himself.

He never inquired where the orders came from, or who gave them...not even why; without exception he submitted to God, to the civil rulers, and to the voice of conscience.

When God sends an angel to charge him with the care of Mary, in spite of the mystery which surrounds Her maternity and troubles his humility, he obeys; when he is told to flee into Egypt under painful circumstances, well calculated to fill him with worry and anxiety, he obeys without the slightest word of objection. On his return, he has no idea where to go; naturally he heads for Bethlehem, since the Child had been born there and God had not revealed otherwise.

Not until he has reached the very gates of Judea does God advise him in a dream to return to Nazareth. Surely God could have warned him in advance, but it pleases Him to see these sacrifices accepted out of obedience. In every situation, Joseph's obedience is as simple as his faith, as humble as his heart, as prompt as his love; it neglects nothing; it is universal.

He fulfills all his duties: duty before all—such is his rule of conduct. If necessary, he would have sacrificed the happiness of being with Mary; actually he did sacrifice the rest and quiet of Nazareth, at the call of duty.

To the civil rulers and to everyone who had authority over him, he was obedient; their orders he looked upon as being the orders of God, because he knew that they took God's place in the government of society. He obeyed all the laws without privilege or exemption, for he wanted to fulfill all justice.

Such ought to be our obedience, if we are to share in the merits of Christ's Eucharistic obedience. It should be our special virtue as servants. We ought to glory in observing the law without privilege like our Master and like Saint Joseph, our model. It should be our greatest desire and our supreme happiness.

Thoughts from St. Francis de Sales.— When the angel ordered Joseph to take the Mother and Child and flee into Egypt until he should tell him to return, he was sparing in his words, treating Joseph like a true religious. "Go and do not come back until I tell you." We learn from the conciseness and simplicity of their converse how we must embark on the sea of Divine Providence without food, without rudder or sail, in a word, without any provisions, leaving the success of our affairs to the Lord, without a worry or a fear for the future.

Poor Saint Joseph could well have objected, "Must I leave immediately? If I am to take the Mother and Child, tell me, if you can, how I will find food for Them on the journey? For you know full well that we have no money." But he says nothing; he confides entirely in God's foresight to help him obtain their meager sustenance, either from his trade or from the alms they will receive. Certainly the first religious were remarkable for their confidence in God to provide for their needs; they left all care of themselves in the Hands of Divine Providence.

But I think it is no less necessary to leave in the Hands of Divine Providence the care of our spiritual life and of our perfection; for it is nothing else than our excessive solicitude for ourselves that makes us lose our peace of mind and puts us into strange and changeable moods. When we commit a fault, however small it may be, we think everything is lost; is it any wonder that we fail at times? But I am so often troubled with dryness that I feel that I am not close to God, Who is so full of consolations. We must, then, like Saint Joseph, be calm in our trials and leave it to our Lord to free us from them, when it pleases Him to do so.

(by Chorpenning—*Just Man*, from pp. 55 & 216)

The Holy Family remained in exile in Egypt for seven years.

Let us consider now the anxiety and fright that Joseph suffered at the time when King Herod was looking for the Child to kill Him. Joseph was so unprepared for this news that, according to the Armenians, he fled the city as soon as he could with his Wife and left Her hidden in a cave. Then he went back to the city to look for some provisions and things for the journey, and he was an eyewitness to the slaughter of the Holy Innocents.

Afterwards, St. Joseph returned from the city with a few things for such a long journey, filled with fear and fright, and with this anxiety, the Holy Family began its flight from King Herod. And since Joseph was afraid that they would be overtaken, he became uneasy when he saw soldiers on the road, fearful that they would tear the Child from Mary's arms, as he had seen them do to others in the city.

In order to go to Egypt, they traveled through the desert and through towns. In the desert, they had to be on the watch for tigers, lions, snakes, beasts, wild animals, and robbers. The towns were inhabited by Gentiles, who were archenemies of the Israelites; since Joseph did not carry a halbred (weapon) nor were troops close by to guard the King, he could not be sure of anything.

In Egypt, Joseph had neither relative nor friend, house nor vineyards, nor any other human means to support his family than the work of his hands. The Holy Family must have felt especially the pain of being deprived of the Temple and its feasts, ceremonies, and sacrifices. In our own age, this is what is most painful for those who find themselves living outside Catholic countries.

(by Cristiani—*The Father of Jesus*, from p. 44)

The 40 league journey to Egypt took four or five days.

Dionysius Exiguus, the scholarly monk who, in the beginning of the sixth century, calculated the starting point of the Christian era, lacked the tools in our possession today for making this calculation. He set the year 1 of the new era to correspond with the year 753 after the founding of Rome (A.U.C.). It is known that Herod died in the year 449 A.U.C. Hence, there is a discrepancy of at least four years, and perhaps five or six, in the establishment of the era. If we agree that Christ was born on December 25 in the year 5 before our era, the flight into Egypt should have occurred in the beginning of the year 4 when Jesus was between two and two and a half months old.

A month later, a little before Easter of the year 4, Herod died a wretched death. It is possible that the Holy Family lived in Egypt only a short while—a few months at most.

(by Gasnier—*Joseph the Silent*, from p. 115)

Egypt was the nearest foreign country—its frontiers could be reached in four or five days. To reach the central cities, six days more of travel were needed.

The Apocrypha have it that when the Holy Family arrived in Egypt, the idols fell from their pedestals and were broken to bits. "Behold the Lord...will enter into Egypt, and the idols of Egypt shall be moved at His Presence" (Isa. 19:1).

What is certain is that in Egypt the Holy Family experienced isolation, loneliness, and all the ills that followed from the circumstances in which they found themselves.

But the little family did not reveal the true cause of their exile. As an extra precaution, they took care not even to pronounce the name of their ancestral village. They in no way regretted being in need. Jesus, at His birth, had given them an example. They knew it was of His free choice He had been born in a neglected stable. They found comfort in remembering that the life of poverty and privation He shared with them was according to His will, and they in turn were happy to prolong for themselves the mystery of Bethlehem.

(by Healy Thompson—*Life And*, from pp. 300, 305 & 323)

The Holy Family cannot have traversed the desert in less than 15 days, and that, too, amidst continual perils of wild beasts and robbers, and all the sufferings of exposure and privation incidental to traveling through so desolate a region.

The Gallican Martyrology says that St. Aphrodisius made a house available to the Holy Family for seven years.

Memphis and even Hermopolis and Alexandria are said by some writers to have been the abode of the Holy Family, as well as old Cairo, situated between Memphis and Matarieh. At this place, the spot to which they are believed to have retired, is now enclosed within the Monastery of St. Sergius. They may have made a sojourn in these various places, but the many religious memories which have clung to Matarieh, and which cannot be recognized elsewhere, seem to confirm that most reliable tradition which we possess on this subject. In Matarieh, there still exists a sycamore of enormous girth where the Holy Family is said to have rested.

It would appear from history that Herod's miserable death occurred about a year and a half after the massacre of the Innocents. Hence, Epiphanius concludes that the Holy Family's exile lasted two years. Nicephorus extends the term to three years. But it must be allowed that the general tradition of the Church—and such tradition is never to be lightly set aside, even when probabilities seem to tell against it— allots seven years to their sojourn in Egypt. St. Francis of Sales, indeed, is of the opinion that it was five, while Baronius even prolongs their absence to the ninth year.

Jesus, from His tenderest infancy, displayed such divine beauty and grace in His countenance, in His every look, and in His whole behavior, that the mere sight of Him ravished all hearts.

The children and the women of Matarieh were the first to know this wonderful and Heavenly Child; the report spread, and then both men and women came to see Him, not only from the immediate neighborhood, but from other towns and villages. Jesus had two Apostles to aid Him in His mission...Mary and Joseph; and who can calculate the power and the grace that accompanied their words and their every act? Whoever, indeed, beheld the Divine Infant and then lifted up their eyes to look at Mary and Joseph, said in their hearts, "These are truly angels of Paradise."

Doctors have gathered from Oriental traditions that the Egyptian women, seeing Mary so beautiful, so gracious, so modest, and so discreet, conceived a great love for Her, and numbers of them would come to visit Her and bring Her presents. They had such confidence in Her, it is said, that in their bodily infirmities and other afflictions, they had recourse to Her assistance, and in their sorrows sought and found consolation from Her lips.

They would also bring their sick children to Her, and She would gently lay Her hand on their heads, or would place them near to Her Divine Son, and they were healed. The Saracens, afterwards, would say that no woman on whom Mary laid Her hand ever died in childbirth.

(by Levy—*Joseph, the Just Man*, from p. 60)

While all men would contribute to the death of the Savior, only one, St. Joseph, was to save Him from death in His infancy. Yet, it will be understood that a sword of sorrow pierced the heart of St. Joseph. The journey of one hundred and eighty miles would entail untold sacrifice and hardship. Saintly, obedient Joseph "arose and took the Child and His Mother by night, and retired into Egypt; and He was there until the death of Herod" (Matt. 2:14).

One thing that stands out in the life of St. Joseph is his simple, unquestioning prompt obedience. It was sufficient for him to know that God wanted something done. He never stopped to question. He acted immediately.

Whilst Holy Scripture does not tell us by what road the Holy Family fled into Egypt, it is reasonable to suppose that St. Joseph chose a direct route to Gaza on the Mediterranean, which would have taken about ten hours' travel. After another dismal nine days' journey through the little Arabian desert, they would arrive at the River Nile, which they were obliged to cross.

According to tradition, it was at Heliopolis, which is near Cairo, that the Holy Family abode during their exile in Egypt.

(by Llamera—*Saint Joseph*, from p. 142)

Many would be the physical as well as mental tribulations of this journey which would take several days, and, of the time spent in exile—probably about a year.

(by Meinardus—*The Holy Family*, from pp. 6 & 22)

According to Coptic tradition, the Holy Family resided in Egypt for three and a half years.

Both the Eastern and Western traditions are unanimous that the journey of the Holy Family in Egypt was accomplished by ass.

(by O'Carroll—*Joseph, Son of David*, from p. 99)

Tradition mentions Heliopolis as the town where the Holy Family took up their abode. This was still a hundred miles journey for them. If the Holy Family went to Cairo, the journey would have taken them three weeks.

Modern scholarship rejects the view that the Holy Family remained seven years in Egypt. It is fairly certain that Herod died in the year 4 B.C. Allowing two years in Bethlehem to include all between the Nativity and the coming of the Magi, we have, on the assumption that Our Lord was born in 6 B.C., not more than three years, probably less, for the exile in Egypt. Fr. Prat thinks it may have lasted at most for 18 months, but also very much less—even a few months or a few weeks.

(by O'Carroll—*The King Uncrowned*, from p. 60)

Crisis reveals character. The flight into Egypt now showed to Mary that God had given Her not only a devoted lover and a loyal husband, but a resolute man of action who would shirk nothing in Her defense.

At last the wearisome journey ended at the Nile delta. Where did the Holy Family then choose to live? Tradition tells us that they took up their abode in Heliopolis, which was still a hundred miles journey. But now the journey was easier. They came at last to the city, and settled there with the Jewish Colony, made up of exiles and fugitives. Joseph could set up as a carpenter and be assured of economic stability for his home. At Heliopolis, and later at Memphis, Joseph was able to give the Child and His Mother shelter, dignity, and social security.

(by O'Rafferty—*Discourses*, from pp. 116 & 121)

The coming and the sojourn of the Holy Family in Egypt resulted in the destruction of idolatry and the planting of the seed of the one true faith of Jesus Christ. In fact, there is a tradition of the effect that as soon as the Holy Family set foot upon Egyptian soil, all the statues of the false divinities of that country, as if struck by an invisible hand, fell to earth and were broken in pieces. This is in conformity with the prophetic words of Isaias: "Behold the Lord will descend upon a swift cloud and will enter into Egypt. And the idols of Egypt shall be moved at His Presence, and the heart of Egypt shall melt in the midst thereof" (Isa. 19:1).

It would not be at all surprising to learn that the Divine Child, though only four or five years of age, gave sublime lessons to the other children who surrounded Him, and even to adults. It would be reasonable to believe that He made known to them the folly and malice of idolatry; that He filled them with the love of the One True God, Who rules and governs the whole world; that He animated them to the practice of virtue and the hatred of evil.

Nor was Jesus the only member of the Holy Family who tried to convert the people of Egypt. Mary, too, was an active missionary in this field, especially among the women with whom She associated. And we cannot imagine Joseph standing idly by. No; while working at his trade of carpenter, he lost no opportunity to promote God's honor and glory and his neighbor's material and spiritual welfare.

One of the most glorious titles given St. Joseph by the saints was that of "apostle." According to St. Hilary, he was an apostle because to him was entrusted the office of bringing Christ to the people. And St. Anselm says that he was an apostle because he was active in increasing the number of those who belong to God and to Christ.

In Joseph's work, he came in contact with a great many people, and we have reason to believe that he showed his zeal in speaking to them of the one true faith of Jesus Christ, of God and His goodness, of the true Light which soon was to enlighten the whole world. How great was the blessing bestowed upon Egypt and its people by the Presence of Jesus, Mary, and Joseph!

So blessed was the land of Egypt by the presence of the Holy Family that, after Christ's death, the apostles found it a most fertile field for the preaching of the Gospel. It gradually became one of the great centers of the Christian religion, the land of saints and scholars, the homeland of monks and hermits, who transformed it into a picture of Heaven on earth. Egypt was indeed blessed by nature, but it was blessed still more by grace.

Besides being insanely jealous and ambitious, Herod was a monster of cruelty as well. The massacre of the Holy Innocents alone would suffice to brand him as such. But countless other charges are laid at his door. On the least suspicion, he shed torrents of blood. Among his victims were his wife, their three sons, his brothers, friends, a high priest, all the members of the senate who were the outstanding men of the nation.

Foreseeing that the Jews would celebrate the day of his death with rejoicing, he left orders that on that day, the leading people of the nation should be enclosed and executed, so that instead of rejoicing there might be shedding of tears. Fortunately, however, his order was not carried out. So bloody was his character, that the Roman Emperor, himself, said of him: "It is better to be one of Herod's hogs than one of his sons," because he pardoned his hogs, but he did not pardon his sons.

However, Herod's life of shameful crime was finally punished by God. The Jewish historian, Josephus Flavius, a contemporary, relates that he was inwardly consumed by a burning fire; that he was tormented by hunger that could not be satiated and thirst that could not be quenched; that his bowels were filled with ulcers, and his body with worms; that the odor of his breath was such that no one could approach him. Tormented in mind and body, he experienced a foretaste of the hell that seemed to await him. So unbearable was his condition that, in a rage, he thrust a dagger into his breast, and countless worms exuded from his body.

According to the most probable opinion, five years had elapsed since the Holy Family arrived in the land of Egypt. During that time, St. Joseph must have suffered much. Yet amidst his sufferings, he must have experienced many consolations. It was in Egypt that he saw the Infant Jesus grow; it was there that he saw His Mother Mary clothe Him with a beautiful dress made with Her Own hands; it was there that he witnessed the Infant Jesus place His tiny Feet upon the ground and take His first steps; it was

231.

there that, for the first time, he heard the sound of His Divine Voice; it was there that he heard the Infant, for the first time, call Mary by the sweet name of Mother, and Joseph himself by the loving name of father; it was there he received the first caresses of His tiny Hands, and felt His first kisses on his forehead.

It would be difficult to describe the regret of their newly made Egyptian friends on hearing that news of the departure of this Jewish family, whom they loved so dearly. Joseph's goodness, Mary's sweetness, and Jesus' charm had made such an impression on them, that they would have them still remain among them. But in vain. God had made His will known to them, and it was their duty to obey.

Pious writers tell us that when the hour of departure had arrived, the men and women of Egypt insisted on accompanying the Holy Family a good part of the way. When they were finally requested by St. Joseph not to further inconvenience themselves, with signs of the most tender affection they took leave of the Holy Family and wished them a safe and happy journey. With this most sincere and cordial testimonial of friendship and renewing their thanks and greetings, Joseph, Mary, and Jesus wended their way back to Judea.

(by Patrignani—*Manual*, from pp. 15, 24 & 38)

Joseph remained at least seven years in that idolatrous land.

Do we find in the books of the New Testament a man so frequently honored with the visits of angels as St. Joseph? According to the Gospel, he received at least four.

We may also remark with St. Chrysostom, that the angels always visit St. Joseph in his sleep; and why, he inquires do they not present themselves before him in public, and while awake, as to Zachary and the shepherds? If they wished to honor Joseph, would it not be more glorious to him, that they should visit him with a pomp and retinue worthy of the celestial court? In the eyes of the world, those visits are always considered the most flattering and honorable, which are attended with the greatest pomp and display.

Yet who will believe it? The angels honored St. Joseph infinitely more by appearing to him and disclosing to him the secrets of God in the obscurity of a dream, than they could have done by the most brilliant and imposing demonstrations of respect; for thus they proved how fully convinced they were of the firm and lively faith of a man who, in order to believe the mysteries which they announced to him, needed not to behold with his corporeal eyes those Heavenly ambassadors, all radiant with light and glory. Thus speaks St. John Chrysostom, as also Theophylactus.

The learned and pious Cardinal of Campray, in ecstatic admiration of St. Joseph's great faith, thus apostrophizes him: "O Joseph! O the most just of men! How couldst thou have believed so promptly, so firmly, a mystery so new, so profound, and hitherto unexampled?" But for my part, I am even more astonished at the promptitude with which he executed the orders thus intimated to him, difficult though they were; and I will say to him, with another interpreter: "Be pleased, O glorious saint! Inform me why the angels, who make it a duty to honor your virtues and prerogatives, should not render you some exterior demonstrations of respect, in the intimation of their orders?"

Why not give you time to make preparation for your flight and long exile?... "Take the Child and Its Mother"; thus was the command given. "Fly into Egypt"; thus was announced the manner of performing it. "Remain there until you receive further orders"; thus was intimated to him the duration, or rather the uncertainty of the duration, of his exile, which he had no time either to think of or prepare for. Why not give St. Joseph even a few days' notice? While awaiting an answer, behold! St. Joseph is already on his road, as prompt in obeying the angel's order as was the latter in executing the commands of the Almighty.

It may be asked, what respect did the angel here testify for St. Joseph, for is it not more honorable to command than to obey? To this question I reply, that on this occasion the obedience which St. Joseph practiced, is more worthy of admiration than the authority with which the angel was invested; and it was with a view to his exaltation that the latter commanded him, for he knew how superior Joseph was to the weaknesses and pride of human nature, and what a brilliant example of angelic obedience he was about to exhibit to the world: for, as the angels obey God with promptitude and decided love, so did St. Joseph; he hears the order, rises up, and departs. Oh! What a subject of joy to the angel, to witness this miracle of obedience!

In former days, the angels were constrained to use violence with Lot in order to oblige him to quit Sodom—they were obliged to take him by the arm and put him forcibly outside that sinful city. With Joseph, it was quite the reverse —a word, a mere sign, was sufficient to make him quit his native land; he neither delays nor deliberates, but obeys in silence.

As our Lord would in infancy be conducted into Egypt by St. Joseph's powerful intercession was requisite in order to introduce the faith of the Redeemer into all infidel nations, and as the "Child Jesus," while traveling under St. Joseph's protection, once overturned the Egyptian idols, He still continues, in our days, to employ the arm of His beloved father in order to achieve their destruction.

And may it not have been in order to reward St. Joseph for all the privation and hardships which he had to suffer in a barbarous country, that God has rendered his name so glorious amongst idolatrous nations? And was it not also for the purpose of manifesting to the world this saint's ardent zeal for the salvation of the Egyptians, who once offered an asylum to Mary and Her Son, that the Eternal Father had placed in his hands the conversion of several infidel nations? The reward of his zeal and of his labors was, first, the conversion of a great number of idolatrous nations, such as the Egyptians, effected by his special intercession, and finally, their perseverance in following the light of faith, owing chiefly to the efficacy of his powerful protection.

(by Robert—*Guardian of God's Lilies*, from p. 8)

The "Fathers" attribute to this visit to Egypt of the Divine Child, the spiritual favors and blessings which were afterwards poured out on that country by God, making it for so many ages most fruitful in saints.

(by Sparks—*Dominicans*, from pp. 70, 131 & 162)

It is reasonable that this appearance of the angel was made to Joseph in Jerusalem after the Presentation of Christ in the Temple. Joseph was planning to dwell in Judea, either at Jerusalem or more likely at Bethlehem, but before he could establish his home, the angel warned him to flee into Egypt.

Cardinal Cajetan thinks the slaughter of the Holy Innocents may well have taken place two years later, but why Herod delayed his action so long is unknown. Christ came back to Israel in His fourth year.

Father Natalis Alexander suggests that the flight into Egypt took place, not immediately after the departure of the Magi, but after the Presentation of Christ in the Temple, and after the parents of Christ had returned to Nazareth. This can be gathered from Luke 2:39.

Christ remained in Egypt with Mary, His Mother, and Joseph until the death of Herod. How long they remained there is uncertain. Herod lived, more probably, about a year after the birth of Christ.

Cardinal Gotti distinguishes a twofold journeying to Nazareth; one from Jerusalem after the Purification (Luke) and the second from Egypt after Herod's death (Matt). Christ's stay in Egypt, he thinks, was hardly a year.

(by St. Bridget—*Revelations*, from p. 33)

You may perhaps ask what My Son did all that time of His life before His Passion. I reply that, as the Gospel says, He was subject to His parents, and He acted like other children till He reached His majority. Nor were wonders wanting in His youth: how idols were silenced, and fell in numbers in Egypt at His coming.

(by Suarez—*Joseph of*, from pp. 128, 133 & 135)

The fear of being overtaken and discovered always accompanied those who fled, and made this journey for them a continuous nightmare, and Jerusalem was less than two hours away from Bethlehem. The flight was a rough one, six or seven days long. They would try as much as possible to look like the other travelers, for it is less than likely, despite all the lyrical landscapes, that never having moved out of Nazareth except to go to Jerusalem and Bethlehem, Joseph would risk traveling without the company of those who knew the way and had some experience of it. Looking over his shoulder for pursuit, avoiding embarrassing questions that could arouse suspicions about them or their reasons for being out on the road, Joseph would have his work cut out. It was no picnic.

Regarding their stay in Egypt, there is no agreement, on how long or short this period had been. There is wide margin to choose from between writers. Fr. Pedro de Santamaria y Ulloa indicated a period of seven years, and other erudite commentators like Maldonatus, give them just a few weeks. Moreover, it seems that Herod died at least a year and a half after the birth of Jesus.

Considering what has been established until now with a certain amount of confidence, one is led to conclude that between the birth of Jesus and the death of King Herod, there was a period of between eighteen months and three years. Thus, the stay in Egypt was no longer than two and a half years and no less than a year at least.

(*The Glories of Saint Joseph*, from pp. 98 & 103)

St. Joseph obeyed promptly and without delay. He did not go on sleeping until morning. He did not stay in bed the rest of the night. He got up at once, made known to his holy Spouse the revelation he had received from the angel and, without delay, taking nothing with them, they departed. Thus they were on their way before dawn, perfectly carrying out the command they were given to flee in secret, as the shades of night permitted them to do.

Mary and Joseph obeyed with great joy. The days were long and tiring; they were deprived of ordinary means which might alleviate the hardships of the journey. They hardly gave a thought to their wants. They felt an inner joy that made them insensible to care, absorbed as they were in these two thoughts: it is God's will that they suffer, and for them God's will is the surest consolation; and above all, they have with them the Divine Child. His sweet company did more than charm their loneliness and, in their abandonment, replaced all things they might have lacked. Hence, they did not seek elsewhere the comforts and refreshment most travelers are so eager to obtain.

O Almighty God, Who gave to Mary and Joseph a spirit of such perfect obedience, I beg You through their merits to grant me the same spirit, so that I may obey You like them with complete submission of judgment, with courage, promptness, and joy, desiring only to do Your will and fully confident that Your Divine Providence will never forsake me as long as I shall persevere in uniting my will to Yours (Venerable Louis de Ponte).

What must have been the grief of Joseph on this journey when he saw his beloved Spouse, not used to so much walking, suffer so, carrying in Her arms that dear Child Whom they held in turn as they fled, in constant apprehension of meeting Herod's soldiers at every turn of the road; and all of this in the hardest part of winter with the discomfort of wind and snow!

What had they to eat during the trip? A piece of bread they had brought with them or whatever they might receive as alms. At night they had no place to rest except some wretched hut or an open field under the stars, with, at best, a tree for shelter. St. Joseph was indeed resigned to the

will of the Eternal Father, which was that His
only Son should suffer even from infancy to
expiate the sins of the human race; but it broke
Joseph's heart to hear Jesus cry because of
the cold and the damp.

Finally, consider how much St. Joseph had to
suffer during those seven years he spent in
Egypt, in the midst of an idolatrous, barbarian,
and unknown nation, having no friends or
relatives to help him. St. Bernard said that St.
Joseph had to work day and night to provide
food for his Wife and for the Child, Who Himself
provides food for all men and for all animals on
earth (St. Alphonsus de Liguori).

To be just is simply to be in perfect union
with the will of God and to conform to it in all
events, in prosperity or adversity. No one can
doubt that St. Joseph was perfectly obedient
to God at all times and occasions.

(by Valtorta—*Poem, Vol. 1*, from p. 188)

And nearby on a mat on the ground, there
is the Child Jesus. I think He must be two
years old, or two and a half at the very most.
He is playing with some little pieces of carved
wood, which look like little sheep or little
horses, and with some clear wood shavings, less
curly than His golden curls. With His little
plump hands He is trying to put those wooden
necklaces onto the necks of His little animals.

He is quiet and smiling. Very beautiful. His
little Head is a mass of very thick little golden
curls; His skin is clear and slightly rosy; His

Eyes are live and bright, of a deep blue color. The expression of course, is different, but I recognize the color of the Eyes of my Jesus: two beautiful dark sapphires. He is wearing a kind of a long white shirt which must certainly be His tunic, with short sleeves.

At present He has nothing on His Feet. His tiny sandals are on the mat and they, too, are being used as a toy by the Child, Who is placing His little animals on the mat, and then pulls the sandal by the strap as if it were a little cart. The sandals are very simple: a sole and two straps, one of which is coming from the point and the other from the heel of the sole. The one coming from the point then splits at a certain point and one length passes through the eyelet of the strap from the heel, then goes round and is tied with the other piece, forming thus a ring at the ankle.

A little farther away, sitting also in the shade of the tree, there is our Lady. She is weaving at a rustic loom and watching the Child. I can see Her white slender hands moving backwards and forwards throwing the shuttle on the weft while Her foot, shod in a sandal, is moving the pedal. She is wearing a tunic the color of mallow flowers: a rosy violet like certain amethysts. She is bareheaded, and so I can see that Her hair is parted, forming two simple plaits which gather at the nape of Her neck. Her sleeves are long and rather narrow. She has no other ornament except Her beauty and Her most sweet expression. The color of Her face, of Her hair and Her eyes, the form of Her face are always the same every time I see Her. She looks very young now. She looks about twenty years old.

At a certain moment, She gets up and bends over the Child, puts His sandals back on again, and ties them carefully. She then pats Him and kisses His little Head and His beautiful Eyes. The Child prattles and She answers. But I do not understand the words. She then goes back to Her loom; She covers the fabric and the weft with a piece of cloth, picks up the stool on which She was sitting and takes it into the house. The Child follows Her with His Eyes without troubling Her when She leaves Him alone.

Obviously Her work is finished, and it is almost evening. In fact, the sun is setting on the barren sand, and a huge fire invades the whole sky behind the far away pyramid.

Mary comes back. She takes Jesus by the hand and lifts Him from His mat. The Child obeys without any resistance. While His Mother picks up His toys and the mat and takes them into the house, He toddles on His well-shaped little legs towards the little goat and throws His arms around her neck. The little goat bleats and rubs her head on Jesus' shoulder.

Mary comes back. Now She is wearing a long veil on Her head and is carrying an amphora in Her hand. She takes Jesus by the hand, and They both start walking, turning round the little house towards the other side.

I follow them admiring the gracefulness of the picture. Our Lady adjusts Her step to the Child's, and the Child toddles and trips along beside Her. I can see His rosy heels moving up and down, with the typical grace of children's steps, on the sand of the little path. I notice that His little tunic does not reach down to His feet, but only to half His calf. It is very clean and simple and it is held tight to His waist by a little white cord.

I see that on the front of the house the hedge is broken by a rustic gate, which Mary opens to go out onto the road. It is a poor road at the end of a town or a village, whatever it may be, where it ends up with the country that here is formed of sand and some other houses, as poor as this one, with some scanty kitchen gardens.

I do not see anybody. Mary looks towards the center of the town not towards the country, as if She were waiting for someone; She then moves towards a vessel or well, whatever it may be, which is some ten meters further up, and on which some palm trees form a shady circle. Over there some green herbs can be seen on the ground.

I can now see a man coming along the road; he is not very tall, but is well built. I recognize Joseph, who is smiling. He looks younger than when I saw him in the vision of Paradise. He may be forty years old at most. His hair and beard are thick and black; his skin is rather tanned; his eyes are dark. An honest pleasant face, inspiring confidence.

When he sees Jesus and Mary, he quickens his step. On his left shoulder he has a kind of saw and a kind of plane, and he is holding in his hand other tools of his trade, not exactly like the ones we use now, but almost similar. He is probably coming back after working in somebody's house. He is wearing a tunic the color of which is between hazel and dark brown; it is not very long—it reaches a good bit up from his ankles—and its sleeves are short. I think he is wearing a leather belt at his waist. It is the proper tunic of a workman. On his feet he has sandals tied at his ankles.

Mary smiles and the Child utters cries of joy and He stretches out the Hand which is free. When the three meet, Joseph bends down and offers the Child a fruit which I think is an apple, by its color and shape. He then stretches his arms and the Child leaves His Mother, and cuddles in the arms of Joseph, bending His little Head into the cavity of Joseph's neck; he kisses Him, and is kissed by Him. A scene full of loving grace.

I was forgetting to say that Mary had promptly taken Joseph's work tools, to leave him free to embrace the Child.

Then Joseph, who had crouched down to the ground to be at the same height as Jesus, stands up, takes his tools with his left hand and holds little Jesus tight to his strong chest with his right arm. And he moves towards the house, while Mary goes to the fountain to fill Her amphora.

After entering the enclosure of the house, Joseph puts the Child down, takes Mary's loom into the house, and then he milks the goat. Jesus watches all these activities carefully, and in particular, the closing up the little goat in a little closet in one side of the house.

It is now getting dark. I can see the red of the sunset becoming violet on the sands which seem to be trembling because of the heat. The pyramid looks darker.

Joseph goes into the house, into a room which must be his workshop, the kitchen, the dining room all in one. The other room is obviously the bedroom. But I do not go in there. The fire is lit in a low fireplace. There is a carpenter's bench, a small table, some stools, some shelves with two oil lamps and some kitchenware on them. In a corner, there is Mary's loom. And a great deal of order and cleanliness. A very poor dwelling, but very clean.

And this is a remark I wish to make: in all the visions concerning the human life of Jesus I have noticed that both He and Mary, as well as Joseph and John, are always tidy and clean, both in their garments and their bodies. They wear modest and simple garments, but they are so clean that they look like gentlemen in them.

Mary comes back with the amphora and the door is closed on the rapidly growing dusk. The room is illuminated by a lamp which Joseph has lit and placed on his bench, where he now starts working on some little boards, while Mary is preparing supper. Also the fire illuminates the room. Jesus, with His little Hands leaning on the bench and His little Head turned upwards, is watching what Joseph is doing.

They then sit down at the table after saying their prayers. Obviously they do not bless themselves with the Sign of the Cross, but they pray. It is Joseph who says the prayers, and Mary answers. I do not understand anything at all. It must be a psalm. But it is said in a language which is entirely unknown to me.

They then sit down at the table. The lamp is now on the table. Mary is holding Jesus in Her lap, and makes Him drink some of the goat's milk, into which She dips some small slices of bread, which She has cut off from a little round loaf. The crust of the loaf, as well as the inside, is very dark; it looks like rye bread or bread made with barley. It certainly contains a lot of bran, judging by its color. In the meantime, Joseph eats some bread and cheese, a small slice of cheese and a lot of bread. Then Mary sits Jesus on a little stool near Her, and brings some cooked vegetables to the table—they appear to be boiled and dressed as we use them nowadays—and She also eats some of them after Joseph has helped himself.

Jesus is nibbling happily at His apple, and He smiles displaying His little white teeth. Their supper ends with some olives or dates. I cannot tell exactly which, because they appear to be too light to be olives and too hard to be dates. There is no wine. The supper of poor people.

But there is so much peace in this room that not even the sight of the most solemn royal palace could give me as much. And how much harmony!

Jesus does not speak this evening. He does not explain the scene. He has taught me with the gift of His vision and that is enough. May He be always and equally blessed.

(26th January 1944—Jesus says:)

The things you see teach you and others the lesson. It is a lesson of humility, resignation, and good harmony. A lesson given as an example to all Christian families, and particularly to the Christian families in this especially sorrowful age. You have seen a poor house. And what is more saddening, a poor house in a foreign country.

Many people, only because they are fairly good Catholics who pray and receive Me in the Holy Eucharist, pray and receive Me for "their" needs, not for the needs of their souls and for the Glory of God—because only seldom those who pray are not selfish—many people would pretend to have a prosperous, happy, easy material life, well-protected even from the least pain.

Joseph and Mary had Me, True God, as their Son, yet they did not even have the meager satisfaction of being poor in their own country where they were known, where at least there was their "own" little house; and the problem of a dwelling did not add a harassing thought to their many problems, in the country where, as they were known, it was easier for them to find work and provide for the needs of their lives. They are two refugees just because they had Me. A different climate, a different country, so sad in comparison with the sweet countryside of Galilee, a different language, different habits, living amongst people who did not know them, and who generally distrusted refugees and people they did not know.

They are deprived of those comfortable and dear pieces of furniture of "their" little house, of so many humble and necessary things they had there, and which did not seem to be so necessary, whereas here in the void that surrounds them, seem even beautiful, like the luxurious things that make the houses of rich people so charming. And they felt nostalgia both for their country and for their home; they worried about the poor things they had left behind, about the little kitchen garden where probably no one would take care of their vines and their figs, and the other useful plants. And they had to provide every day for food, clothes, fire and for Me, a Child, Whom they could not feed with the same food they took themselves. And they were sad at heart, because of their homesickness, because of the uncertainty of the future, and the lack of trust of people who are reluctant, particularly at first, to accept the offer of work of two unknown people.

And yet, as you have seen yourself, that house is pervaded with serenity, smiles, harmony; and by mutual consent, they endeavor to make it more beautiful, even in its scanty little kitchen garden, that it may be more like the more comfortable one they had to leave behind. They have only one thought: that the land may be less hostile and less unpleasant for Me, since I come from God. It is the love of believers and relatives which reveals itself in many ways: from the little goat they purchased with many hours of extra work, to the little toys carved in scraps of wood, to the fruit purchased only for Me, while they denied themselves a morsel of food.

O beloved father of mine on the earth, how loved you have been by God, by God Father in the Most High Heavens, by God Son, Who became the Savior on the earth!

In that house there is no quick temper, no sulkiness, no grim faces; neither is there any reproach against each other, and least of all against the God Who has not loaded them with material wealth. Joseph does not reproach Mary as being the cause of his discomfort; neither does Mary reproach Joseph because he is incapable of procuring greater worldly goods. They love each other in a holy way, that is all. And, therefore, they do not worry about their own comfort, but only about the comfort of their consort. True love is not selfish. And true love is always chaste, even if it is not perfect in chastity as the love of the two virgin spouses. Chastity united to charity yields a suite of other virtues and therefore two people who love each other chastely become perfect.

The love of Mary and Joseph was perfect. Therefore it was an incentive to every other virtue, and in particular to charity towards God; blessed every hour, notwithstanding His holy will is painful for the flesh and the heart; blessed because, above the flesh and above the heart, the spirit was more lively and stronger in the two saints, and they exalted the Lord with gratitude because they had been chosen as guardians of His Eternal Son.

In that house they prayed. You pray too little in your homes nowadays. The sun rises and sets, you start your work, and you sit at the table without a thought for the Lord, Who has granted you to see a new day, and then to live and see a new night, Who has blessed your work and has made it the means for you to purchase the food, the fire, the clothes, the house which are so necessary for your human lives. Whatever comes from Good God is "good." Even if it is poor and meager, love gives it flavor and body, the love that allows you to see in the Eternal Creator, the Father Who loves you.

In that house there is frugality and it would be there even if there was plenty of money. They eat to live. They do not eat to satisfy their gluttony, with the insatiability of gluttons and the whims of epicures who fill themselves to the extent of being sick and squander fortunes on expensive food, without giving one thought to those who are without or with little food, without considering that if they were moderate, many people could be relieved of the pangs of hunger.

In that house they love work, and they would love it even if there was plenty of money, because the working man obeys the command of God and frees himself from vice, which like tenacious ivy clenches and suffocates idle people, who are like immovable rocks. Food is good, rest is serene, hearts are happy, when you have worked well and you enjoy the resting time between one job and the next one. Neither in the houses nor in the minds of those who love work, can many-sided vice rise. And, in its absence, love, esteem, reciprocal respect prosper, and tender children grow in a pure atmosphere and they thus become the origin of future holy families.

Humility reigns in that house. What a lesson of humility for the proud. Mary, from a human point of view, had a thousand reasons to be proud and to be adored by Her spouse. Many women are proud only because they are a little better educated, or of nobler birth, or of a wealthier family than their husbands. Mary is the Spouse and the Mother of God, and yet She serves— and does not expect to be served—Her consort, and She is full of love for him. Joseph is the head of the family, judged by God so worthy of being the head of a family, as to be entrusted by God with the guardianship of the Word Incarnate and the Spouse of the Eternal Spirit. And yet he is anxious to relieve Mary of Her work, and he takes care of the most humble jobs in the house, so that Mary may not get tired; not only, but whenever he can, he does his best to please Her and make Her house more comfortable and Her little garden more beautiful.

In that house, order is respected: supernatural, moral, material. God is the Supreme Head and He is worshipped and loved: *supernatural order.* Joseph is the head of the family and he is loved, respected, and obeyed: *moral order.* The house is a gift of God, as well as the clothes and the furnishings. The Providence of God is shown in everything of God, Who supplied wool to sheep, feathers to birds, grass to meadows, hay to animals, grains and branches to birds; Who weaves the dress of the lily of the valley. The house, the dresses, the furnishings are accepted with gratitude, blessing the Divine Hand that supplies them, looking after them with respect as gifts of the Lord, without any bad humor because they are poor without ill use, without abusing Divine Providence: *material order.*

You did not understand the words they exchanged in the dialect of Nazareth, neither did you understand the words of the prayer. But the things you saw are a great lesson. Meditate on them, you all who now suffer so much because you failed in so many things towards God; also in those things in which the holy spouses never failed, the spouses who were My Mother and father.

And you, rejoice remembering little Jesus; smile thinking of His little steps of a child. In a short time you will see Him walking under the Cross. And then it will be a vision of tears.

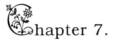

Chapter 7.

Living In Nazareth

(by Agreda—*City (Incarnation)*, from pp. 347, 358,
& 364; *(Transfixion)*, from pp. 5, 23, 26 & 28)

The humble but blessed house of Joseph contained three rooms, which occupied nearly all its space and formed the exclusive dwelling place of the two spouses. In one room Saint Joseph slept, and in another he worked and kept the tools of his trade of carpentering; the third was ordinarily occupied by the Queen of Heaven and was also Her sleeping room. It contained a couch made by the hands of Saint Joseph.

The two holy spouses lived alone in their house, having no servants of any kind, not only on account of their humility, but in order more fittingly to hide from any witnesses the wonders, which passed between them and which were not to be communicated to outsiders. Likewise, the Princess of Heaven did not leave Her dwelling, except for very urgent causes in the service of God or Her fellow-man.

Although he labored for others, as did also his Heavenly Spouse, yet never did they ask for any wages, or set a price on their work, leaving the payment of wages entirely in the hands of their employers and accepting it not as a just return for their labors, but as a freely given alms. When they at times had nothing to eat, they would pray and the Host High sent the holy angels to provide food for them.

In prayer they asked God to show them His will and pleasure regarding the rearing of the Infant God. Together they heard an audible Voice saying: "I have come from Heaven to the earth in order to exalt humility and discredit pride, to honor poverty and contemn riches, to destroy vanity and establish truth, and in order to enhance worthily the value of labor. Therefore, it is My will that exteriorly you treat Me according to the humble position which I have assumed, as if I were the natural Child of both of you, and that interiorly you acknowledge Me as the Son of My Eternal Father, and bestow the reverence and love due to Me as the Man-God."

They both concluded that according to the limited means allowed them by their poverty, they were to expend whatever they could afford in the service of the Infant God without going into excess or failing in anything; for the sacrament of the King was to be concealed in humble poverty, though at the same time, they wished to exercise their burning love as far as was possible.

Saint Joseph, in exchange for some of his work, accepted two pieces of woolen cloth, such as his Heavenly Spouse had previously described to him, the one white, the other mulberry-colored mixed with grey, both of them of the best quality he could find. Of these the

Heavenly Queen made the first little dresses of Her most holy Son, while She prepared the swathing clothes and shirts from a piece of linen which She Herself had spun and woven. Being woven by such hands, it was a most delicate piece of cloth, originally begun as a gift to the Temple. Saint Joseph gathered such flowers and herbs as he could find from which, together with other aromatic materials, the zealous Mother extracted fragrant essences. With these She sprinkled the sacred vestments of the Victim of sacrifice which She awaited; then She folded and laid them away in a chest which was later taken with them to Bethlehem.

From the time of their return from Egypt until His public preaching, during the 23 years of Their stay in Nazareth, the Incarnate Word and His holy Mother occupied Themselves in the hidden sacraments of all the mysteries of the evangelical law and of His doctrine. As the Divine Child grew larger, He sometimes helped Saint Joseph as far as His strength would permit.

Jewish men, not the women and children, were obliged to present themselves before the Lord in the Temple of Jerusalem three times each year. Twice a year Saint Joseph went to Jerusalem by himself, while on the third occasion, the Holy Family would go together to the feast of Pasch, which lasted seven days. The Child Jesus desired that they journey on foot, to assume hardships in the service of His Eternal Father, and for our advantage; and with much pleasure He would speak of the delight with which He accepted these hardships for the glory of the Eternal Father and for the good of men.

(by Aumann—*Compendium*, from p. 126)

St. Joseph shows all of us how to be servants of the Word rather than be masters over others. His hidden and silent oblation of self can serve as an antidote to a self-seeking generation, interested only in self-fulfillment without sacrifice.

(by Baij—*Life of*, from pp. 263, 268, 273 & 295)

Happy to return again to Nazareth from Egypt, Joseph found that some people there had an antagonistic attitude toward him. They said: "You have been most vile indeed, even worse than Herod, for you knew of the decree and yet you informed no one, while using your secret knowledge solely for your own benefit. However, God will punish you, you selfish creature! He will bring it about that your Son shall perish even as ours had to perish! We will find a way to kill Him."

The Holy Family endured all this with an invincible patience. Joseph had recourse to Jesus with the complaint: "Oh my precious, beloved Son! Is it really possible that trials are repeatedly to break in upon us? It was my belief that You would be cordially received by our townspeople, but now I see that, instead of this, You are being envied and persecuted.

I had hoped for the peaceful enjoyment of Your most beloved company, but now I behold fresh oppressions arising."

Jesus reminded Joseph that it was not the time for rest and consolation; moreover, that it was most appropriate to always have some trial to bear. Only in the Heavenly homeland could he expect full consolation. God the Father ordained there always be some affliction for Joseph during his life here on earth, in order to prove his fidelity and love. The saintly Joseph bowed his head in reply to this, and made himself completely submissive to the divine will.

Certain individuals who were given to idleness, came into Joseph's workshop to talk, only to find themselves completely unnoticed by him. Joseph was characterized as being an inept and feeble-minded person. When this became known, he thanked God that these people considered him to be mentally deficient. It pleased him, in his humility, not to be esteemed by anyone but to be depreciated. He considered these offenders his benefactors. Nor was he mistaken in his attitude, for this was truly an occasion of great merit for him, and he was able to enrich his soul with imperishable treasures.

Consequently, he prayed much for them and, when he was accosted by them and treated abusively, either by word or deed, he presented towards them an even more cheerful countenance than usual. He greeted them politely and in his heart only wished them well. He was able to obtain many graces for their souls precisely because of this behavior of his, which was so pleasing to God, that He readily granted him anything that he requested. The realization of what great satisfaction he was giving God

enabled Joseph to practice virtue with great
joyfulness of soul.

Even from among those who were well-
disposed towards him, Joseph had to put up with
a great deal of disparagement. Their comments
were well-meaning, for they admonished him
to desist from any further wandering about in
other cities as he had done. Others derided him
and called him a tramp, in addition to accusing
him of being a man of little consideration
for having taken his Spouse so far away
from home. They declared that She, Who was
so wise, so distinguished, and so lovable,
would only be exposed to further calumniations. Therefore, he should establish himself
permanently in Nazareth. By this time he must
have accumulated a considerable amount of
experience, they asserted, and so must surely
be a mature man!

These remarks penetrated deeply into Joseph's
soul. In order not to reveal his secret, he was
compelled to remain silent and permit himself
to be considered guilty of these accusations,
and of being an irresponsible person. His face
flushed with shame as he proceeded to thank
these people for their good will, and to beg
them to be indulgent with his poor power
of comprehension. Within his heart, he made
an offering of all this to God and declared
himself to be ready to suffer much more out
of love for Him. "Inasmuch as I have been so
blessed and favored by You, oh my God,"
he cried, "it is only fitting that I should be
depreciated by men. Moreover, it is enough
for me to be able to please You and to fulfill
Your divine will. Behold, I am prepared even
to leave my native land again if You should
wish it! I would gladly subject myself again not
only to all the pains and deprivations, but also
to all the abuses and calumniations of men

who put a faulty interpretation upon my actions." Actually, Joseph was at all times ready to accomplish the divine will in everything. For him, it was synonymous with peace, a peace which he found so abundantly in fulfilling its demands.

Then the Heavenly Father desired that His Only-Begotten Son humble Himself by rendering His services to Joseph in the workshop. Joseph rejoiced exceedingly over his own good fortune, for he had already learned in Egypt what a great blessing it was to work in the company of Jesus. Even though Jesus knew what Joseph needed, He rarely performed tasks directly, because He wanted to be commanded to do so by Joseph, and, thereby, practice humility and submissiveness.

Many of the neighbors noticed Jesus was helping Joseph and were impelled to go over to observe Him more closely. The unusual attractiveness of the Divine Youth astounded them, and they declared that Joseph was indeed fortunate and blessed, and declared: "It would have been a most unspeakable atrocity to have slain such an appealing and lovable Child." A considerable number of them begged Joseph to forgive them for the unjust abuse that they hurled at him previously. Joseph thanked God for having transformed the hearts of his enemies.

Joseph was a bit disturbed, due to the fact that by taking Jesus with him, Mary would be deprived of His Presence, so he mentioned this to Her. She admonished him not to be distressed because She always found Her happiness in fulfilling the divine will.

The large number of people who stopped by in the beginning, definitely interfered with

Joseph's enjoyment of the adorable Presence of his beloved Jesus. Yet, he never made any complaints. His love for his neighbor was such that, instead, he rejoiced over the fact that others were receiving comfort. Indeed, he was willing to be deprived completely of the Presence of Jesus in order to benefit others and provide them with spiritual consolation, if the Heavenly Father so wished.

It was Joseph's policy to be content with whatever recompense each customer freely offered to him. No complaint ever fell from his lips, even though some unconscientious individuals gave him little. Then he retained for himself only as much of his earnings as was necessary for their livelihood; the rest he distributed to the poor. It was gratifying for him to labor in order to give alms to beggars. Of course, Jesus and Mary derived much satisfaction from it.

In spite of all the work he did, Joseph continued to maintain his usual daily schedule in his other activities. He spent a definite period of time in the recitation of the divine praises and in personal intercourse with God. Though he felt the strain of his work most intensely, God blessed his efforts, and he accomplished more than other men of his trade. Inasmuch as he had as his Helper in the shop, the King and Ruler of all the angels, it follows that the angels themselves did not consider it to be beneath their dignity to lend their assistance now and then, as the occasion demanded, in order to satisfy those people who wanted their particular articles completed on short notice.

The first article made by Jesus was a cross. Since there existed within Joseph's heart, definite forebodings of what was to occur with the passage of time—that his Jesus would be crucified—and since he had obtained a clear illumination concerning this from the Heavenly Father, his heart was already afflicted and penetrated by a most poignant sorrow. This became greatly enhanced as he watched Jesus completing His small cross.

After this first project of His was completed, Jesus turned to Joseph and declared: "Dearest father, observe the means whereby the salvation of mankind is to be accomplished." He said this joyfully, together with a yearning that the much longed-for time would soon arrive. At these words of Jesus, Joseph's strength seemed to leave him. He would have succumbed under the intensity of the anguish which he now felt, had it not been for the help of divine grace. As it was, he was merely able to say in reply: "Oh, my dearest Jesus!" Shaken to the depths, he began to weep bitterly. However, Jesus fortified him with the reminder that the Heavenly Father's will must be done, and so Joseph once more became resigned. The pain, however, remained embedded in his heart.

Jesus talked with Mary and Joseph concerning His eventual sufferings. These remarks caused Joseph to collapse. The Mother of God was Herself transfixed by intense grief; She did not succumb, but remained in full possession of Her powers in order to endure uninterruptedly these sorrowful pangs within Her heart.

The intensified interior anguish with which Joseph now found himself stricken was to endure for the remainder of his life, in spite of the encouragement and support that Jesus would give him. Although he was not destined to be a witness to the actual sufferings of the Savior, he, nevertheless, experienced something of the bitterness connected with them. By means of his meditations upon these sufferings which were in store for the Savior, he had the opportunity of gaining much merit.

Jesus never did anything without Joseph's approval. He did not even leave the shop to go and see His Mother without Joseph's express permission. Joseph was amazed at the Savior's great humility, and endeavored to emulate Him. The sight of Divinity Itself being thus submissive to his commands only made him seek to abase himself all the more. Hence, when Jesus could not see him do so, he would prostrate himself on the ground and adore Him, or when Jesus left the workshop, he would kiss the floor where the Sacred Feet had rested, or he would lovingly put to his lips those articles which Jesus had touched with His Sacred Hands.

Indeed, the members of the Holy Family actually competed with each other in the practice of humility and the other virtues. Joseph strove earnestly to be a faithful and precise imitator of Jesus and Mary. Though already very virtuous, he recognized that he was, nevertheless, very much inferior to Them. Hence, he often humbled himself and said to his holy Spouse: "Oh, how ashamed I feel of my wretchedness when I see You and Jesus, so rich in virtue and merits. I am indeed poor and miserable. I ought to be a most perfect imitator of each One of You, but I realize that I am far from it. Oh, my beloved Spouse, obtain for me the graces I need." In this manner, Joseph advanced to an ever greater fullness in grace.

(by Binet—*Divine Favors*, from p. 8)

St. Justin, in his dialogue with Triphon, adds that the Child Jesus acted as His adopted father's little Apprentice, assisting him to make yokes and ploughs.

(by Cirrincione—*St. Joseph, Fatima*, from p. 19)

According to Jewish custom, a male child remained in his mother's care until he was five years of age; then the father took a more active part in his upbringing. Thus St. Joseph would have introduced Jesus to the *Psalms*, taken Him to the synagogue on the Sabbath, walked with Him during leisure hours. When he was busy in the workshop, he would let the Boy watch him, explain what he was doing, and let Him fetch a tool and help sweep up at the end of the day. No doubt they had a little patch of land outside the town where they grew vegetables, and the Boy would till the soil at the side of His father.

Jesus' reply: "How is it that you sought Me. Did you not know I must be about My Father's business?" Was Jesus, in His reply to Mary, leading Her to begin to think of His real career 18 years later? Clearly, at the moment, She probably did not grasp that suggestion, namely, that Jesus was saying to Her: "I have chosen My second career, that of Teacher, like the teachers among whom You found Me. *This* is My Father's business, the business I spoke to You about, for I shall not always be a Carpenter."

(by Chorpenning—*Just Man*, from pp. 39, 48, 148, 157, 162, 173,179, 189, 214 & 247)

Joseph is set ablaze with the fire of divine love by Jesus, the Heavenly and Divine Cupid. Not only did the Christ Child's embraces infuse Joseph with the fire of divine love, so, too, did His kisses that were fiery arrows that penetrated the saint's heart.

It is because of the great love with which he was inflamed and that he showed in his service to Mary and Jesus, that Joseph can also be said to be like the Seraphim, whose ministry is to love God without ceasing.

St. Joseph is a role model who teaches that the contemplative and active life must be blended and harmonized, and that love is not the same as romantic daydreams, but must be enfleshed in a life of self-sacrifice and service to others that unfolds in the circumstances of the real world and in the profoundly human context of marriage and family.

It is noteworthy that once St. Joseph was depicted as a young man in art, his face resembled that of the adult Christ. This reflects the idea, widespread in the tradition of devotional writing on Joseph, that this saint was a mirror of God the Father.

The term "Body of Christ" refers to three interrelated and inseparable realities: the humanity of Christ, the Eucharist, and the Church. Joseph's mission was to care for, protect, and guide the Word made flesh for

the 30 years that preceded His public
ministry. As Doze has observed, "Joseph is
an important name in the Bible: it determined
not only a person but also a role. Joseph,
either in person or by a mysterious spiritual
presence which can only be hinted at, is
in charge of keeping watch, then and now,
over the Body of Christ."

Work was the daily expression of love in
the life of the Family of Nazareth.

St. Augustine, speaking of the Patriarch
Joseph, and even more so our St. Joseph, says
this: "Joseph was chaste in body and pure
in heart, beautiful of face and even more
beautiful in spirit, and this beauty never
harmed him because he always kept his
appetites subject to his reason.

Universal justice is to render to all what
is their due. The human person owes God
reverence as Creator, love as Father, and fear
as Judge. With respect to the neighbor,
obedience is owed to superiors, benevolence
to equals, kindness to subordinates. With
regard to oneself, there is the obligation to
preserve purity in thought, truthfulness in
word, and right intention in deeds. And when
a person does not fail in any of these nine
obligations, then that individual is just and
lives uprightly.

St. Joseph had God Himself as his Son, and
Jesus and the Virgin Mary as his Neighbors,
with Whom he interacted constantly and
from Whom he learned the uprightness of
justice. It is clear that St. Joseph fulfilled
all the obligations of justice, and therefore
he was enriched with grace, endowed with
wisdom, and perfect in every virtue.

Art often visualizes theology. The color of the clothing that Joseph wears when he is depicted in art also has a particular symbolism. Joseph is most frequently shown wearing a green robe with a yellow cloak. These colors serve to highlight some of Joseph's principal virtues. Jesus epitomized charity, symbolized by red; Mary exemplified faith, represented by blue; and Joseph, hope, signified by green. Joseph's hope is closely related to his constancy in the midst of adversity. Yellow symbolizes magnanimity, and in the case of Joseph, this virtue is manifest in his care of the Holy Family. Pope John Paul II sums up the existence of Joseph's magnanimity with regard to the Holy Family in these words: "Joseph surrendered his whole existence to the demands of the Messiah's coming into his home."

A person who overcomes strong opponents of obstacles is called "strong." Joseph conquered the devil; he conquered a tyrannical king; he conquered himself, surrendering to the angel when he revealed to him the mystery of the Incarnation; he despised the world, trampling it underfoot; he conquered his appetites and all that is contrary to virtue. This holy man was an example of fortitude for the martyrs, who, with their eyes fixed on Saint Joseph, had the strength to suffer a thousand deaths not to lose Christ. Joseph must have had a superabundance of all the gifts of the Holy Spirit.

The Virgin Mary told St. Bridget, speaking of the poverty in which they lived, that: "The surplus from our household, apart from what was necessary for a plain meal, we distributed to the poor, and Joseph served Me with such devotion that I never heard him speak an angry word, nor any vanity nor complaint.

He was most patient in the midst of our
extreme poverty, diligent in his work so that he
could support us, most meek with those who
criticized him, most obedient to whatever
I wished, most prompt in defending Me against
those who spoke ill of Me, a most faithful
witness to the wonders of God, and dead to
the world and the flesh to such a degree that
he desired nothing that was not of Heaven.
He believed with so great a faith in the divine
promises that he continually said; 'Oh, that I
might see fulfilled every detail of God's will!'
Joseph did not usually interact with many
people, because his complete desire was to serve
the Lord, and thus he enjoys much glory in
Heaven."

In his great mercy, Saint Joseph supported
the first two poor Persons, spending himself,
both physically and spiritually, in Their service;
he also defended from Herod's anger the
Divine Redeemer, so that dying upon the cross,
He would redeem the world and found the
Church. Thus it can be said that, after Christ,
Who died for the Church, and the Virgin, Who
was the Mother of the Church's Redeemer,
Saint Joseph gave to the Church the greatest
alms that She has received from any saint.

The histories of St. Joseph state that, both in
Egypt and in Nazareth, as well as in the other
places where he lived, if there were neighbors
who were at odds with and would not speak
to one another, they would appeal to Joseph,
who, with a few words, would make peace.

The universal office of angels, according to
what can be deduced from Sacred Scripture, is to
serve the divine Majesty as spirits that are sent
on their ministry for the benefit of those who
are to inherit salvation (Hebrews 1:14). And since
this Lord is infinite, thousands upon thousands

upon millions attend His Presence (Daniel 7:10); and, according to what the Book of Job says: "There is no numbering of these soldiers of God." (Job 25:3).

The angels cannot be jealous because being blessed in glory, they are confirmed in grace; but, if they were, they would envy no one as much as Mary and Joseph. But instead of envy, the angels are filled with admiration and praises of God, seeing these two souls occupied in such a sublime service and ministry.

After the divine mystery of the Incarnation was revealed to the glorious St. Joseph, he lived with his Spouse a little less than six months in Nazareth.

Of all creatures, Saint Joseph was the man most like Christ and His Mother, the Virgin, in countenance, speech, complexion, habits, inclination, and way of life.

(by Chorpenning—*The Holy Family*, from p. 11)

The Pseudo-Bonaventure extols poverty as "the highest virtue...the Heavenly pearl for which it appears one must exchange everything," and "the main foundation of the whole spiritual edifice." It is the hallmark of the Holy Family's life: "Saintly poverty shines in them, guiding us to love and follow it."

(by Cristiani—*The Father of Jesus*, from pp. 56 & 59)

The devout Jew set aside several times each day for prayer. It was customary to pray in the morning and in the evening, and also at the "noon" of the Psalmist, that is, at the sixth hour, as it was then called.

Until the child reached the age of five, he was given entirely to his mother's care, but after the age of five, it was the "father's" duty to see to his child's religious and moral education.

(by Deiss—*Joseph, Mary, Jesus*, from p. 14)

The carpenter's trade (*tekton*) was held in high esteem. For example, among the Talmudic adages concerning a matter difficult to explain or understand, it is said, "This is a thing not even a carpenter—it being implied 'as educated as he might be'—can explain." The work *tekton* could also be applied to an artisan who worked in iron or stone. In brief, we may suppose that Joseph, and later Jesus, were good craftsmen in the village, well-skilled in everything that concerned their trade.

(by Doze—*St. Joseph: Shadow*, from p. 19)

Another noteworthy admirer of Joseph in the 18th century is St. Alphonsus Liguori, founder of the Redemptorists. He meditates on an important idea: the growth of love in the heart of Joseph, of love for Mary, of love for Jesus. ...When texts speak to us of "growth" (and we know that this is the very meaning of the name of Joseph, "increasing it"), what can we think of that is more worthy of growth than love?

"Among humans, the effect of living together is that we usually end up by having only a very mediocre love for each other because, as relationships are kept up, we become more and more aware of each other's shortcomings. On the contrary, as St. Joseph continued to live with Jesus, he constantly grew in admiration for His holiness. We can thereby understand what burning love he managed to have for Him, having lived in this intimacy, which defies description, for no less than 25 years, as is generally believed."

(by Emmerich—*Life of Blessed*, from p. 343)

I saw the Holy Family preparing as promptly and obediently for their journey home as they had done when warned to flee into Egypt.

(by Emmerich—*Life of Jesus*, from pp. 323 & 330)

There were three separate rooms in the house at Nazareth, that of the Mother of God being the largest and most pleasant; in it

Jesus, Mary, and Joseph met to pray. I very seldom saw them together at other times. They stood at prayer, their hands crossed upon their breast, and they appeared to speak aloud. I often saw them praying by a light. They stood under a lamp that had several wicks, or near a kind of branched candlestick fastened to the wall, and upon which the flame burned. They were most of the time alone in their respective rooms, Joseph working in his. I saw him cutting sticks and laths, planing wood, and carrying up a beam, Jesus helping him. Mary was generally engaged sewing or knitting with little needles, at which She sat on the ground, Her feet crossed under Her, and a little basket at Her side. They slept alone, each in a separate room. The bed consisted of a cover which in the morning was rolled up.

I saw Jesus assisting His parents in every possible way, and also on the street and wherever opportunity offered, cheerfully, eagerly, and obligingly helping everyone. He assisted His foster-father in his trade, or devoted Himself to prayer and contemplation. He was a model for all the children of Nazareth; they loved Him and feared to displease Him.

At the age of eight years, Jesus went for the first time with His parents to Jerusalem for the Pasch, and every succeeding year He did the same. In those first visits, Jesus had already excited attention in Jerusalem among the friends with whom He and His parents stayed, also among the priests and doctors. They spoke of the pious, intelligent Child...of Joseph's extraordinary Son, and would recognize Him again the next year. So Jesus had already some acquaintances in the city when, in His 12th year, He made the journey for the fifth time.

After being lost and found in the Temple, our Jesus was always like a teacher among

His companions. He often sat among them instructing them or walked about the country with them.

(by Filas—*Joseph Most Just,* from pp. 48 & 53)

Only Mary and Joseph lived for so long a time in the intimate company of God made man, and only Joseph daily beheld the joint example of Jesus and Mary—God Himself, and God's most perfect Creature. Bernardine of Siena expresses the idea thus: "If we wretches often can make progress by living with holy men who, compared to the Virgin, are nothing, what tremendous progress should we not attribute to Joseph, who lived with the Virgin! How much perfection must have accrued to him by living with God, blessed Jesus."

St. Francis de Sales gives St. Joseph this tribute: "Although it is true that Mary possessed every virtue in a higher degree than is attainable by any other pure creature, yet it is quite certain that the glorious St. Joseph was the being who approached most nearly to that perfection... All Her virtues and perfections were absolutely reflected in St. Joseph, so that it almost seemed as if he were as perfect and possessed all virtues in as high a degree as did the glorious Virgin."

(by Filas—*St. Joseph, After*, from p. 33)

We see imitable qualities of Joseph when we meditate on the full import of Mary's words when Christ is found in the Temple. Mary says to Jesus, "Son, Thy father and I have been seeking Thee with sorrow in our hearts." Why would Mary, at such a moment, have so spontaneously uttered these words of union with Her husband, unless it was one of Her deepest convictions that Her husband loved Her as no other human could have loved? We see the example of Joseph, in the fact that Jesus was subject to him. The fact is mentioned with awe in all Christian centuries, that he who was least in dignity in that Holy Family, was greatest in authority, entrusted by God with authority over the Son of God. Joseph would exercise it with all the respect due such authority.

(by Gasnier—*Joseph the Silent*, from pp. 29 & 155)

It was at Nazareth he became betrothed to Mary, and we have reason to think that it was there also that he was born and spent his early years. Some commentators hold that he was born at Bethlehem, but in that case it would be hard to explain why, on his arrival there with Mary at the time of the census, no relative, no friend, no house was open to receive them and they were obliged to seek shelter in an inn.

Who were Joseph's relatives at Nazareth? Again, there are no documents to tell us. However, a certain historian called Hegesippus, who lived in Palestine at the beginning of the second century and who might have been able to follow up the traditions kept in the surroundings themselves, writes that Joseph had a brother named Cleophas. It is supposedly that Cleophas, an uncle of Jesus, who had married the Mary of whom the Gospel speaks as being the "sister" of the Virgin, and who was probably the mother of the four "brothers" of the Savior—James, Joseph, Simon, and Jude—and of three sisters, whose names are not given.

St. Joseph was favored in that, from morning till evening, he lived with Jesus in closest intimacy. He worked with Him. They took their meals together, slept in the same room, prayed together.

Like a tree planted near the running brook of which the Psalmist sings, whose leaves stayed green and whose fruits never failed, Joseph lived always at the source of all grace, all life. His faith grew stronger and stronger, his love deeper and deeper. The Gospels opened out before his eyes in a manner familiar, continual, concrete.

And in the measure in which Christ revealed Himself to Joseph, his obedience to God became more perfect. Like Jesus Himself, his food and drink was the Father's will.

The more plausible derivation of the name Nazareth is En-Nazira, meaning the guardian, but a tradition coming down from St. Jerome says the name signified "City of Flowers." It is true that its springtime beauty made it look like a vast bouquet of many-colored flowers.

In their home, there was no luxury and very little comfort was to be found is such dwellings. Straw mats were scattered on the hard earthen floor. The wooden furniture was simple, like that of the people round about: bedrolls, clothes chests, household utensils, pitchers, a hand mill for grinding wheat, a rug or two, and cushions for visitors.

(by Griffin—*Saint Joseph & Third*, from pp. 105, 165, 265 & 364)

John Paul II said: "Work was the daily expression of love in the life of the Family of Nazareth."

Three times a year, St. Joseph and Mary made a pilgrimage to Jerusalem with the Child Jesus.

St. Joseph was truly and fully a father... the most perfect of fathers. He received his mission from God, and was given authority over the Child. Authority is taken from the Latin word "augere," which means to make grow.

St. Joseph, by welcoming Mary, his Spouse in Her virginal vocation, allowed Her to respond fully to God's plan, which made Her the Mother of the only Son of God. The father's role is not only to feed, educate, protect, and provide a mother for the child; it is also to introduce the child into human society, to give him, as it were, a social identity.

But the picture grows lifelike when we think of the holiest Three sitting crosslegged around a low table on the beaten mud floor of their home. They are dressed quite simply because they live in a semi-tropical climate. The mother has a head veil, the father and the boy wear a sort of turban, flowing down to protect their necks from the sun.

For garments, they wear an innermost "sindon," a sort of long shirt stretching to the knees. Over this is the tunic, ankle-length with slit skirt for facility in walking. A band of cloth at the waist gives the garment pleasing lines, and its appearance is helped even more by the striped reds and browns that are favorite colors.

Joseph wears a two-forked beard. Both Joseph and the Boy Jesus have two long locks of hair, ringlets framing their faces on each side, to agree with the contemporary custom. Mary's hair is made up in tresses.

They are eating their evening meal as we observe them. No silverware, not even wooden spoons are on the table. With their fingers, they delicately sample the boiled mutton with its pottage seasoned with mint. Joseph hands Jesus and Mary cucumbers or pomegranates of clusters of raisins—all favorite dishes. They have two beverages available, goat's milk and wine, kept in goatskin "bottles"—actually, sewed skins—from which the drinks are poured.

Their house looks so poorly furnished, but for the times it represents the living quarters of a middle-class village artisan. Of stone block, with the outer room extending back into the hill as a cave, it is low, perhaps windowless, getting its light through the open doorway or from the flickering lamp whose wick rests in a saucer of olive oil. There is little furniture to be seen, except for the gaily-colored mats folded along the wall. These will later be spread on the floor as night approaches, for beds, as we know them, are not the custom here.

The three are barefoot, because they are at home. Their sandals are placed side by side at the doorway, ready for use outside the house.

(by Healy Thompson—*Life And*, from pp. 96, 152,
158, 170, 177, 182, 339, 351 & 368)

Joseph, indeed, was poor, but he was not a beggar because he worked at a trade which implied manual labor, and his state in life should not be regarded as either mean or contemptible. With the Hebrews, who still retained many of the simple and primitive customs of the Patriarchs, the profession of an artisan, if not noble or distinguished, was yet far from being esteemed as the lowest. The arts were respected as useful to society, and a good artificer was preferred to the richest merchant.

Moreover, every father of a family was bound by the law to make his children learn some trade, even if they did not require them to practice it, in order that they might not take to dishonest practices or become a burden to others. Accordingly, we find that St. Paul, born in possession of the freedom of a Roman citizen and a learned doctor in the law, which he had studied at the feet of Gamaliel, had been taught the art of tent-making, which he afterwards practiced when an Apostle, that he might be a charge to no man.

The merit of Joseph, then, did not consist in his having been born poor and living a life of poverty, neither was it on this account that God chose him for His representative in the house of His Son on earth, but because he willed and loved to be poor, seeing that God Himself so willed and disposed it. He was inwardly sensible of the perfection which lay in embracing a life of poverty, even as if he had a prescience that the moment was at hand when voluntary poverty would become one of the most splendid ornaments with which a creature could deck itself in the eyes of its Creator.

Joseph and Mary went to establish themselves in Nazareth, where the Blessed Virgin owned a small house, inherited from Her parents, along with some slender possessions in Sephora and in Carmel. We have good reason to believe that the holy spouses never contemplated retaining the whole of the patrimony which Mary inherited from Her parents, and which, moderate as it was, would probably have sufficed to raise them above the level of actual poverty.

Joseph knew, says the pious and learned Gerson, that he was the head of Mary, because the husband is the head of the wife. Nevertheless, his veneration for Her was so profound that he considered himself unworthy to be Her companion, or even to kiss the ground on which She had walked; and he was always on the watch to render Her some service, although unrequested, even as might some most devoted servant rather than spouse. And then he loved Her so exceedingly, with a love like what the Heavenly Spirits feel for each other, and would have readily given his heart's blood for Her; and as yet he knew not Her incomparable dignity!

Mary (says Isloano) gave honor to Joseph, not only as Her husband, but as Her tutor and guardian; She never departed a hair's breadth from his wishes; She never determined on anything without his advise, never moved a step without his permission, nor undertook anything without his consent. In everything, She depended on his will, for in the will of Joseph She recognized the most holy will of God. They were one heart and one soul—what concord, then, what tranquillity, what peace reigned between them!

St. Bernardine of Siena wrote: "Since the Virgin comprehended how great was conjugal unity in spiritual love, and knew that this spouse had been given Her directly by the Spirit of God, I believe that She sincerely loved Joseph with the entire affection of Her heart;" and Isidoro Isolano adds that: "The love of the saints is the most ardent, the most perfect, and the holiest of loves." John of Cartagena, indeed, argues that eminent sanctity of Joseph above all the saints from the very fact of Mary's most ardent love of him; for "knowing" he says, "the obligation that lay upon Her to love Her spouse, She loved St. Joseph more than all the patriarchs and prophets, martyrs, apostles, and angels."

What felicity for Joseph, and what an honor, to enjoy the whole love of Her who with a single glance of Her eye could enhance the joy of the angels of Paradise! Now it is that we can realize how the Evangelist, desiring to express the highest encomium of Joseph, comprised it in these few words; "Joseph, the husband of Mary." The "being Mary's spouse" was the foundation and basis of all his dignity.

St. Gabriel bowed low before the Virgin of Nazareth, and said, "Hail, Full of Grace, the Lord is with Thee. Blessed art Thou among women."

After the Annunciation, Joseph as yet knew nothing of the sublime dignity to which his Spouse had been exalted. Mary met him as usual, with the same loving reverence, kneeling down to wash his feet when he returned wearied with his labors; but we believe that he must have experienced an undefined impression of veneration for Her, and would have preferred to cast himself humbly at Her feet.

If favored souls are sometimes sensibly conscious of the Presence of the Blessed Sacrament in our churches, how much more must holy Joseph, whose spiritual senses were so delicate and refined, have felt his heart burn within him with divine charity, from the nearness of Him Who now dwelt in Mary as His living Tabernacle!

But She said nothing; perhaps was even more silent than was Her custom. She went about Her usual employments; She prepared the frugal meal, and all was the same, yet not the same, for a glory must have shone in the countenance of the august Mother, and a fragrance of Paradise have pervaded that lowly dwelling.

But why did not Mary confide in Joseph, for previously he had been the depositary of all Her thoughts? First, because the secret which the angel had revealed to Her She understood to have been intended for Herself alone, wherefore She would not communicate it, even to Joseph, fearing to go beyond the Divine will. Moreover, the Virgin was possessed of much discretion and forethought. If She made known to him that the Son of God had become Incarnate within Her, She knew, indeed, that he would believe Her, but She knew also his humility and reverent spirit, and may have thought that, awed by so much majesty, he would perhaps retire and leave Her. She waited therefore until the mystery should be divinely manifested to him; and finally, being Herself perfect Mistress of humility, She dared not utter any word which would turn to Her Own praise.

It may have taken them three days to reach the city where Elizabeth and Zachary dwelt, which is commonly supposed to be Hebron.

In favor of the claims of Aim Karem, are the Sanctuary of the Visitation of Mary to Elizabeth existing there, and another pointed out as the birthplace of John the Baptist, as also the spot where he was concealed from the rage of Herod, and the desert and grotto where he abode from his tenderest years. But no written record remains to testify to any ancient tradition on the subject. The general opinion of doctors is that the city of Juda mentioned by St. Luke is Hebron, the ancient Cariath-Arbe, a sacredotal city, and one of the cities of refuge.

Some writers believe that Joseph remained with Mary the three months in the house of Zachary.

All the males in Israel were bound by the Mosaic Law to appear three times yearly before the Lord...that is, at the Feast of the Pasch, at Pentecost, and at the Feast of Tabernacles.

In Heaven, the saints behold nothing but what is lovable. Such also was Joseph's life on earth; full of light, burning with love, and plunged in ineffable delight.

When Jesus was displaying the first rays of His glory before the Doctors of Israel, and in the very midst of His divine instructions, a word from Mary made Him leave all, and meekly return with Her and Joseph to Nazareth. It is scarcely necessary to observe that when our Lord says His hour was not come, we are to understand that it would not have come but for His Mother's intercession. What a light is here shown on the wonderful potency of prayer and, above all, on Mary's influence with Her Son!

(by John Paul II—*Guardian*, from pp. 10 & 18)

Besides offering a salutation which recalled that of the angel at the Annunciation, Elizabeth also said: "And blessed is She who believed that there would be a fulfillment of what was spoken to Her from the Lord" (Lk. 1:45). These words were the guiding thought of the Encyclical *Redemptoris Mater*, in which I sought to deepen the teaching of the Second Vatican Council, which stated: "The Blessed Virgin advanced in Her pilgrimage of faith, and faithfully preserved Her union with Her Son, even to the cross," preceding all those who follow Christ by faith.

Now at the beginning of this pilgrimage, the faith of Mary meets the faith of Joseph. If Elizabeth said of the Redeemer's Mother, "blessed is She who believed," in a certain sense this blessedness can be referred to Joseph as well, since he responded positively to the Word of God when it was communicated to him at the decisive moment.

One can say that what Joseph did, united him in an altogether special way to the faith of Mary. He accepted as truth, coming from God, the very thing that She had already accepted at the Annunciation.

Joseph is the first to share in the faith of the Mother of God, and that in doing so, he supports his Spouse in the faith of the Divine Annunciation. He is also the first to be placed by God on the path of Mary's "pilgrimage of faith." It is a path along which—especially at the time of Calvary and Pentecost—Mary will precede in a perfect way.

The path that was Joseph's—his pilgrimage of faith—ended first, that is to say, before Mary stood at the foot of the cross on Golgotha, and before the time after Christ returned to the Father, when She was present in the upper room on Pentecost, the day the Church was manifested to the world, having been born in the power of the Spirit of Truth. Nevertheless, Joseph's way of faith moved in the same direction: it was totally determined by the same mystery, of which he, together with Mary, had been the first guardian.

The Incarnation and Redemption constitute an organic and indissoluble unity, in which "the plan of revelation is realized by words and deeds which are intrinsically bound up with each other." Precisely because of this unity, Pope John XXIII, who had a great devotion to Saint Joseph, directed that Joseph's name be inserted in the Roman Canon of the Mass—which is the perpetual memorial of Redemption—after the name of Mary and before the apostles, popes, and martyrs.

At the Circumcision, Joseph names the Child "Jesus." This is the only Name in which there is salvation (cf. Acts 4:12). Its significance had been revealed to Joseph at the moment of his "annunciation": "You shall call the Child Jesus, for He will save His people from their sins" (cf. Mt 1:21). In conferring the Name, Joseph declares his own legal fatherhood over Jesus, and in speaking the name, he proclaims the Child's mission as Savior.

(by Levy—*Joseph, the Just Man*, from pp. 66, 76 & 130)

When Joseph heard that Archelaus reigned in Judea in the place of Herod, his father, he was afraid to go thither. He prayed for guidance and the angel appeared to him for the fourth time to direct him. "Being warned in sleep," the Gospel tells us, "he retired into the quarters of Galilee...and dwelt in a city called Nazareth that it might be fulfilled which was said by the prophets; 'that He shall be called a Nazarene'" (Matt. 2:22, 23).

The Bishop of Nottingham, England, wrote in 1887 during the Holy Season of Advent: "In the Holy House of Nazareth, the Child was the Teacher of His parents, not taught by them. The Eternal Wisdom of God could learn nothing from any creature, even in His human nature. Divine light, and teaching, and grace poured forth from His every act and word into the souls of His father and Mother. Yet, while He thus enlightened them—the two most perfect of His creatures—His every look and word were those of a docile and obedient Child.

"He followed their directions and obeyed their commands, and also the commands of His Heavenly Father, sent, not to Him directly, but to them for Him. He sat at their feet, hearing them and asking them questions, as He did with the priests in the Temple, while they always hung upon His words, and pondered them in their hearts, and wondered at His wisdom and at His answers.

"How marvellous must have been that school of Heavenly Wisdom, in which Mary and Joseph were but pupils, where even the Virgin of Good Counsel, the Seat of Wisdom Herself, and Her dear spouse Joseph, the Just Man, the son of David, did not always comprehend the Word that was said, but had to ponder divine mysteries in their hearts, waiting for further illuminations of the Holy Spirit!

"What perfect and consummate wisdom was there breathed forth! What inconceivable perfection and holiness of life was there displayed! The angels who looked on in adoring admiration might have paraphrased the words of the prayer taught to the Apostles, and have besought God that His will might be done by them in Heaven, as it was done by Jesus upon earth.

"For thirty years was Jesus subject to His parents, and for thirty years did that Paradise of Delights, the Holy House of Nazareth, continue to offer to us a model of every Christian virtue, or which at least according to their measure, every home should imitate.

"Dear children in Christ, visit in spirit that Holy House. Consider its poverty, and the rudeness and simplicity of its furniture. Behold also the exquisite cleanliness, order, and neatness which is manifested in every detail. Though poor, it is bright and cheerful, made so by the looks and words of loving hearts, and the labors of loving hands. The Eternal God, and the Queen of Heaven and Her spouse, chose not to have earthly magnificence around them. Had they possessed it, they being perfect, would have sold what they had, and given to the poor.

"They chose the better part of voluntary poverty, working with their hands that even so they might have wherewith to give to those who were in need. They knew how many of the houses of their neighbors must be poor and destitute. Therefore, they took their part in poverty and destitution, to show that the deepest poverty can be enriched and made happy by the love of God and man.

"How can we sufficiently admire the unremitting, uncomplaining, self-sacrificing toil of Joseph, who was honored by the Eternal Father with the office of governing and working for His Eternal Son and the ever-blessed Virgin Mother! How shall we wonder at the sweet, gentle, assiduous labors of Mary, watching over the comfort of Her husband and Her Child, never forgetting nor omitting anything which might cheer or alleviate their earthly lot, and brightening their home with Her beautiful and loving smiles!

"How shall we adore the gracious Child, advancing daily in wisdom, and age, and grace with God and man, manifesting ever more and more to His parents' wondering eyes the hidden perfections of His Godhead, and captivating their love by His reverent obedience and sweet attentions, and gentle loving ways!

"What a school of love was there! Jesus, the ocean of created love and charity; Mary, full of grace and love as much as was possible to a pure Creature; Joseph, the guardian-father of Jesus, the virgin-husband of Mary, the companion and disciple of Both, and filled by God with that supreme love which such offices required.

"Every kind of created tenderness was there. There was the ineffable mutual love of husband for Wife and of Wife for husband, intensified as well as purified by the virginity of both. There was the love of father and the love of Mother for their Child; for He was the Child of both, preordained to be the recompense and bond of their virginal union. There was the love of the Child for His parents, intense and perfect, as must have been every kind of love in the Sacred Heart of God.

"There was the pattern of charity, piety, and mutual service and kindness, which should be imitated in every Catholic home. There was also a pattern of religious observance and of the worship of God. We read in the Holy Scriptures how perfectly our Lord and His parents observed the Law of Moses, even when they might have justly claimed to be dispensed from it.

"We know He and His Blessed Mother and Saint Joseph were ever engaged in unceasing love and contemplation of the Divinity. We can imagine, then, something of the solicitous attention, the reverence, and the devotion of the prayerful life of the Holy Family in their humble home. Prayer of the heart without ceasing, prayer in common many times a day, prayer undistracted, prayer made with adoring reverence in the visible Presence of God, prayer enriched with the divine blessing of Him Who prayed.

"There also was the virtue of temperance in its perfection. In Jesus and Mary is found no evil passion to restrain, and in Joseph, a saint already made perfect in self-denial. Yet it lost nothing of its perfection or of the fullness of its practice. Obedience, self-sacrifice, humility, mortification of the appetites, meekness, chastity, modesty, sobriety—all concurred to the holiness and happiness of that home."

St. Francis de Sales.—"There is no doubt that St. Joseph was more valiant than David and wiser than Solomon; nevertheless, seeing him so humbly working in his carpenter's shop, who would have imagined (unless enlightened supernaturally) that he was endowed by God with such marvellous gifts, so closely and carefully did he keep them concealed! But what must not his wisdom have been, seeing that God committed to his charge His all-glorious Son and chose him to be His guardian!

"If earthly princes consider it a matter of so much importance to select carefully a tutor fit for their children, think you that the Eternal God would not, in His almighty power and wisdom, choose from out of His creation the most perfect man living to be the guardian of His divine and most glorious Son, the Prince of Heaven and earth? There is, then, no doubt at all that Saint Joseph was endowed with all gifts and graces required by the charge which the Eternal Father willed to commit to him, over all the domestic and temporal concerns of our Lord, and the guidance of his family, which was composed of three persons only, representing to us the mystery of the most Holy and Adorable Trinity.

"Not that there is any real comparison in this matter, excepting as regards our Lord, Who is one of the Persons of the most Blessed Trinity, for the others were but creatures; yet still we may say that it was a trinity on earth representing in some sort the most Holy Trinity, Mary, Jesus, and Joseph—Joseph, Jesus, and Mary—a trinity worthy to be honored and greatly esteemed!

(by Neuzil—*Our Lady of America*, from p. 29)

Joseph said, "I was king in the little home of Nazareth, for I sheltered within it the Prince of Peace and Queen of Heaven. To me They looked for protection and sustenance, and I did not fail Them. I received from Them the deepest love and reverence, for in me They saw Him, Whose place I took over Them.

"So the head of the family must be loved, obeyed, and respected, and in return be a true father and protector to those under his care.

"In honoring, in a special way, my father-hood, you also honor Jesus and Mary. The Divine Trinity has placed into our keeping the peace of the world. The imitation of the Holy Family, of the virtues we practiced in our little home at Nazareth, is the way for all souls to that peace which comes from God alone, and which none other can give."

(by O'Carroll—*The King Uncrowned*, from p. 95)

Visitors to the Holy Land and archaeologists reconstruct Nazareth in outline for us, as a group of small houses, strung together in narrow streets in a beautiful and fertile part of Palestine, possibly the most delightful site in all that land, a verdant space with hills about it that easily took on a wooded cover. The inhabitants derived sustenance easily from the flocks which fed on its surrounding pastures and from the vines, olives, and corn that grow with singular richness in its soil. Houses were small and frequently two would have use of the same small courtyard.

In this wise, communal intercourse was normal. The sanctity of the home was held in respect but it would never completely envelop and conceal one of the family. Jesus was a villager Who took His part in the public ritual and public activities of this small community. Joseph was a man known to all by reason of his trade.

(by O'Rafferty—*Discourses*, from pp. 58 & 123)

The High Priest was inspired by God to insist that, despite their vow of virginity, Mary and Joseph consent to be united in marriage. When the year following the ceremony of their espousals came to an end, their marriage took place in Jerusalem. They were surely accompanied to the Temple by their relatives and friends. There, before the High Priest, they pledged each other fidelity until death did them part, and were blessed by him. Then they proceeded to the nuptial chamber, preceded according to custom by harpists and flutists and youth who shouted in joy, waving boughs of myrtle and palms, which they strewed along the bridal path.

As the nuptial cortege reached Joseph's house, where the wedding feast was prepared, the happy couple entered full of joy, while the guests intoned a hymn of gladness: "Blessed are they who come in the name of the Lord." Joseph and Mary were then seated at the table in places of honor which, despite their great humility, they could not decline. What a beautiful spectacle! It has much in common with the Marriage Feast at Cana of Galilee. Surely the marriage of Joseph and Mary is a model for all Christian marriages!

No sooner were the ceremonies of that joyful day concluded that Joseph and Mary renewed their vow of virginity, and promised to live together like the angels of Heaven. Then, after spending some few days in Jerusalem, they returned to Nazareth to the humble house which Mary inherited from Her parents, Joachim and Anne.

After their stay in Egypt, acting on the angel's warning which Joseph received in his sleep, he and Mary calmly and quietly took the road

that led to Nazareth, from which they had
been absent for so many years. Who can fathom
the feelings which were theirs when they came
within view of that dear city where Mary was
born, and where the Son of God became Man
and began to dwell among us? Who can describe
the reception which the people of Nazareth
began to prepare for the Holy Family as soon
as word reached them that they were about
to arrive among them? We can imagine how
their old friends rushed out of their homes to
greet them and bid them welcome, as well as
to admire the Child Jesus, Who was now six
or seven years old, and Whose beauty was
beyond description. The Holy Family finally took
possession of their little home, which belonged
to them, and having arranged everything to
their satisfaction, they resumed their way of life
so humble and so perfect.

(by Patrignani—*Manual*, from p. 16)

O admirable Virgin! In the house at Nazareth,
You, as well as Jesus, placed all Your glory
and happiness in obeying Joseph in all things:
the slightest intimation of his wishes was a
command in Your estimation; his will was the
rule and guide of all Your actions, thoughts, and
affections. In short, it was Your highest ambition
to descend to the lowest and most servile offices,
in order to testify to Joseph the extent of that
affection so justly due to the best of husbands;
to show Your respect for so zealous and
honorable a protector, and Your readiness to
obey one whom You might well designate the
most tender of fathers.

(by Robert—*Guardian of God's Lilies*, from pp. 9 & 12)

The great St. Jerome and the Blessed Theodoret tell us that St. Joseph was a carpenter by trade. St. Hilary and St. Peter Chrysologus say he wrought in iron, as a smith. But it is most likely that he wrought both in iron and in wood. This opinion St. Augustine favors by saying, "He and Jesus made ploughs and yokes for oxen."

St. Joseph was supremely happy because in all things he sought to know and to fulfill perfectly God's Holy Will. When trials came to him, he bowed his head, and kept on doing his work the best he knew how. He did not always know where that Will would lead him, as far as this earthly life was concerned, but he was sure that if he followed it, it would guide him straight to the Kingdom of God.

(by Rondet—*Saint Joseph*, from p. 100)

For Joseph to safeguard Mary's virginity under cover of marriage, it was needful that he should be pure as an angel, so that his virtue could in some sort correspond to the purity of his Maiden Bride. To protect the Savior Jesus amid the dangers of His Childhood, it was needful that Joseph should be immovably faithful, with a faithfulness that could not be shaken by the threat of any adversity. To cherish

the secret entrusted to him, it was needful that
Joseph should be specially humble, avoiding the
public gaze, withholding himself from the world,
loving to be hidden with Christ Jesus.

(by Sabat-Rivers—*Saint Joseph Day*, from p. 6)

Joseph was the man whom Scripture does not
record a single word, who never puts himself
forward, but who is always there when he is
needed.

(by St. Bridget—*Revelations*, from p. 33)

No uncleanness appeared upon Jesus, nor
entanglement in His hair. When He came to more
advanced years, He was in constant prayer, and
obediently went up with us to Jerusalem and
elsewhere to the appointed feasts; so wonderful
then were His sight and words, and so acceptable,
that many in affliction said: "Let us go to Mary's
Son, by Whom we may be consoled."

But increasing in age and wisdom, wherewith
He was replete from the first, He labored with His
Hands in such things as were becoming, and
spoke to us separately words of consolation and
divinity, so that we were continually filled with
unspeakable joy. But when we were in fear,
poverty, and difficulty, He did not make for us
gold and silver, but exhorted us to patience, and
we were wonderfully preserved from the envious.

Necessaries were occasionally furnished to us by the compassion of pious souls...sometimes from our own labor, so that we had what was necessary for our actual support, but not for superfluity, for we only sought to serve God.

After this, He conversed familiarly with friends, who came to the house, on the law and its meanings and figures; He also openly disputed with the learned, so that they wondered, saying: "Ho! Joseph's Son teaches the masters; some great Spirit speaketh in Him."

Once, as I was thinking of His Passion, seeing My sadness, He said: "Dost Thou not believe, Mother, that I am in the Father, and the Father in Me? Wast Thou sullied when I entered Thee, or in pain when I came forth? Why art Thou contracted by sadness? For it is the will of My Father that I suffer death; nay, My will with the Father. What I have of the Father cannot suffer; but the flesh which I took of Thee shall suffer, that the flesh of others may be redeemed, and their spirits saved."

He was so obedient that when Joseph by chance said: "Do this or that," He immediately did it, because He so concealed the power of His divinity that it could not be discerned except by Me, and sometimes by Joseph, who both often saw an admirable light poured around Him and heard angelic voices singing over Him. We also saw that unclean spirits, which could not be expelled by tried exorcists in our law, departed at the sight of My Son's Presence.

Our Lord's Appearance

Such as My Son is in Heaven, you cannot behold. But hear what He was in Body in the world. He was so beautiful of countenance that

293.

no one looked Him in the Face without being consoled by His aspect, even if heartbroken with grief. The just were consoled with spiritual consolation; and even the bad were relieved from worldly sadness, as long as they gazed upon Him. Hence, those in grief were wont to say: "Let us go and see Mary's Son; we shall be relieved for that time."

In His twentieth year, He was perfect in manly strength and stature. Amid those of modern times, he would be large, not fleshy, but of large frame and muscle. His hair, eyebrows, and beard were of a light brown, His beard a hand's width long. His forehead not prominent or retreating, but erect. His nose moderate, neither small nor large; His eyes were so pure that even His enemies delighted to look upon Him; His lips not thick, but clear red. His chin was not prominent or over long, but graceful in beautiful moderation. His cheeks modestly fleshy, His complexion clear white and red. His bearing erect, and His whole Body spotless.

(by Stein—*The Tapestry*, from p. 38)

The Blessed Virgin Mary said to St. Bridget, "St. Joseph was so reserved and careful in his speech that not one word ever issued from his mouth that was not good and holy, nor did he ever indulge in unnecessary or less charitable conversation. He was most patient and diligent in bearing fatigue. He practiced extreme poverty. He was most meek in bearing injuries. He was strong and constant against My enemies.

"He was the faithful witness of the wonders of Heaven, being dead to the flesh and the world, living only for God and for Heavenly goods, which were the only things he desired. He was perfectly conformed to the divine will and so resigned to the dispositions of Heaven that he often repeated: 'May the will of God be ever done in me!' He rarely spoke with men, but continually with God, Whose will he desired to perform. Wherefore, he now enjoys great glory in Heaven."

(by Stramare—*Saint Joseph,* from pp. 135, 149 & 152)

St. Joseph chiefly tended toward the contemplation of truth. Joseph was in daily contact with the mystery hidden for ages, which dwelled under the roof of his house.

While one takes delight in the vision of the thing loved, the delight itself in the thing seen excites love all the more. That is why Gregory says that when one sees the beloved, he is more intensely enkindled with love for him. And this is the ultimate perfection of the contemplative life; that divine truth is not only seen, but is also loved.

God will demand less from many, more from others; from some He will demand all. From Joseph, God did indeed demand all, unconditionally. And Joseph responded with a dedication without equal, making himself the servant of Jesus with the love of a father. He placed himself effectively at the service of Jesus as a total sacrifice, making himself a holocaust to God's will, taking upon himself all the tasks and responsibilities of the family, and renouncing the most legitimate human aspirations.

St. Joseph speaks little, but he lives intensely, never shirking any responsibility which the will of God places on him. He presents an example of attractive availability to the divine call, of calm in every event, of complete trust flowing from a life of superhuman faith and charity and from the great means of prayer... One who has faith does not tremble, does not rush events, does not disturb his neighbor.

Of course, because of the work in which he was occupied, St. Joseph is especially presented as a model of holiness to the class of people that constitutes the overwhelming majority of mankind. By his life of most faithful fulfillment of daily duty, he left an example to all those who must earn their bread by the work of their hands, and he deserves to be called the just man, the living example of that Christian justice which must reign in social life.

(by Suarez—*Joseph of Nazareth*, from p. 145)

Every year His parents went to Jerusalem. Nazareth is some seventy miles from Jerusalem by the most direct route. As Passover drew near, several families would join together to make the pilgrimage, keeping one another company and helping each other. They would break journey each evening after making fifteen or twenty miles; Jerusalem would be about four days away, and coming from as far up-country as they did, they would stay there for a whole week before making their way back to Galilee.

(*The Spiritual Doctrine*, from p. 214)

Jesus wished, by His example, to instruct the Blessed Virgin and Saint Joseph, who alone were more important in His eyes than all other creatures.

(by Valtorta—*Poem, Vol. 1*, from pp. 91, 194 & 206)

Joseph is a handsome man in the prime of life. He must be 35 years old at most. His face is framed by his dark brown hair and a beard of the same color and his eyes are very sweet and very dark, almost black. His forehead is large and smooth, his nose thin and slightly aquiline, his cheeks are roundish of a brown hue, but not olive-colored, on the contrary they are rosy near the cheek-bones. He is not very tall, but he is strong and well-built.

Before sitting down, he offers Mary two eggs and a bunch of grapes, somewhat withered, but well-preserved. And he smiles saying: "The grapes were brought to me from Cana. I was given the eggs by a Centurion for some repair work I did to his cart. A wheel was broken and their carpenter fill ill. They are new laid. He took them from the hen house. Drink them. They will do You good."

Mary gets up at once to fix something to eat for Joseph. She comes back from the kitchen with some milk, some olives, cheese, an apple and some bread. "I have nothing else," says Mary. "Take an egg." But Joseph does not want it. The eggs are for Mary. He eats with relish his bread and the cheese, and he drinks the lukewarm milk. He then accepts an apple. And his supper is over.

The First Working Lesson Given to Jesus

I see my little Jesus appear as sweet as a ray of sun on a rainy day; He is a little Child about five years old, completely blond and most beautiful in His simple blue dress which reaches down to half His well-shaped calves. He is playing with some earth in the little kitchen garden. He makes little heaps with it and on top He plants little branches as if He were making a miniature forest, with little stones He builds little roads and then He would like to build a little lake at the foot of His tiny hills. He therefore takes the bottom part of an old pot and inters it up to its brim and then fills it with water with a pitcher which He dips into a vessel, which is certainly used either for washing purposes or to water the little garden. But the only result is that He wets His dress, particularly its sleeves. The water runs out of the chipped pot which is probably also cracked and...the lake dries up.

Joseph appears at the door, and for some time he stands very quietly watching the work of the Child and smiles. It is a sight, indeed, that makes one smile happily. Then, to prevent Jesus from getting more wet, he calls Him. Jesus turns round smiling, and when He sees Joseph, Jesus runs towards him with His little Arms stretched out. Joseph, with the edge of his short working tunic, dries the little Hands which are soiled and wet, and kisses them.

And then there is a sweet conversation between the two. Jesus explains His work and His game, and the difficulties He met in it. He wanted to make a lake like the lake of Gennesaret. (I therefore suppose that they have either spoken to Him about it or they had taken Him to see it.) He wanted to make a little one for His own delight. This was Tiberias, there was Magdala, over there Capernaum. This was the road that one took to Nazareth, going through Cana. He wanted to launch some little boats in the lake; these leaves are boats, and He wanted to go over to the other shore. But the water runs away...

Joseph watches and takes an interest, as if it were a very serious matter. He then proposes to make a small lake the following day...but not with an old cracked pot, but with a small wooden basin, well coated with pitch and stucco, in which Jesus would be able to launch small real wooden boats which Joseph would teach Him how to make. Just then, he was bringing Him some small working tools, suitable for Him, that He might learn to use them, without any fatigue.

"So I will be able to help you!" Jesus says, smiling.

"So You will help me, and You will become a clever Carpenter. Come and see them."

And they go into the workshop. Joseph shows Him a small hammer, a tiny saw, some very small screwdrivers, a plane suitable for a doll, which are all lying on the bench of a budding carpenter: a bench suitable for little Jesus' size.

"See, to saw, You must put this piece of wood like that. You then take the saw like that, and making sure that You do not catch Your fingers, You start sawing. Try..."

And the lesson begins. And Jesus, blushing with the effort and pressing His lips together, saws the piece of wood carefully and then planes it, and although it is not perfectly straight, He thinks it is nice. Joseph praises Him and with patience and love teaches Him how to work.

Mary comes back. She had certainly gone out, and She looks in at the door. Joseph and Jesus do not see Her because She is behind them. Mother smiles seeing how zealously Jesus is working with the plane and how loving Joseph is in teaching Him.

But Jesus must have perceived Her smile. He turns round, sees His Mother and runs towards Her, showing Her the little piece of wood not yet finished. Mary admires it, and She bends down to kiss Jesus. She tidies up His ruffled curls, wipes the perspiration on His hot Face, and listens with loving attention to Jesus, Who promises to make Her a little stool so that She will be more comfortable when working. Joseph standing near the tiny bench, with one hand resting on his side, looks and smiles. I have thus been present at the first work lesson of my Jesus...and all the peace of this Holy Family is within me.

Later... Jesus is a handsome young Boy, 12 years old, well-built, strong but not fat. He looks older that His years, because of His complexion. He is already tall; in fact He reaches up to the shoulders of His Mother. His Face is a rosy round Face of a Child and later, in His youth and then in His manhood, it will get thinner and thinner. His lovely blond hair is already somewhat darker than when He was a little Boy.

"Here is our Son," says Mary, lifting Her right hand which is holding Jesus' left one. She seems to be introducing Him to everybody and confirming the paternity of the just man who is smiling. And She adds: "Bless Him, Joseph, before leaving for Jerusalem. There was no ritual blessing for His first step in life, because it was not necessary for Him to go to school. But now that He is going to the Temple to be proclaimed of age, please bless Him. And bless Me with Him. Your blessing..." (Mary sobs softly) "will fortify Him and give Me strength, to detach Myself a little more from Him."

Mary bends down and takes Joseph's hand and kisses it. She is the respectful, loving Spouse of Her consort.

Joseph receives the sign of respect and love with dignity; he then lifts the hand which She has kissed and lays it on the head of his Spouse and says to Her: "Yes. I bless You, oh blessed One, and I bless Jesus with You. Come to me my only joys, my honor and essence of my life." Joseph is solemn. With his arms stretched out and the palms of his hands turned down above the Two Heads which are bent down, both blond and holy, he pronounces his blessing: "May the Lord look upon You and bless You. May He have mercy on You and give You peace. May the Lord give You His blessing... And now let us go."

~~~~~~~~

Jesus says:

I have consoled you, My dear soul, with a vision of My childhood, which was happy in its poverty, because it was surrounded by the love of two saints, the greatest the world ever had. They say that Joseph was My foster-father.

Oh! If, being a man he could not feed Me with milk, as My Mother Mary did, he worked very hard, indeed, to give Me bread and comfort, and he had the loving kindness of a real mother. From him I learned—and never had a pupil a kinder teacher—I learned everything that makes a man of a child, and a man who is to earn his own bread.

If My intelligence, that of the Son of God was perfect, you must consider and believe that I did not want to deviate from the attributes and attainments of My own age group ostentatiously. Therefore, by lowering My divine intellectual perfection to that of a human intellectual perfection, I submitted Myself to having a man as My teacher, and to the need of a teacher. If I learned quickly and willingly, that does not deprive Me of the merit of submitting Myself to man, neither does it deprive the just man of the merit of being the person who nourished My young mind with the ideas which are necessary to life.

Not even now that I am in Heaven, can I forget the happy hours I spent beside Joseph, who, as if he were playing with Me, guided Me to the point of being capable of working. And when I look at My putative father, I see once again the little kitchen garden and the smoky workshop, and I still appear to see Mother peep in with Her beautiful smile which turned the place into Paradise and made us so happy.

How much families should learn from the perfection of this couple who loved each other as nobody else ever loved! Joseph was the head of the family, and as such, his authority was undisputed and indisputable; before it the Spouse and Mother of God bent reverently and the Son of God submitted Himself willingly. Whatever Joseph decided to do, was well done; there were no discussions, no punctiliousness, no oppositions. His word was our little law. And yet, how much humility there was in him! There never was any abuse of power, or any decision against reason only because he was the head of the family. His Spouse was his sweet adviser. And if in Her deep humility She considered Herself the servant of Her consort, he drew from Her wisdom of Full of Grace, light to guide him in all events.

And I grew like a flower protected by vigorous trees, between those two loves that interlaced above Me, to protect Me, and love Me.

No. As long as I was able to ignore the world because of My age, I did not regret being absent from Paradise. God the Father and the Holy Spirit were not absent, because Mary was full of Them. And the angels dwelt there, because nothing drove them away from that house. And one of them, I might say, had become flesh and was Joseph, an angelical soul freed from the burden of the flesh, intent only on serving God and His cause, and loving Him as the seraphim love Him. Joseph's look! It was as placid and pure as the brightness of a star unaware of worldly concupiscence. It was our peace, and our strength.

Many think that I did not suffer as a human being when the holy glance of the guardian of our home was extinguished by death. If I was God, and as such I was aware of the happy destiny of Joseph, and consequently I was not sorry for his death, because after a short time in Limbo, I was going to open Heaven to him... as a Man, I cried bitterly in the house now empty and deprived of his presence. I cried over My dead friend, and should I not have cried over My holy friend, on whose chest I had slept when I was a little Boy, and from whom I had received so much love in so many years?

Finally I would like to draw the attention of parents to how Joseph made a clever workman of Me, without any help of pedagogical learning. As soon as I was old enough to handle tools, he did not let Me lead a life of idleness, but he started Me to work and he made use of My love for Mary as the means to spur Me to work. I was to make useful things for Mother. That is how he inculcated the respect which every son should have for his mother and the teaching for the future carpenter was based on that respectful and loving incentive.

Where are now the families in which the little ones are taught to love work as a means of pleasing their parents? Children, nowadays, are the tyrants of the house. They grow hard, indifferent, ill-mannered towards their parents. They consider their parents as their servants, their slaves. They do not love their parents and they are scarcely loved by them. The reason is that, while you allow your children to become objectionable overbearing fellows, you become detached from them with shameful indifference.

They are everybody's children, except yours, oh parents of the twentieth century. They are the children of the nurse, of the governess, of the college...if you are rich people. They belong to their companions; they are the children of the streets, of the schools...if you are poor. But they are not yours. You, mothers, give birth to them and that is all. And you, fathers, do exactly the same. But a son is not only flesh. He has a mind, a heart, a soul. Believe Me, no one is more entitled and more obliged than a father and a mother to form that mind, that heart, that soul.

A family is necessary: it exists and must exist. There is no theory or progress capable of destroying this truth without causing ruin.

A shattered family can but yield men and women who in future will be more perverted, and will cause greater and greater ruin. And I tell you most solemnly that it would be better if there were no more marriages and no more children on the earth, rather than have families less united than the tribes of monkeys, families which are not schools of virtue, of work, of love, of religion, but a babel in which everyone lives on his own, like disengaged gears which end up by breaking.

Broken families. You break up the most holy way of social living and you see and suffer the consequences. You may continue thus, if you so wish. But do not complain if this world is becoming a deeper and deeper hell, a dwelling place of monsters who devour families and nations. You want it. Let it be so.

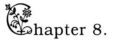

hapter 8.

Joys and Sorrows of St. Joseph

(by Agreda—*City (Transfixion)*, from p. 133)

Saint Joseph, although he was not so very old at the time when our Blessed Lady reached Her 33rd year, was much broken and worn out, as far as his body was concerned; for his continual cares, his journeys, and his incessant labors for the sustenance of his Spouse and of the Lord had weakened him much more than his years. This was so ordained by the Lord, Who, wishing to lead him on to the practice of patience and of other virtues, permitted him to suffer sickness and pain.

From that time on, he rested from the hard labor of his hands, by which he had earned a livelihood for all three. They gave away the carpenter tools as an alms, not wishing to have anything superfluous or useless in their house and family. Being thus at leisure, Saint Joseph occupied himself entirely in the contemplation of the mysteries of which he was the guardian and in the exercise of virtues. As he had the happiness and good fortune of continually enjoying the sight and the intercourse of the Divine Wisdom Incarnate, and of Her, Who was the Mother of It, this man of God reached such a height of sanctity, that, his Heavenly Spouse excepted, no one ever surpassed him, and he far outstripped all other creatures.

The Blessed Lady, and also Her Most Holy Son, attended upon him and nursed him in his sickness, consoling and sustaining him with the greatest assiduity; and hence, there are no words sufficiently expressive of the humility, reverence, and love which all this caused in the simple and grateful heart of this man of God. He thus became the admiration and joy of the angels and the pleasure and delight of the Most High.

(by Baij—*Life of*, from pp. 162, 175, 177, 180, 221, 289 & 292)

The Divine Infant looked lovingly at Joseph and spoke appealingly to his heart. He revealed to him how willing He was to suffer, so that the will of the Heavenly Father might be accomplished, and for the redemption of mankind. In addition, He interiorly declared to him: "Other sufferings await Me. I already embrace them now, and I long to show the world how much I love My Heavenly Father and all mankind. After all, it was to save men that I came down from Heaven upon this earth, assumed human flesh, and became man. I shall willingly accept sufferings, and even choose death so that, thereby, the work of man's redemption may be accomplished."

The favor which the divine Savior granted
Joseph, that of hearing Jesus speak interiorly
to him, brought with it much consolation and
satisfaction; it filled Joseph with love and
trust. Inasmuch as he now realized that the
Savior would have much to suffer and will
finally have to die to complete the work of
mankind's redemption, he was saddened afresh.
In this manner, Joseph's joys and consolations
always happened to be accompanied by some
distress and suffering. Due to his complete
abandonment to the divine will, he accepted
with equal readiness either consolations or
tribulations. His countenance always bore a
peaceful and contented expression.

He would weep when he saw the sufferings
of the Divine Infant, but he was able to rejoice
at the manifestations of divine favor, and
he was indeed jubilant over being able to see
his Savior in mortal flesh. He would often
become enraptured by the beauty of the Infant
Jesus, but it was exceedingly painful for him
to be compelled to leave the Infant whenever
he himself had to go to work, for he wished
his eyes could remain fixed forever upon this
exclusive Object of his love.

Sometimes Joseph would soliloquize in the
following manner: "Joseph, consider the great
blessing that is yours! Consider how fortunate
you are! What a consolation is yours in thus
living together with the Mother of the Messiah,
the Mother of the One Who has been expected
for so many hundreds of years! Not only that,
but you are even permitted to have the company
of the Messiah Himself! Furthermore, it will
be your privilege actually to be considered as
the one possessing the status of 'father' to the
Incarnate Word.

"Oh, what a grace! How many patriarchs
and prophets have yearned to see Him and did

not attain to it! How many have sighed for this coming! King David desired to see Him and to venerate the spot upon which His Feet would rest. You, however, are able not only to see Him, but actually to enjoy His immediate Presence. Nay more, you are even able to take Him up into your arms! You have the happiness of being His guardian, and of being designated as His provider. Oh, what a tremendous grace, a grace which your own mind could never have conceived, and one which you have in no way merited!"

As he spoke thus to himself, Joseph became overwhelmed with love and gratitude toward his Divine Savior. He hastened to Mary, cast himself at Her feet and earnestly begged Her to give thanks to God in his behalf, saying: "My Spouse, I ask that You, Who are the worthy Mother of the Savior, speak to God for me. Do me the favor of rendering thanks to our God for having deigned to choose me as Your consort, and for having raised me to such a high dignity. I myself cannot thank Him adequately.

"I feel overwhelmed by His graces and favors, but at the same time, I am beset with confusion, since I do not deserve all this and do not know how to thank my God for such an extraordinary and immense favor. Offer to Him my willing servitude and my entire being, and tell me what I must to do please Him, for I am beside myself when I think of His great gifts and singular favors. Oh my Spouse, You know only too well my lowliness and unworthiness; hence, I again ask that You speak for me."

Mary rejoiced as She saw Joseph's deep gratitude, and She assured him that his earnest protestations were most pleasing to God, and that by these acknowledgments of the many benefits and graces he had received, he was making it possible for himself to receive additional graces and favors. She also promised not to be remiss on Her part in complying with his request, that She give praise and thanksgiving to God for His divine bounty towards him.

Joseph was afflicted with sorrow when the prophet Simeon spoke to Mary, because he was, to a certain extent, aware what these words implied. He tried to subdue his feelings of anguish, but he nevertheless, succumbed and wept bitterly. Thenceforth, these words of the prophet Simeon were indelibly imprinted upon his heart. They caused him constant affliction. The Mother of God, however, was even more penetratingly affected by them, since She was able mentally to foresee and visualize all that was to come. Hence, the sword of sorrow remained imbedded in Her virginal heart throughout Her entire life.

The prophetess Anna also spoke to Mary, and foretold the sufferings and death of Her Son. Joseph, however, did not fully comprehend all that was said, or he would have died of anguish. He was already so distressed by Simeon's words that God had to assist him with His grace, in order to prevent him from fainting away. Mary, on the other hand, kept Her sorrow buried within Herself.

Although these things were already perfectly and clearly known to Her, still when Simeon and Anna uttered, in so graphic a manner, these prophecies concerning the future sufferings and death of Her Son, there was inflicted upon Her anew a most painful blow. She not only kept all this to Herself, but even proceeded to console Her sorrowing spouse.

Joseph felt himself strongly impelled to talk over these things more fully with Mary, but presently they had to remain for some time in the Temple, where they presented, as offerings, the gifts they received from the Eastern kings. Mary kept pressing Her divine Babe to Her breast, rendering unto Him at the same time continual acts of love, thanksgiving, and sympathy. She pleaded with Her Jesus that, in His graciousness, He would grant some comfort to Joseph in his grave distress. The Divine Infant saw to it that Her petition was granted.

Amid sighs and tears, Joseph attempted to explain to his most holy Spouse all that happened to him while they were in the Temple. He revealed to Her the mysteries that God had permitted him to contemplate, and he described to Her the anguish with which he was afflicted as a result of Simeon's prophecy. He often reiterated: "Oh my innocent Spouse, how immense will be Your sorrow! I don't know what the future holds for me, but if I should have to witness Your great sufferings, how would my heart ever be able to bear it?"

As he said this, Joseph wept disconsolately. Mary consoled him, telling him not to fear, for God would always stand by them with His providential care and would support them with His grace. "God is with us," She said, "and we must not give way to fear; let us abandon ourselves completely to His most holy will. For the present, let us rejoice over the fact that we have ransomed our Jesus, and He is now completely ours, enabling us to enjoy His companionship and to partake of His lovableness and sweetness. The mere thought that Jesus is with us and belongs to us, should serve to sweeten every bitterness."

These words comforted Joseph tremendously, but Jesus now wished to grant him the additional consolation of His intimate Presence. He again made it known to His Mother that He wished to be given to Joseph. The saint received the Divine Infant with great jubilation of heart, and embraced Him, saying: "Oh my Incarnate God! You now belong entirely to us. We have indeed ransomed You for the future salvation of all mankind, but for the present, it will be our privilege alone to know You, rejoice in You, and carry You in our arms!"

While the saint was speaking to Him in this manner, the Infant Jesus nestled up close and caused Joseph to experience the sweetest joys of Paradise. The saint stood there for a time as if transported, his spirit ravished by this eminent bliss; after all, was it not God Himself that he was holding in his arms? Mary was happy, too, to see Her spouse so greatly consoled, and She gave thanks to God.

Presently, as the overjoyed Joseph once again gazed upon the Divine Savior, he was moved by the realization of the great graces and favors that had been granted to him and he wept. The Divine Infant caressed him and spoke to his heart, making it quite evident how very much He loved him, and how pleased He was with him.

Whereupon, Joseph exclaimed: "Oh my Savior, how shall I repay Your immense goodness to me? Oh, what a happiness it is for me to bear You in my arms! Who would ever have conceived that You would deign to treat the lowliest of Your servants with such tremendous favors and distinctions? Simeon had no further wish than to die, once he had borne You in his arms. What then shall I seek or desire, my Lord, I who have the happiness so often of embracing You, and of holding You thus pressed closely to my breast? I do not seek to die as long as it is given to me to possess the delights of Your Presence, and as long as I can remain with You and provide for Your wants and necessities.

What more can I desire, than to love You increasingly, to serve You faithfully, and to see to it that all creatures shall come to know You, love You, and thank You for Your many benefits, especially for Your becoming man in order to redeem mankind? These things alone do I seek, my Savior, and these alone do I yearn for and plead for. Oh, grant that these earnest petitions and desires of mine may be fulfilled."

Now the Divine Infant rejoiced that Joseph was thus inflamed with love for Him and so earnestly concerned for His greater glory and for the welfare of all mankind! He manifested His pleasure by the smiling and loving look He bestowed upon Joseph. There was in the Divine Infant's glance, however, not only love, but majesty as well. Joseph was now inflamed all the more with grateful love for God.

Handing the Infant back to His Mother, he declared: "Oh Virgin most pure, take Your Son, the God-man. In Your most chaste arms, He most surely always receives His greatest satisfactions. Since He has bestowed upon You all those favors whereby You would always be pleasing and agreeable to Him, and so it is to be expected that He should find in Your embrace His most fitting repose and most complete contentment." The Mother of God abased Herself at these words, yet at the same time, She also confirmed them, inasmuch as She repeated that hymn of praise which She had sung for the first time when She visited Her cousin Elizabeth, namely: the *Magnificat*.

There were some people who had been stirred up by the devil to make offensive remarks against the saintly Joseph. They proclaimed that it had been an immense folly to have given the delicate maiden Mary as Spouse to a man like him, since he had shown no concern for Her, but instead had allowed Her to suffer. They accused him of not recognizing what a precious Spouse he had obtained, and declared that upon him would rest the blame for Her premature death resulting from Her many sufferings.

These remarks were as so many swords piercing the heart of the loving Joseph, for he knew how much he loved his Spouse, and how grateful he had been to God for having given Her to him. He was aware also, that he had rendered to Her all the care and attention that he owed to Her. To these slanderers, Joseph replied: "You are mistaken, for I do appreciate the blessing of having so precious and worthy a Spouse, but my poverty does not permit me to do for Her all that ought to be done, and this is very painful for me. Her generosity, however, is so immense that She is content with what She receives, and desires nothing more." He said that with utmost calmness, and with a cheerful demeanor, never once becoming excited, although he would certainly have had plenty of reason for doing so.

God permitted these trials and enmities so that Joseph would practice the virtues of humility, meekness, patience, and charity, and he practiced them generously and joyfully, for he knew that this would be pleasing to God. In doing so, he always acquired for himself more grace and more love. It also made Mary very happy to see Her spouse so saintly and virtuous. She was ever faithful in petitioning God to assist him and to grant him in increasing measure grace and strength, and above all, love.

In answer to Her prayers, Joseph's heart glowed so intensely with love and with longing to see his God loved by all men, that he often exclaimed amid tears: "Oh my God, why are You not loved by everyone? What could I do that might help to bring all creatures to acknowledge You and love You? How is it possible that You, Who are Infinite Goodness, Immeasurable Perfection, and Unfathomable Beauty are not loved by all men?" With these words, Joseph went into ecstasy for several hours, delighting in the grandeur and the perfection of God. He became more keenly aware of how much God really deserved to be loved, and being thus on fire with most holy love, he now had the urge, as he told Mary, to go through the whole village announcing and praising the glories of God. Mary restrained him, saying: "Let us give praise to God in the name of all."

Together they sang in praise of Him, and with this, Joseph was somewhat mollified. "May You be ever blessed, my Spouse," he said to Her, "for loving God as much as You do! It is certainly fitting that You thus give to Him what is really due to Him. May You love Him ever more, and, thereby, make amends for that multitude of souls who have no love for Him. Love Him also for me, since You have a heart with such a great capacity to love, whereas my own is so small, and has such a meager capacity for loving Him."

Mary's heart was actually being consumed by Her love. As he gazed fixedly upon Her, Joseph noticed Her countenance become flushed and radiant, as from the brightest of lights, which further stimulated this divine love within his own heart. Upon seeing Joseph so full of enthusiasm, Mary placed the Divine Infant in his arms. Joseph pressed the holy Child to his bosom and thereby provided full satisfaction to his love-hungry heart.

The saint would quite often rest a bit with the Infant Jesus thus in his embrace, and Mary, in contemplating this picture, could observe how happy the Divine Infant was to be in Joseph's arms. She noticed how Her spouse's soul was refreshed by this contact with his beloved God, causing him to enjoy a Heavenly peace and sweetness.

The Divine Child was growing rapidly, and Joseph's love for Jesus was steadily increasing, so that his heart was veritably being consumed by his love for Him. It seemed to him that the Child was becoming ever more gracious and comely, and the desire to contemplate Him would, again and again, take possession of him.

If, however, Joseph's love was so intense, equally so was the pain that he experienced due to the fact that his Jesus was not recognized as being God, and that on the contrary, He was being seriously offended. This consideration caused him to spend whole nights bewailing the blindness of so many pagan souls, as well as their offenses against his Lord.

When the Boy Jesus was lost in Jerusalem, Joseph's heart was pierced by a twofold sorrow when he saw Mary's anxiety, and, yet could offer Her no consolation. For three days, Mary and Joseph searched without any alleviation of their distress. By this time, the afflicted Joseph was finding it almost impossible to continue living in such intense anguish, and his distress was evident. Nevertheless, even in the midst of this most bitter anguish, he never lost patience, and in his excessive misery, he still praised God for His condescension and for the divine ordination which were permitting this great tribulation. He continued practicing interiorly all of the virtues, but particularly this virtue of submission to the divine dispensations.

It is well nigh impossible to conceive the joy that Joseph experienced upon seeing Jesus again, and upon listening again to His words of wisdom. He noticed that all the outstanding men of learning were gathered there, and that the Temple servants were standing about listening in astonishment to Jesus. He saw how they all wondered at the graciousness and wisdom of this Youth.

He felt an inexpressible elation and remarked to himself: "Behold, now my Jesus will be known and accepted for what He is, the true Messiah. Since He is expounding the Scriptures to them so wonderfully and wisely, and is also making it so evident to them that the Messiah has indeed come, they will necessarily love Him. The fact that He is so very rich in wisdom, grace, and eminent virtue, even in His youthful years, must surely make them recognize that He is the promised Messiah of the Law. I trust that they will be enlightened by His divine wisdom, and that every one of them will acknowledge Him as such."

Because of their pride and ambition, the words of Jesus made little impression upon them. Though God did not withhold His enlightenment from them, nor prevent them from recognizing the truth, yet, through their own fault, His grace remained inefficacious in them.

Mary spoke to Jesus, but Joseph remained silent, being too overcome with consolation to speak. He was quite satisfied just to have again found his All, and he could not get his fill of the satisfaction which he derived from contemplating the Savior. In his joy, he wept.

317.

(by Bl. Eymard—*Month of St. Joseph*, from p. 77)

Because Saint Joseph was associated with Mary in Her glorious privileges, he also had to suffer like Her, and his heart, too, was pierced by seven swords. These seven great afflictions were like the stations of the Sorrowful Way that he had to tread in company with Jesus. He suffered continually in his heart; but at certain times his agony became doubly acute, taking on a new intensity, turning the knife in its own wounds.

1. His first great trial was the torturing doubt he felt at Mary's pregnancy. About to abandon Her without saying a word, he wondered, "What will become of this young girl, little more than a Child? Who will take care of Her? Still the law enforces separation, and respect for it obliges me to leave Her." What terrible anguish for so loving and devoted a heart as Joseph's, a heart that loved Mary more than we can understand.

2. He was deeply hurt when Bethlehem rejected him and forced him to seek refuge in a stable. He grieved not for himself, but for that young Mother, Queen of Angels, and for the Infant, his God, Who was coming into the world. What smote him hardest was the injury done Them and the privations his loved Ones would endure in the stable. He did not know how many days and nights they would have to stay there. God was leading him like a blind man, keeping him always dependent, and this uncertainty redoubled his distress.

3. The Circumcision of Jesus. What a shock to Joseph to think that he himself would make the Infant-God suffer and would shed the first drops of His Blood. How his heart ached at the sight of that wound, the Blood that flowed from it, and the tears of the divine Mother.

4. The prophecy of the aged Simeon. When Joseph learned that a sword would pierce Mary's soul, he fathomed the full meaning of Isaiah's prophecy concerning the sufferings and humiliations of the Messias. From that moment on, he bore the sorrow of both Mary and Jesus. The thought of Their sufferings never left him, but became a daily torture which he shared with Them.

5. The hurried flight into Egypt. Who can imagine the fears, the terrors of that journey? God filled Joseph with dread, so that he might abandon himself to Providence. In that strange land, on those deserted roads, Joseph endured constant anxiety, apprehending every misfortune. He had the heart of a father, the tenderest of hearts. There he was, a poor old man, charged with protecting alone the Treasure of God the Father, against the enemies that might at any instant attack It.

6. On his return from Egypt, another misfortune was awaiting him. For fear of Archelaus, Joseph was obliged to conceal the Child Jesus again. There was no rest for Joseph, no peace; he escaped one danger only to encounter another.

7. The loss of Jesus in the Temple. So great was Joseph's anguish, so bitter were his tears, that the Holy Spirit was willed to immortalize them in Mary's words: "My Son, why has Thou treated us so? Think, what anguish of mind Thy father and I endured, searching for Thee." He was all the more racked with worry as, in his humility, he accused himself of negligence in caring for the Father's sacred trust.

These were the seven great sorrows of Saint Joseph. He endured them in silence, humility, and love, neither having nor desiring any human consolation. He suffered, not for himself, but for Jesus, for Mary, for the world, for us. Blessed suffering that united him to the redemptive work of the Savior.

(by Gasnier—*Joseph the Silent*, from pp. 105 & 165)

Simeon addressed himself to Mary alone. He was not afraid to foretell to this young Mother the terrifying events of the future: "Behold, this Child is destined for the fall and the rise of many in Israel, and for a sign that shall be contradicted. And Thy Own soul a sword shall pierce" (Luke 2:34-35).

In this prophecy and its fulfillment, Joseph was to have no share. Simeon seemed to wish to spare him the sorrowful knowledge of what would take place on Calvary, since he would not then be present.

But all the same, Joseph's heart was sword-pierced. He had understood the prophecy. How could he not grieve in knowing of the agonies his Son and his Spouse were one day to bear? And besides, the blow dealt him was the more cruel, because the words—precise, exact—were nevertheless so vague, he was left to imagine, to fear all kinds of torments.

Jesus was to suffer contradiction. What could it mean? Would He be rejected by the nation that had so long awaited His coming? Would men be divided into two opposing camps? The one blaspheming, the other falling on their knees? The one finding salvation, the other being lost?

Then the words concerning Mary were no less a torture. She, too, was to undergo measureless sufferings, all kinds of misfortunes!

How must Joseph have wished that all these could fall on him instead of on Them! Let his own mission become a torment; he could bear it. But Mary—so sweet, so pure, so holy. Could it be possible that God had destined Her for sufferings such as those!

It hurt him to have been spared by the old man, whose words, nevertheless, had wounded him to the quick. Engraved in his soul, they saddened his life. He could no longer look at his Child, his Wife, without thinking of the unknown agonies that They would have to undergo. Dreading for Them the prophet's sword, he went his way with a wound in his heart that would not heal.

Those Christians who want to penetrate into the mystery which is Joseph will find in his life, as in that of Mary, a series of seven joys and seven sorrows.

The first was his indescribable anguish when he saw in his Betrothed the signs of approaching Motherhood. His heart was torn at the thought of losing Her, but when the angel had assured him that Her fruitfulness was of the Holy Spirit, the frightful nightmare was changed into a song of praise to God, a redoubled respect and tenderness for Her.

The second time his heart was pierced as by a sword when, at the birth of Jesus, all the doors in Bethlehem were closed against him and he had to shelter Mary in a stable. But how joyful was the compensation when Mary had put the newborn Infant into his arms and he had pressed Him against his heart, knelt in adoration before His crib and seen those sent by God, the shepherds and the Magi, do as he.

The third sword thrust came when, as father of the Child, he had been obliged to circumcise the Infant and cause the tears of pain and the Blood of the wound to flow. But then, at the same moment it was he, Joseph, who was the first to pronounce the Name of Jesus as he imposed it on the Child—that Name which through all ages men would lovingly repeat over and over again. Enlightened on the meaning of that name, he foresaw the work of salvation to be wrought through the Blood of this Little One.

The old man Simeon was the cause of the fourth sorrow when, drawing back the veil of the future, he announced that Jesus would be a sign of contradiction to men, and that Mary's Own heart would one day be transfixed. But a joy, too, followed and consoled Joseph: Jesus would be the light of all nations and the glory of Israel.

The fulfillment of Simeon's prophecy was not long in coming, for Joseph's fifth sorrow was the flight into Egypt. Like hunted beasts, to save Jesus from Herod's fury, the Holy Family fled through the desert into exile. But the desert itself flowered for Joseph, since he could pour himself out in service for the Two he loved.

Hardly had they returned to Palestine when he learned that Archelaus, as cruel and blood-thirsty as his father, ruled in Judea. He dared not return to Bethlehem. A sixth sorrow. But his anxiety was turned to joy when the angel of the Annunciation came again as ambassador from Heaven to tell him to take Jesus and Mary to Nazareth and settle there once more in their happy home.

The seventh sword pierced Joseph's heart when he thought he had lost Jesus in Jerusalem and when for three days he sought Him with indescribable anguish, conjuring up with what perils He might be threatened. But what joy on finding Him! His love then was enriched as a result of his suffering during the days in which they had been separated.

Such were Joseph's memories. Trials indeed had not been wanting, but God had blessed him with overwhelming joys.

He rehearsed in his heart the words Tobias had heard: "Because thou wast acceptable to God, it was necessary that temptation should prove thee" (Tob. 12:13). Far from repining, he had made use of his crucifying sufferings to grow in virtue and strengthen his loving fidelity.

As for his joys, he told his God that they were far beyond his merits; that he had been treated with divine munificence; that his life could not be long enough to render proper thanks. He was God's servant, well content to carry out His designs; well content to leave this earth when such should be His good pleasure.

(by Healy Thompson—*Life And*, from p. 347)

Our Lord revealed to Jeanne Bénigne Gojos, a nun of the Order of the Visitation, who lived in the 17th century and had a great devotion to the Sacred Humanity, that the pain which both Mary and Joseph suffered was so great that without His secret assistance, they could not have survived. Their sorrow, He said, was simply incomprehensible, and that He alone could understand it. From His revelations to this holy soul, we also gather that this third dolor of our Lady was one of the chief sufferings of our Blessed Lord Himself. Fr. Faber in the book *The Foot of the Cross*, believes it may have been Mary's greatest sorrow.

When Joseph and Mary lost Jesus, the Doctors in the Temple, says St. Luke, "were astonished at His wisdom and His answers." And truly His divine loveliness was in itself sufficient to entrance them. A kingly majesty was on His youthful Brow. His beautiful Hair rested on His Shoulders; and we are told that it never grew beyond the length suitable for man, and, moreover, that not one Hair of His adorable Head ever fell from it until plucked out by the cruel Roman soldiers. His Eyes were radiant with the light of truth and the fire of charity.

What was He saying, and what had they asked? No doubt, it had reference to the promised Messias, the expectation of Whose Advent was general in Israel at that day. The same favored soul whom we have already quoted says that He was rectifying their erroneous notions concerning a glorious and warlike Deliverer, Who was to restore political independence to their nation and give them sovereignty over their enemies and oppressors. He was pointing out the prophecies, by them overlooked, which spoke of the humiliation and sufferings of the Messias; and, had the hearts of the listeners been as open to grace, as were their eyes and ears to the charm of what they saw and heard, they must have recognized the predicted Liberator in the marvellous Boy Whose Wisdom so astonished them.

Nevertheless, we may hope some good seed may have been sown in the hearts of more than one among them, which was later to bear fruit. We are reluctant to think that He, Who accorded to His Apostle Peter a miraculous catch of no less than 3000 souls at his first sermon, would Himself on this occasion, when He mysteriously forestalled His own future public ministry by occupying Himself thus early about His Eternal Father's interests, have drawn no single one into His net, and that bare admiration and wonder were all that He succeeded in eliciting.

Be this as it may, we cannot penetrate the secret counsels of God, nor expect always to see what we call the reasons of things. Even in the natural world we are constantly at fault in this respect; how much more should it be so in the higher region of grace, in the invisible things of God, and the secret dispensations of His Providence!

Even Mary and Joseph are said to have wondered on seeing Him. There was something new to them in His Voice, manner, attitude, and bearing. Never had they seen Him like that before. Doubtless, they stood for a moment looking on, silent for very joy and awe.

(by John Paul II—*Guardian*, from p. 21)

Mary asked: "Son, why have you treated us so? Behold, Your father and I have been looking for You anxiously" (Lk. 2:48). The answer Jesus gave was such that "they did not understand the saying which He spoke to them." He had said, "How is it that you sought Me? Did you not know that I must be in My Father's house?" (Lk. 2:49-50).

Joseph, of whom Mary had just used the words "Your father," heard this answer. That, after all, is what all the people said and thought: Jesus was "the Son (as was supposed) of Joseph" (Lk. 3:23). Nonetheless, the reply of Jesus in the Temple brought once again to the mind of his "presumed father" what he had heard on that night twelve years earlier: "Joseph...do not fear to take Mary your Wife, for That Which is conceived in Her is of the Holy Spirit." From that time onwards, he knew that he was a guardian of the mystery of God, and it was precisely this mystery that the twelve-year-old Jesus brought to mind: "I must be in My Father's house."

(by Levy—*Joseph, the Just Man*, from p. 72 & 81)

It is reasonable to suppose that St. Joseph, well versed in Holy Scripture, had knowledge of the prophecies regarding the Passion of his Foster-Son; that He was the promised Redeemer, Who would be rejected by His own people, condemned to death, and crucified. Pondering these events surely must have caused him profound sorrow.

Yet, amidst sorrow, there can be joy; joy in a realization that whatever happens—sin excepted—is the Will of our Heavenly Father.

Spiritual writers also enumerate seven joys in the life of Saint Joseph, namely: the assurance given to him by the Angel that Mary was innocent and that She had conceived miraculously; the adoration of the shepherds; the conferring of the Name "Jesus"; the adoration of the Magi; the announcement of Simeon that the Child would be the "resurrection of many in Israel": the message of the angel bidding the Holy Family to return from Egypt; and the finding of Jesus in the Temple.

In truth, there must have been great rejoicing in Heaven when Jesus, forty days after His Resurrection, ascended triumphantly into Heaven, accompanied by all the just who had lived from the beginning of creation, and had been redeemed through the promise of Mankind's Savior. Foremost among these was His beloved foster-father, St. Joseph, who, standing at the right hand of Jesus, was led by Him to occupy a place which, with the sole exception of that destined for Mary, his holy Spouse, was the highest in Heaven.

(by Neuzil—*Our Lady of America*, from p. 28)

As St. Joseph ceased speaking, I saw his most pure heart. It seemed to be lying on a cross which was of brown color; it appeared to me that at the top of the heart, in the midst of the flames pouring out, was a pure white lily. Then I heard these words: "Behold this pure heart so pleasing to Him, Who made it."

Then St. Joseph himself said, "The cross upon which my heart rests is the cross of the passion, which was ever present before me, causing me intense suffering.

327.

(by Patrignani—*Manual*, from p. 54)

In Jesus only, can true and solid happiness be found, even on Earth; Joseph knew this well; he also knows that the sinner's misery springs from the misfortune of having lost Jesus! Joseph himself experienced that grievous torment; his anguish was great on that occasion, though his own conduct was irreproachable; he can, therefore, more feelingly sympathize with poor sinners; he is more alive to the misery of their condition, and consequently a more strenuous advocate in their behalf. In the company of Mary, he will conduct them to the Temple, where after three days' careful search and heartfelt grief, they will have the happiness of finding Him! "If you seek Him, you will find Him with Joseph and Mary," says Origen.

(by Petrisko—*St. Joseph and the Triumph*, from p. 188)

Finally, it is again noted how St. Joseph must have struggled in the terrifying days before finding Jesus in the Temple, when it is said that St. Joseph could neither eat nor sleep.

(by Robert—*Guardian of God's Lilies*, from p. 134)

Great Saint Joseph, son of David,
Foster father of our Lord,
Spouse of Mary, ever virgin,
Keeping o'er Them watch and ward.

In the stable thou didst guard Them
With a father's loving care;
Thou by God's command didst save Them
From the cruel Herod's snare.

Three long days in grief and anguish,
With His Mother sweet and mild,
Mary Virgin, didst thou wander
Seeking the beloved Child.

In the Temple thou didst find Him;
Oh, what joy then filled thy heart!
In thy sorrows, in thy gladness,
Grant us, Joseph, to have part.

Clasped in Jesus' arms and Mary's,
When death gently came at last,
Thy pure spirit sweetly sighing
From its earthly dwelling passed.

Dear Saint Joseph, by that passing,
May our death, like thine, be blest;
And with Jesus, Mary, Joseph,
May our souls forever rest.

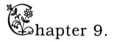hapter 9.

Death of St. Joseph

(Agreda—City (Transfixion), from pp. 142, 150.
161 & 165)

Along the royal highway of the Cross, the Lord led the spouse of His blessed Mother, Saint Joseph, whom He loved above all the sons of men. In order to increase his merits and crown before the time of his meriting should come to an end, He visited him in the last years of his life with certain sicknesses, such as fever, violent headaches, and very painful rheumatisms, which greatly afflicted and weakened him.

In the midst of these infirmities, he was suffering from another source, more sweet, but extremely painful, namely, for the fire of his ardent love which was so vehement, that the flights and ecstasies of his most pure soul would often have burst the bounds of his body if the Lord, Who vouchsafed them, had not strengthened and comforted him against these agonies of love. In these sweet excesses, the Lord allowed him to suffer until his death, and on account of the natural weakness of his extenuated body, this exercise was the source of ineffable merits for the fortunate saint, not only because of the sufferings occasioned, but because of the love by which these sufferings were brought about.

Joseph never complained either of these, nor of any of the other trials, nor ever asked for any relief in his wants and necessities. He bore all with incomparable equanimity and greatness of soul. Our Lady served his meals on bended knees, and when he was much disabled and suffering, She took off his shoes in the same posture.

In the last three years of his life, when the infirmities increased, our Queen attended upon him day and night. Her only other employment was in the service and ministration due to Her most holy Son. Jesus sometimes joined and assisted Her in the care of Her holy spouse, whenever He was not engaged in other necessary works. There was never a sick person, nor will there ever be one, who was so well nursed and comforted. Great was the happiness and worth of this man of God, Saint Joseph, for he alone deserved to have for his Spouse Her, Who was the Spouse of the Holy Spirit.

Already eight years Saint Joseph had been exercised by his infirmities and sufferings, and his noble soul had been purified more and more each day in the crucible of affliction and of divine love. As the time passed, his bodily strength gradually diminished and he approached the unavoidable end, in which the stipend of death is paid by all of us children of Adam (Heb. 9:27).

Mary prayed for Joseph's soul, and Jesus answered: "My Mother, thy request is pleasing to Me, and the merits of Joseph are acceptable in My Eyes. I will now assist him and will assign him a place among the princes of My people (Ps. 115:15), so high that he will be the admiration of the angels and will cause them and all men to break forth in highest praise. With none of the human-born shall I do as with Thy spouse." The great Lady gave thanks to Her sweetest Son for this promise; and, for nine days and nights before the death of Saint Joseph, he uninterruptedly enjoyed the Company and attendance of Mary or Her Divine Son.

One day before he died, being wholly inflamed with divine love on account of these blessings, he was wrapped in an ecstasy which lasted 24 hours. The blessed Trinity commissioned and assigned him as the messenger of our Savior, to the holy Patriarchs and Prophets of Limbo and commanded him to prepare them for their issuing forth from this bosom of Abraham to eternal rest and happiness. When Saint Joseph awoke from this ecstasy, his face shone with wonderful splendor, and his soul was entirely transformed by his vision of the essence of God.

The Redeemer of the world gave him His benediction, saying: "My father, rest in peace and in the grace of My Eternal Father and Mine; and to the Prophets and Saints, who await thee in Limbo, bring the joyful news of the approach of their redemption." At these words of Jesus, and reclining in His Arms, the most fortunate Saint Joseph expired, and the Lord Himself closed his eyes.

It is necessary to mention that the long sickness and sufferings which preceded the death of Saint Joseph were not the sole cause and occasion of his passing away; for with all his infirmities, he could have extended the term of his life, if to them he had not joined the fire of intense love within his bosom. Love was the real cause of the death of Saint Joseph. Death is but a sleep of the body and the beginning of real life.

The most fortunate of men, Saint Joseph, reached the age of 60 years and a few days. At the age of 33, he espoused the blessed Virgin and he lived with Her a little longer than 27 years as Her husband. When Saint Joseph died, She had completed the first half of Her 42nd year, for She was espoused to St. Joseph at the age of 14. The 27 years of Her married life completed Her 41st year.

The manner of Joseph's death was a privilege of his singular love, for his sweet sighs of love surpassed and finally put an end to those of his sickness, being far more powerful. As the Objects of his love, Christ and His Mother, were present with him always, and as Both of Them were more closely bound to him than to any of the woman-born, his most pure and faithful heart was unavoidably consumed by the loving effects of such a close union.

(*Ante-Nicene*, from p. 389)

At length, by increasing years, the old man arrived at a very advanced age. He did not, however, labor under any bodily weakness, nor had his sight failed, nor had any tooth perished from his mouth. In mind also, for the whole time of his life, he never wandered; but like a boy, he always in his business displayed youthful vigor, and his limbs remained unimpaired, and free from all pain. His life, then, in all, amounted to 111 years, his old age being prolonged to the utmost limit.

Now Judas and Simeon, the elder sons of Joseph, were married, and had families of their own. Both the daughters were likewise married, and lived in their own houses. So there remained in Joseph's house, Judas and James the Less, and My Virgin Mother. I moreover dwelt along with them.

It came to pass thereafter, when he returned to his own house in the city of Nazareth, that he was seized by disease, and had to keep to his bed. This disease was very heavy upon him, as he had never been ill, as he now was, from the time of his birth.

As soon as I pronounced the Amen, a great multitude of angels came up, and I ordered two of them to stretch out their shining garments, and to wrap in them the body of Joseph, the blessed old man. I spoke to Joseph, and said: "The smell or corruption of death shall not have dominion over thee, nor shall a worm ever come forth from thy body. Not a single limb of it shall be broken, nor shall any hair of thy head be changed. Nothing of thy body shall perish, O My father Joseph, but it remain entire and uncorrupted, even until the banquet of the thousand years."

(by Baij—*Life of*, from pp. 311, 321, 332 & 338)

Joseph's increasing anguish regarding the future sufferings of the Savior, as well as his expanding love for God, reached such proportions that his physical strength began to be seriously affected, and it was a great strain upon him to work. He gave the impression of being exhausted and depressed. Jesus did the most difficult work Himself, and otherwise made Joseph's labors lighter. His mere Presence was a consolation to the saint and strengthened him to such an extent, that he could at least manage the lighter work.

Jesus proceeded to console Saint Joseph and declared that he had in reality exerted himself excessively in the past and did all that he could. Wherefore, he should now be at peace, as it was proper for him at times to rest awhile. He urged him to bear with this situation cheerfully, since it was God's will that he be in this state of weakness. Thus consoled, Joseph accepted generously this decline in his physical powers. His spiritual powers, on the other hand, became all the stronger, so he actually practiced all the virtues with perfection and was making great advances in grace and in love for his God.

Now that the saint found himself increasingly incapacitated for work, he began to meditate extensively on the divine perfections. There was enkindled within him an ardent desire for death, so that he might enjoy seeing God face to Face. His gaze would wander Heavenwards and remain fixed for several hours. He wished for the day to arrive when the mission of man's redemption would be accomplished, since through it, he would merit entry into the Heavenly mansions.

In spite of his condition, the saint never omitted his regular prayers. On the contrary, he increased them. He spent many hours on his knees, pleading with the Heavenly Father for the welfare of souls and asking that everyone accept the true Messiah when He revealed Himself for the world through His preaching. This fact had already been revealed to Joseph through divine revelation.

As a consequence of these holy conversations, the fires of love burned ever brighter within the saintly Joseph. Often he was so overcome that he fainted away and became still weaker.

Joseph continued to grow noticeably weaker. He no longer had any appetite for food and did not wish to eat. Only the spiritual nourishment provided by prayer and by the divine discourses, given by his Savior, were pleasing to him. Jesus managed to persuade him to take some nourishment, and Mary prepared the food for him according to his taste. To this, Jesus added His grace and His blessing. The saint proceeded to eat, but only enough to sustain life.

One night, Joseph became afflicted with most violent pains. He bore these with unflinching patience, offering them up to God in reparation for his sins; at least this was his assertion, though actually, he had never committed any sin.

The angel of the Lord spoke to him in his sleep, and transmitted to him a message from God, which proclaimed that the time for his death was drawing near and consequently, he should put himself in readiness for it by the extensive practice of virtue and acquisition of merits. Furthermore, he was told that God would yet try him with a malady that would bring with it most excruciating pains. The angel encouraged Joseph to be patient and assured him that by his patience and abandonment in this trial, he would give a great deal of satisfaction to God.

His holy Spouse again manifested Her exceedingly great affection for him and indicated that She was prepared to bear this burden of suffering for him, if this should please the Heavenly Father. Joseph would not give his consent to this. He wished to bear these sufferings alone, out of a desire to imitate to some extent his Savior, Who would be subjected to so many grievous afflictions.

Extremely violent pains presently gripped Joseph in his intestines. At times he succumbed completely, occasioned on the one hand by the pain, and on the other by his burning love for God. Heart palpitation was present.

Though Joseph truly desired to be liberated from the bonds of the flesh, the thought that he would be compelled to part from Jesus and Mary also tormented him. By means of this painful illness, God delivered Joseph from every earthly attachment. Even his love for Jesus and Mary, though holy and comparatively perfect, was purified, for it did have its self-gratifying elements.

It was God's will that His faithful servant should be more severely tried, so that he might acquire even greater merit. Thus, He now permitted Joseph to experience great interior desolation. He took from him his delight in spiritual things. One night, while still in this state, Joseph's pains once more gripped him with great intensity. He cried out again to God for assistance, but now he did not experience the same consolation as formerly. He felt that he was in a state of complete abandonment.

Jesus allowed Joseph to remain in his miseries so that he might be able to accumulate more merit, (thus to be in the highest place in Heaven, next to our Lady).

God wished to test Joseph's faithfulness to an even greater extent by now permitting the devil again to tempt him. This occurred during the following night while the saint was still in this afflicted condition and deprived of all support. Upon being again subjected to an attack of most excruciating pain, he was at the same time seriously tempted to impatience and despair.

One can, indeed, imagine in what a state the saint must have been. Nevertheless, he persevered in his loyalty to God and manifested an unconquerable patience. He defeated the enemy by his undaunted courage and by exciting in himself acts of confidence in God, even when it seemed to him that God had forsaken him. He persisted in his appeals to God's kindness and generosity, and remained confident that in virtue of them, God would come to his aid. Joseph, therefore, practiced most heroic virtue in this struggle.

After the saint persevered for several hours in this great trial, he made a fervent recommendation of himself to God. It was then that Jesus again came to visit him, and it was at the sight of Jesus that the devil vanished, disconcerted and defeated by reason of Joseph's virtue.

Since Joseph endured so much anxiety and distress by reason of his illness and his other trials, and since he enriched himself so extensively with merits through the practice of virtue, above all, through his invincible patience, it now pleased the Most High to grant him greater consolation and joy than ever before, and give him evidences of His love for him.

Moreover, an angel came while the saint was still immersed in his sufferings and abandonment, to inform him that it was God's intention to release him from this great trial, and to bestow upon him many additional graces. The angel assured Joseph that, during the time of trial God had imposed on him, he had not only acquired much merit, but gave immense satisfaction to God by the manifestation of his loyalty and love for Him.

Upon awakening, Joseph perceived a most delightful and melodious chanting, evidently celestial, which stirred him to the depths of his heart. He was simultaneously refreshed with consolation, as he now experienced the intimate, and loving visitation of God, Himself, Who, in most affectionate terms, invited him to an intimate and loving union with His Own Spirit. The consolation which Joseph experienced on this occasion was so great, that his blessed soul seemed as if immersed in a sea of joy.

Joseph wished to die on a day and at an hour similar to that on which Jesus Himself was to die, inasmuch as he would not be physically present on that dread occasion. God granted this favor to Joseph. After this, the saint was again smitten with his former pains, but now he glorified in his tribulations, thanking God for His clemency in permitting him to suffer and accumulate greater merit.

Since the final moment of Joseph's life had now arrived, the Son of God invited Joseph's blessed soul to depart from his body, so that it might be taken up in His Own most holy Hands, and from thence be committed to the angels who were to escort it into Limbo.

In response to this sweet invitation, the blissful Joseph breathed forth his soul in a vehement act of love for God, calling out the sweetest Names of Jesus and Mary.

The saintly Joseph was 61 years old age at the time of his death. His dead body was surrounded by a wonderful radiance and also emitted a delightful odor. This eminent attractiveness also remained unchanged, and he seemed truly to resemble an angel of Paradise, wherefore, everyone who saw him was also moved to venerate him.

The blessed corpse was escorted by Both Jesus and Mary, and also by some other devout women who were rendering consolation to Joseph's holy Spouse. In nature, a rather pleasant mood prevailed. The air was clear and mild, and even the birds apparently sang more than they had ever done before, astonishing everyone. All who were there had, moreover, detected the sweet fragrance which emanated from Joseph's venerable body. The burial ceremonies were performed according to the custom of the Hebrews.

At precisely the same time in which Joseph passed from this life, many other persons died in Nazareth, and in other places where the Mosaic Law was observed. However, while these people were still in their death agony, God had made this fact known to Joseph. Even though he himself was then at death's door, Joseph wished to carry out his assignment as Patron of the Dying. He made his usual fervent supplications to God in their behalf, and again pleaded earnestly for their eternal salvation. God again heard his prayers, and in His goodness gave to all these dying men a true compunction for their sins. They thus owed their deliverance to Joseph's merits and prayers.

Furthermore, by granting his petitions, God wished to comfort His most faithful servant. Indeed, how could God ever have refused to hear the prayers of such a saintly soul, one who had loved Him so intensely and had served Him so faithfully, who had obeyed His commands so humbly and submissively, who had observed His Law so exactly, and who had imitated so extensively the good example that Jesus and Mary gave to Him?

When the Savior of the world gloriously and victoriously arose from the dead on the third day following His painful death, He thereafter, proceeded to deliver and to take with Him from Limbo, those souls which had been confined there. Joseph's glorified soul was, by the power of God, again reunited to his blessed body. The latter thereby also became glorified, i.e., it became endowed with all the properties appertaining to a glorified body, just as it will be for all the saints when they arise on the day of universal judgment.

Saint Joseph made his entry into Heaven together with the Savior on the occasion of His remarkable Ascension. There the saint now occupies, in virtue of his virginity and great purity of soul, a most distinguished throne near to the unspotted Lamb of God, and very close to that occupied by the Queen of Angels and of Men, Whose faithful and pure spouse he had been in life, and Whom he had more closely resembled than had any other creature.

341.

(by Binet—*Divine Favors*, from pp. 11 & 99)

The date of St. Joseph's death is uncertain; we know only that it took place before the Passion of Our Lord Jesus Christ. What an entrancing sight to behold him expire, one hand in that of Jesus, the other in that of our Lady; breathing forth his blessed spirit on the Bosom of the Savior God! To die thus is not to lose life, but to overcome death.

From songs, Gerson passes to tears. He supposes, according to the general opinion, that St. Joseph died before the time of the Passion, for otherwise the Savior would not, on the cross, have recommended His Mother to St. John. He then continues: "It is my belief that when St. Joseph was dying, he was assisted by Jesus and Mary, and that, since virtue makes natural affection more perfect, Jesus wept for His foster-father and served him in his last illness, consoling and strengthening him for the final passage. I believe that his holy Spouse mingled Her tears with those of Her Son, weeping with tenderness for Her well-beloved spouse, and thanking him affectionately for all the services that he had rendered Her.

And why should not Jesus have shed tears at the death of Joseph, His father, as He afterwards shed them at the death of Lazarus, His friend? But who can describe to us the feelings of the holy Patriarch, when he saw himself the object of such tears? Who can make us understand the divine consolations with which Jesus inundated his soul, and the words of sweetness addressed to him by the most holy Mother of God, his Spouse? Never did man repeat with more truth those touching words: "Lord, into Thy hands I commend my spirit," since, with humble confidence, he committed his into the Hands of the Son of God, Himself, Who had chosen him to be His guardian and His father.

Could there be a death more holy, or in more holy Company?

(by Chorpenning—*Just Man*, from pp. 49, 51 & 223)

Love was the cause of Joseph's death. For Francis de Sales, the list of saints who died of love is long—the martyrs, St. Mary Madgalen, SS. Peter and Paul, St. Catherine of Siena, St. Francis of Assisi, St. Charles Borromeo, St. Stanislaus Kostka, St. Teresa of Avila, to name only a few—but chronologically Joseph was the first.

Again, Joseph becomes the prototype for Teresa of Avila. It is commonplace in Teresian hagiography that divine love was the cause of her death. Teresa's death was miraculous in that it did not result from natural causes, though her constitution had been weakened by illness. Rather, she died in ecstasy, in a transport of spiritual love for God, during which she uttered terms of endearment to her Spouse and willingly gave up the ghost. Evidence was provided not only by witnesses, but also by Teresa's own prediction beforehand and confirmation afterward in an appearance to her conventual sisters. This view of her death as supernatural became canonical and was included in the official acts and bull of her canonization, as well as in the lessons of her Office.

In an engraving of her death, Saint Teresa reclines on her deathbed holding a cross, Christ appears above, together with the Virgin Mary and Saint Joseph, while a white dove emerges from Teresa's body and flies up toward Him. The inscription that accompanies the engraving refers explicitly to the ecstatic nature of Teresa's death: "She was wounded by the most fervent force of love."

Joseph was already dead when Christ began to preach. If he were not dead, Joseph would have been present when the Redeemer died on the cross, because he would not have left his Spouse alone at the foot of the cross, nor would Christ have entrusted His Mother to the beloved disciple, and he would have been present at the wedding feast at Cana.

St. Joseph died when Christ was 29 years old, not long before He was baptized by St. John the Baptist. And although in these matters there is insufficient evidence, still it does not take much to be persuaded that this was the case, because Joseph's office was to serve and to support Jesus and His Mother according to the poverty that They chose in this world. And so we read that the Redeemer, until He began to preach, spent His time in silence and in prayer, and did not engage in human commerce. To take care of the business affairs involved in the carpentry trade—looking for work, buying wood, and selling what was made—God permitted St. Joseph to live until the time when Christ went out to begin preaching. Although Christ would work at home in the carpenter's trade, He would not engage in these business matters. In this I hold as certain the opinion of Trujillo.

(by Emmerich—*Life of Jesus*, from p. 330)

As the time drew near for Jesus to begin His mission of teaching, I saw Him ever more solitary and meditative; and toward the same time, the 30th year of Jesus, Joseph began to decline.

When Joseph was dying, Mary sat at the head of his bed, holding him in Her arms. Jesus stood just below Her near Joseph's breast. The whole room was brilliant with light and full of angels. After his death, his hands were crossed on his breast, he was wrapped from head to foot in a white winding sheet, laid in a narrow casket, and placed in a very beautiful tomb, the gift of a good man.

Only a few men followed the coffin with Jesus and Mary; but I saw it accompanied by angels and environed with light. Joseph's remains were afterward removed by the Christians to Bethlehem, and interred. I think I can still see him lying there incorrupt.

Joseph had of necessity to die before the Lord, for he could not have endured His Crucifixion; he was too gentle, too loving. He had already suffered much from the persecution Jesus had had to support from the malice of the Jews from His 20th to His 30th year; for they could not bear the sight of Him. Their jealousy often made them exclaim that the carpenter's Son thought He knew everything better than others, that He was frequently at variance with the teachings of the Pharisees, and that He always had around Him a crowd of young followers. After Joseph's death, Jesus and Mary moved to a little village of only a few houses between Capharnaum and Bethsaida, where there were friends of the Holy Family.

(by Gasnier—*Joseph the Silent*, from pp. 169 & 175)

So far as we know, it was not of old age that Joseph died. Since he may be considered to have been but a little older than Mary at the time of their marriage, he could not have been over sixty at the time of his death.

There is not even a tradition concerning Joseph's burial place, nor is there any spot where his relics are venerated. Silent in life, silent in death, he was stripped of all things not essential to true glory.

He, above all, was that saint who understood, as Bossuet says, "That to be hidden in Christ Jesus is of all glories the greatest." He had sought not what the world admires, but what was pleasing to his Lord. If in effacing himself before the Divine will he had already procured for himself the greatest of joys, these were only a prelude to the marvelous rewards with which God would crown him.

According to his self-abasement, so would his exaltation be. Because he did not try to appear before men, he would be glorified in their sight. Because he loved to be hidden and unknown, God would make his light to shine for all the world to see. But God wished to leave to men to discover his greatness, to become ever more aware of his radiance as if to prove in his case the truth of Jacob's prophecy concerning that other Joseph of the Old Testament: *Joseph accrescens*—Joseph destined to be raised on High.

Then came the great heralds of this devotion to Joseph. In the 14th century, Cardinal Pierre D'Ailly composed the first theological treatise on St. Joseph. His disciple, Gerson, chancellor of the University of Paris, in a rigorous doctrinal thesis, enumerated the reasons men had for honoring the saint. Later, the Franciscan, Bernardino of Siena, the great preacher of the 15th century, Isadore of Isolanis of the 16th century, and still more the reformer of Carmel, Saint Teresa of Avila, in the same century, all contributed by their great influence, their teachings, their writings, and their example to make the devotion popular.

From that time on, the honor paid by Christians to St. Joseph has never ceased to grow and be enriched. It looks as if the Church wished to repay with interest the tribute of honor which She was so long in according him.

(by Griffin—*Saint Joseph, Theo,*, from pp. 19, 34 & 39)

In all probability, Joseph died before Our Lord begins His public career; certainly before the wedding feast at Cana.

Tradition has always believed that it was necessary for Joseph to disappear from the scene or he would have been an obstacle to the preaching of Christ. Think how confusing it would have been for Christ to be preaching about His Heavenly Father if Joseph were close at hand! There is every reason to suspect that the multitudes would have thought He was speaking about Joseph. In order to obviate such difficulties, the early death of Joseph was convenient. Joseph had to decrease that the Kingdom of God on earth could increase.

Today it can be affirmed that it is the common teaching of the Church that Joseph occupies a very special place in Heaven, because of his exceptional holiness, that is second only to the place occupied by the Mother of God.

Mary was raised far above all created nature—does this mean that Pope Leo XIII was teaching that Mary is holier than the angels themselves? It does, and this has been the common teaching of the Church for many centuries. But, what is more pertinent to this study of ours: does this mean that Joseph is also higher in dignity and holiness than the angels? Leo does not explicitly say this, but he certainly supplies the premise from which such a conclusion can legitimately be drawn. Pope Pius XI, in his characteristically incisive and clear language, dispelled any doubt that might still linger when he wrote: "...between Joseph and God we do not see, and we can not see, anyone except Mary with Her Divine Motherhood."

On May 26, 1960 Pope John XXIII, in his homily for the Feast of the Ascension of our Lord, made a statement that the Assumption of Saint Joseph is worthy of pious belief (*cosi piamente noi possiamo credere*). He also stated that he believed the same privilege was accorded to Saint John the Baptist. This is the first time that a Pope has ever made a public statement of the subject and the fact should offer great reassurance to those who feel it would be contrary to their religious sentiments to imagine Christ refusing Joseph this crowning grace. Pope John's words are a guarantee that such a belief is truly prudent and therefore can no longer be classified as a "pious exaggeration."

(by Healy Thompson—*Life And Glories*, from p. 410)

St. Jerome, indeed, was of the opinion that Joseph's sepulchre was included within the limits of the garden of Gethsemane, and that it was not without a mystery that Jesus made the choice of that spot for prayer, especially to engage us to seek to have Joseph near us when we are in our last agony, and hence to enjoy the consolation of his patronage at that dread hour.

(by Llamera—*Saint Joseph*, from p. 261)

The holy Patriarch died before Christ began His public ministry. This belief, although not expressly stated in the sacred text, can be found implicitly in the Gospel itself. In the first place, when Christ, His Mother and His disciples were invited to the wedding at Cana, no mention is made of St. Joseph. This, we believe, would not have happened if the saint were still living. Second, this same silence prevails during the whole time of Christ's preaching. Third, while Christ was preaching on one occasion, He was informed: "Thy Mother and Thy brethren are without, and wish to speak with Thee" (Matt. 12:47), but there is no mention of St. Joseph. Fourth, there is no doubt that he died before the Passion of our Lord, because the blessed Virgin would otherwise not have been given into the care of Saint John at the foot of the Cross.

349.

(by Patrignani—*Manual*, from p. 103)

The bonds of affection which united this blessed Mother and Her Divine Son to holy Joseph, were not severed by his death. Both in anguish closed his eyes, and Both paid him the tribute of Their tears; for let not any one deem it unworthy of Jesus that He should weep on such an occasion.

Surely His affection for Joseph was much more tender and lively than that which He afterwards felt for His friend Lazarus? If His groans and tears at the tomb of Lazarus astonished the spectators, and elicited from them the remark; "Behold, how He loved him!", is it not very reasonable to suppose that such mournful demonstrations were far more justly due to the deceased person, who was not only a friend, but also His guardian and His adopted father? So, those persons who visited the mortal remains of Saint Joseph might also have said of Jesus: "Behold, how He loved him." Thus reasons John Eckius, a pious contemplative.

Gerson adds, that Jesus Himself washed this virginal body, that He crossed the hands over the breast, that He afterwards blessed it, in order to preserve it from the corruption of the tomb, and charged the angels to guard it until it should have been laid in Joseph's ancestral sepulchre, between the Mount of Sion and that of Olives. The general opinion is that he died about the age of 60, and before our Divine Lord quitted Nazareth in order to receive Baptism from St. John the Baptist.

(by Stein—*The Tapestry*, from pp. 27, 30 & 60)

St. Jerome (340-420) was of the opinion that St. Joseph's sepulchre was included within the limits of the Garden of Gethsemane. And it was no mystery that Jesus made the choice of that spot for prayer, especially on the night of His Agony. Possibly, He desires us to seek St. Joseph when we are in our last agony, and to enjoy the consolation of his patronage at that dread hour.

Tradition says that Joseph went to Jerusalem with Mary and Jesus to celebrate the Feast of the Unleavened Bread, the Pasch, which was always kept at the full moon following the 14th, then died on the 19th of March, as the Church holds. The Roman Martyrology says, "In Judea, the birthday of St. Joseph, spouse of Blessed Mary the Virgin, Confessor." Had St. Joseph died in Nazareth, the notation would have been Galilee, not Judea.

Tradition holds that the tomb was in the Valley of Josaphat, which was thought to be in the Cedron (Kidron) Valley on the eastern side of Jerusalem. According to John 18:1, "Jesus went out with His disciples across the Kidron valley. There was a garden there, and He and His disciples entered it." (This was the evening of the Agony.)

Venerable Bede (c.672-735) considered that it was probably by Divine disposition that St. Joseph's death occurred at the season of the Pasch, in order that, according to his desire, he might be buried with his ancestors.

351.

The Bollandists (followers of Jean de Bolland (1596—1665), Flemish hagiologist, (which means a recorder of the lives of saints), maintained that the now-empty tomb of Joseph was in the Valley of Josaphat. This theory prevails to the present day.

(by Valtorta—*Poem, Vol. 1*, from p. 223)

Jesus is working at a large carpentry bench. He is planing some boards which He then rests against the wall behind Him. He then takes some kind of stool, clamped on two sides by a vice. He frees it from the vice, and He looks to see whether the job is perfect. He examines it from every angle.

He is by Himself. He works diligently, but peacefully...no abrupt or impatient movement. He is precise and constant in His work. Nothing annoys Him...neither a knot in the wood which will not be planed, nor a screwdriver (I think it is a screwdriver) which falls twice from the bench, nor the smoke floating in the room from the fireplace, which must irritate His Eyes.

While He is busy making something, which I think is part of a wheel, His Mother comes in, rushing towards Jesus, saying: "Oh! Jesus! Come, come. He is very ill!" He leaves His work, takes His apron off, and goes out with Her.
The room is poor but tidy. There is a low bed, covered with small mattresses, (I say mattresses because they are thick and soft things, but the bed is not like ours). On it, leaning on many cushions, there is Joseph. He is dying. It is obvious from the livid paleness of

his face, his lifeless eyes, his panting chest, and the total relaxation of all his body.

Jesus goes to Joseph's right-hand side. He lifts quickly and carefully the body which has sunk. He straightens him onto the cushions which He then adjusts together with Mary. He caresses the forehead of the dying man and endeavors to encourage him. Mary is weeping softly, without any noise, but She is weeping. Her large tears run down Her pale cheeks, right down to Her dark blue dress, and they look like bright sapphires.

Then Jesus, bending over the dying man, whispers a long psalm, which begins thus: "Look after me, oh Lord, because I hoped in You..." Then Jesus says: "Thank you, My father on My Behalf and on behalf of My Mother. You have been a just father to Me, and the Eternal Father chose you as the guardian of His Christ and of His Ark. You have been the lamp trimmed for Him, and for the Fruit of the holy Womb; you have had a loving heart. Go in peace, father. Your Widow will not be helpless. God has arranged that She must not be alone. Go peacefully to your rest, I tell you."

Mary is crying with Her face bent down on the blankets (they look like mantles) which are stretched on Joseph's body, which is now getting cold. Jesus hastens to comfort him, because he is breathing with great difficulty and his eyes are growing dim once again.

Jesus says: "Because you have lifted your voice to Him, He will hear you; He will be with you in your last affliction; He will glorify you after this life, showing you even now His Salvation. And in the future life, He will let you enter, because of the Savior Who is now comforting you and Who very soon, oh! I repeat it, He will come very soon and hold you in His divine embrace and take you, at the head of all the Patriarchs, where the dwelling place has been prepared for the Just Man of God, who was My blessed father.

"Go before Me and tell the Patriarchs that the Savior is in the world and the Kingdom of Heaven will soon be opened to them. Go, father. May My Blessing accompany you."

Jesus has raised His Voice to reach the heart of Joseph, who is sinking into the mists of death. His end is impending. He is panting very painfully. Mary caresses him; Jesus sits on the edge of the little bed, embraces him and draws to Himself the dying man, who collapses, and passes away peacefully.

The scene is full of a solemn peace. Jesus lays the Patriarch down again and embraces Mary, Who at the last moment, broken-hearted, had gone near Jesus.

~~~~~
*Jesus speaks:*

I exhort all wives who are tortured by pain, to imitate Mary in Her widowhood: to be united to Jesus. Those who think that Mary's heart did not suffer any afflictions are mistaken. My Mother did suffer. Let that be known. She suffered in a holy way, because everything in Her was holy, but She suffered bitterly.

Those who think that Mary did not love Joseph deeply, only because he was the spouse of Her soul and not of Her flesh, are also mistaken. Mary did love Joseph deeply, and She devoted 30 years of faithful life to him. Joseph was Her father, Her spouse, Her brother, Her friend, Her protector.

Now She felt as lonely as the shoot of a vine when the tree to which it is tied is cut down. It was as if Her house had been struck by thunder. It was splitting. Before, it was a unit in which the members supported one another. Now, the main wall was missing, and that was the first blow to the Family and a sign of the impending parting of Her beloved Jesus.

The will of the Eternal Father Who had asked Her to be a Spouse and a Mother, was now imposing upon Her widowhood and separation from Her Creature. But Mary utters, shedding tears, one of Her most sublime remarks: "Yes. Yes, Lord; let it be done to Me according to Your Word."

And to have enough strength for that hour, She drew close to Me. Mary was always united to God in the gravest hours of Her life: in the Temple, when She was asked to marry; at Nazareth, when She was called to Maternity; again at Nazareth, when shedding the tears of a widow; at Nazareth, in the dreadful separation of Her Son; on Calvary, in the torture of seeing Me dying.

Learn, you who are crying. Learn, you who are dying. Learn, you who are living, to die. Endeavor to deserve the words I said to Joseph. They will be your peace in the struggle of death. Learn, you who are dying, to deserve to have Jesus near you, comforting you. And, if you have not deserved it, dare just the same, and call Me near you. I will come with My Hands full of graces and consolation, My Heart full of forgiveness and love, My Lips full of words of absolution and encouragement.

Death loses its bitterness, if it takes place between My Arms. Believe Me, I cannot abolish death, but I can make it sweet for those who die trusting in Me.

Christ on His Cross, said on behalf of you all: "Father, into Your Hands I commit My Spirit." He said that in His Agony, thinking of your agonies, your terrors, your errors, your fears, your desire for forgiveness. He said it with His Heart pierced by extreme torture, before being pierced by the lance, a torture that was more spiritual than physical, so that the agonies of those who die thinking of Him might be relieved by the Lord, and their spirits might pass from death to eternal life, from sorrow to joy, forever.

Be good and do not be afraid. My Peace will always flow into you, through My words and through contemplation. Come. Just think that you are Joseph, who has Jesus' Chest as a cushion, and Mary as a nurse. Rest between Us, like a child in his cradle.

~~~~~
Mary speaks:

Jesus works miracles also in the humility of a common life. He works them in Joseph opening his spirit to the light of such a sublime truth which he could not understand by himself, although he was just. And after Me, Joseph is the most blessed by this shower of divine gifts.

It is enough if you say with Joseph: "If Jesus is left with me, I have everything," and We will come with Heavenly gifts to comfort your spirit. I do not promise you human gifts or human comfort. I promise you the same consolations as Joseph had: supernatural ones. Because, everybody should know, the gifts of the Wise Men, in the dire necessities of poor refugees, vanished as fast as lightning when we purchased a home, food, and the bare essential household implements necessary for life.

The fact that we had Jesus with us did not procure us any material wealth. He said: "Set your hearts on things of the spirit." All the rest is unnecessary. God provides also food, for men as well as for birds, because He knows that you need food while your flesh is the tabernacle of your soul. But first of all, ask for His grace. First of all, ask for things for your spirit. The rest will be given to you in addition.

All Joseph had from his union with Jesus, from a human point of view, were worries, fatigue, persecutions, starvation. He had nothing else. But as he aimed only at Jesus, all this was turned into spiritual peace and supernatural joy. I would like to take you to the point where My spouse was, when he said: "Even if we should have nothing else, we shall always have everything, because we have Jesus."

It is enough for you to say to Jesus: "Help me!" What you cannot do, He will do in you. Remain in Him, always in Him. Do not wish to come out of Him. If you do not want, you will not come out, and even if your sorrow is so deep as to prevent you from seeing where you are, you will always be with Jesus.

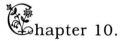

hapter 10.

Patronage of St. Joseph

(by Agreda—*City (Transfixion)*, from p. 166)

I have been informed concerning certain other privileges conferred upon Saint Joseph by the Most High on account of his great holiness, which are especially important to those who ask his intercession in a proper manner.

In virtue of these special privileges, the intercession of Saint Joseph is most powerful; first, for attaining the virtue of purity and overcoming the sensual inclinations of the flesh; secondly, for procuring powerful help to escape sin and return to the friendship of God; thirdly, for increasing the love and devotion to most holy Mary; fourthly, for securing the grace of a happy death and protection against the demons in that hour; fifthly, for inspiring the demons with terror at the mere mention of his name by his clients; sixthly, for gaining health of body and assistance in all kinds of difficulties; seventhly, for securing issue of children in families.

I beseech all the faithful children of the Church to be very devout to him, and they will experience these favors in reality, if they dispose themselves as they should, in order to receive and merit them.

~~~~~

Mary speaks:

On the Last Day, when all men shall be judged, the damned will bitterly bewail their sins, which prevented them from appreciating this powerful means of their salvation, and availing themselves, as they easily could have, of this intercessor to gain the friendship of the Just Judge. The whole human race has much under-valued the privileges and prerogatives conceded to My blessed spouse and they know not what his intercession with God is able to do. I assure you that he is one of the greatly favored personages in the Divine Presence and has immense power to stay the arms of divine vengeance.

In all your necessities, you must avail yourself of his intercession. You should induce many to venerate him. That which My spouse asks of the Lord in Heaven is granted upon the earth, and on his intercession depend many and extraordinary favors for men, if they do not make themselves unworthy of receiving them.

(by Ann—*The Heart of Saint Joseph*, from p. 35)

The secret of Joseph's sanctity was his deep and constant devotion to God the Father. Fathers today might well turn to Saint Joseph as a ready and helpful advocate.

A rather humorous story is related of a significant response by Saint Joseph in one of the Brooklyn homes operated by the Little Sisters of the Poor. The elderly men living there had had no beer to drink for some time, so they placed some empty beer bottles in front of St. Joseph's statue, to remind him of their need.

A priest acquainted with them was riding the subway, when he suppressed a chuckle. A stranger sitting opposite him moved to the space next to him, and asked him to share the joke. The priest told him the story and the stranger promised that, as vice president of a large brewing company, he would see to it that, as long as he lived, the men in the home would never want for beer again. A few days passed, and a large delivery of beer was sent to the men's home of the Little Sisters of the Poor, where God's aged and poor are tenderly guarded and served.

The story of the miraculous staircase attributed to Saint Joseph's workmanship has often been repeated. This marvelous piece of craftsmanship has been inspected by architects from all parts of the United States. Not a nail was used in its construction. Instead, the hardwood has been spliced together at seven places on the inside and nine on the outside. The whole forms a double helix, or spiral. Each section is perfectly fitted into a groove on the adjacent section.

The Sisters of Loreto, of Santa Fe, New Mexico, were unable to provide a staircase to the choir loft of their chapel in the course of its construction (1873-1878). Thus their chapel—Our Lady of Light Chapel—remained incomplete for several years, until an unknown carpenter came to the convent door seeking employment.

The sisters confided their problem of being unable to provide a staircase to their choir loft, due to the limited space available. This proved no problem to the stranger; he was certain he could accomplish the task. The superior and her assistant being forced to leave on an urgent mission, he proceeded with the task.

At the completion of the work and upon her return, the superior of the convent looked to pay the artisan for his service, but he was nowhere to be found. The sisters believed him to have been Saint Joseph, because they had offered their Holy Communion each Wednesday, in Saint Joseph's honor, that he might assist them in their plight concerning the staircase. It is also related that a deaf mute girl was working for the sisters. She and one sister were left behind, when the superior departed on her mission. Upon her return, the superior inquired as to the identity of the carpenter. The mute girl uttered the first word she had ever spoken: "Jose." That is Spanish for "Joseph."

For over 85 years, the staircase was in daily use, both by the sisters and by the students they taught in Loreto Academy. Visitors also were permitted to climb them, and in doing so, experienced a vertical movement with each step, as if walking on a large coiled spring.

Now, over 100 years later, the stairs are used only occasionally, in order to preserve this precious gift from Saint Joseph (and a handrail has been added for safety). Despite the closing of the doors of Loreto Academy about two decades ago, the hotel (the Inn of Loreto) owners who bought it allow the chapel to remain. It is sectioned off from the hotel itself. The wooden spiral staircase may be viewed today by visitors.

Father Jacquinot, of the Society of Jesus, declared: "Towards the end of the world, God will tear asunder the veil concealing from us the marvels of the shrine of Saint Joseph's holy heart; the Holy Ghost will act on the hearts of the faithful, moving them to praise the glory of that exalted person. Religious houses will be consecrated and temples built in his honor, and people will recognize as a special protector that saint who protected Jesus Christ. The Sovereign Pontiffs themselves shall decree, by a holy inspiration from above, that this great Patriarch be solemnly honored throughout the whole spiritual domain of Saint Peter."

(by Aumann—*Compendium*, from p. 125)

But what is so important about practicing devotion to St. Joseph? He was not biologically connected with Christ; he was not given the grace of being conceived immaculate; his holiness is on a lower level than that of Mary.

Nevertheless, I would maintain that the veneration owed to St. Joseph in more than the *dulia* given to the rest of the saints because he was so intimately involved in the mystery of the Incarnation. Therefore, some theologians claim for him the veneration called *proto-dulia*, which is the highest type of veneration given to the saints, but lower than that given to Mary (*hyperdulia*). Likewise, the universal patronage of St. Joseph is beneath that of Mary, but higher than that of any other saint.

(by Baij—*Life of*, from pp. 333 & 341)

God revealed to Joseph that because of his great concern for the dying throughout his life, assisting them and pleading for their salvation with prayers and tears, He was appointing him as their special mediator and patron, and furthermore, that He wished that he would continue to manifest his love for them until the end of time. From his place in Heaven, he would still be able to exercise this role as special intercessor for all those engaged in the struggle with death.

The saint gladly took this service upon himself and he was happy over being permitted to assist everyone in this grave and extreme necessity. He thanked God for having selected him, and from that hour dutifully assumed this responsibility of caring for the welfare of those who are in need at the time of death.

Saint Joseph enjoys in Heaven a glory which is indescribable and which surpasses that of any other saint. This glory cannot be comprehended by merely human understanding, and, hence, actually cannot be made known to the world. However, this glory is indeed recognized, understood, and appreciated by the blessed in Heaven throughout all eternity.

The saint continuously exercises his intermediary function before God on behalf of the dying. He also manifests a deep concern for the welfare of all souls redeemed by the Precious Blood of the Savior. He obtains graces for all, but he manifests a special solicitude for those who honor him. There is no grace that he asks of God, or of the most holy Virgin, which he is not able, subsequently, to obtain.

Saint Joseph supplicates for graces on behalf of all men, but particularly for the afflicted and oppressed, since he himself had to endure so much tribulation during his life on earth. The saint also appears to be especially deferential towards religious. I, therefore, urge all souls, in every state of life, to have a special devotion to this great saint. Marvelous effects will indeed be experienced by doing so.

(by Burkey—*Brindisi*, from p. 129)

To sum up St. Lawrence's teaching, he held that Joseph was absolutely and simply just, endowed with "limitless perfection in each of the different virtues." One final consideration of this holiness remains: Just how did Joseph's sanctity compare with that of others? Lawrence held that Joseph was the third among the predestined, and was predestined even before and above the angels. Because of this, Lawrence held that Joseph was third in holiness among creatures. His principle was that Joseph's "justice arises from predestination." In proof of this, he quotes Rom. 8:30: *Those whom He has predestined, He has called, and...has sanctified.*

Jesus holds the first place of the predestined. Mary the second. And Joseph, it seems to me, undoubtedly holds the third place. Hence he is called Just, and deservedly so. That star is brighter and more splendid which is nearer the sun, the fountain of all light.

Since Christ is the Sun of Justice (Mal 4:2), whichever saint is closer to Christ is endowed with the more perfect sanctity. The Virgin Mary is, therefore, the holiest of all the angels and saints, for She was the closest to Christ. After the Virgin Mary, who is closer to Christ than Joseph? She was Christ's Mother; he was His father—though not a natural father, yet a legal one...a father not by generation but by reason of education, care, affection, and love. Consequently, Joseph appears to me to be clearly the holiest of all the saints. He is holier than the Patriarchs, holier than the Prophets, holier than the Apostles, holier than any of the other saints.

(by Chorpenning—*Just Man*, from pp. 166, 230, 249 & 258)

St. Teresa of Avila said: "The Lord wants us to understand that just as He was subject to St. Joseph on earth—for since bearing the title of father, being the Lord's tutor, Joseph could give the Child commands—so in Heaven, God does whatever he commands."

Teresa's death was accompanied by several supernatural phenomena, one of which was that Christ appeared with the Virgin Mary and St. Joseph...

During four decades as porter at Notre Dame College in Montreal, operated by the Congregation of the Holy Cross, Brother André often spent much of the night on his knees in prayer before a small statue of St. Joseph in his little room near the door; he also became renowned for interceding in the healing of the sick by rubbing them lightly with "St. Joseph's oil," taken from a lamp in the college chapel.

André was convinced that St. Joseph wished to be honored on the land across from the college, known as Mount Royal; however, the landowner refused to relinquish the land. André and some others climbed the steep hill and planted medals of St. Joseph. Suddenly the owner yielded. (Perhaps this is the origin of the popular practice of burying a statue of St. Joseph to help sell a house. On this custom, see Gary L. Smith, "St. Joseph, Realtor?," *The Catholic Digest*, March 1991: 65-68).

(Editor's note: This research of St. Joseph was meant to be a somewhat "scholarly" piece of work, providing truth and fact from all of the best and most important sources. Nevertheless, we have come across many instances where people have had recourse to St. Joseph regarding the sale or purchase of property, even to the point of finding St. Joseph kits being sold in many places for that purpose. Therefore, with all the pervasive evidence, it might be considered remiss to disregard this area of St. Joseph's patronage, so we add this information:

Joan Curcio, a Realtor in the state of Pennsylvania for over 20 years, relates the following: "When I first began this occupation, my dear Aunt Margaret taught me to seek the assistance of St. Joseph. Consequently, I have seen positive results too many times to have any doubts. This seems to be the best procedure:

1) obtain a small inexpensive statue of St. Joseph;

2) have it blessed by a priest;

3) bury it, feet downward, in the front of the land or building;

4) for selling, have the statue facing the street to summon buyers;

5) for enlarging or buying rental property, have the statue of St. Joseph facing the building to extend his blessing upon it;

6) *if the statue is already buried in the wrong direction, go out and turn it around, or if you cannot find it, bury another blessed statue of St. Joseph in the correct position;*
7) *if the property has no soil, bury a blessed medal of Saint Joseph in the seam of the pavement;*
8) *pray to St. Joseph. A suggested prayer is, "St. Joseph, intercede for us";*
9) *leave the statue or medal in the ground permanently.*

Also, if one has undesirable neighbors of any kind, prayers and a Miraculous Medal buried facing that property frequently have been especially efficacious in correcting the situation.")

The Oratory of Saint Joseph, in Montreal, was founded in 1904. Some ten years later, the crypt structures were begun. Decades later, the monumental basilica would be completed, rising to a height of almost 4,000 feet and capable of holding a congregation of more than 10,000 worshippers. Today the Oratory is the worldwide center of the "things of St. Joseph."

St. Joseph often had the opportunity, when he carried Jesus in his arms on journeys or was alone with Him and was regaled with spiritual gifts, to ask favors of God, and nothing that he asked would be denied him. The power of his intercession is second only to that of the Virgin Mary.

(by De Domenico—*True Devotion*, from p. xvii)

On the 13th of October, 1917, our Lady appeared for the sixth time to three children at

Fatima, Portugal. The sun danced in the Heavens and plunged toward the earth and the people believed. Meanwhile, the children saw a series of three visions representing the three parts of the Rosary: the Joyful, Sorrowful, and Glorious mysteries. In the first vision representing the Joyful mysteries, the children saw a vision of St. Joseph carrying the Child Jesus, and both together were blessing the world. No words were spoken, but the vision is itself a silent message about St. Joseph, and an integral part of the Fatima message. In that message, Heaven intended to point the way to the salvation of many souls.

(by Doze—*St. Joseph: Shadow*, from pp. 18 & 25)

A famous Franciscan preacher, St. Leonard of Porto-Maurizio, had St. Joseph as his great source of inspiration; he held him up to all conditions of human existence, to all classes of society. "All Christians belong to Joseph, because Jesus and Mary belonged to him."

He adds: "Rejoice, devout servants of Saint Joseph, for you are close to Paradise; the ladder leading up to it has but three rungs: Jesus, Mary, and Joseph. Here is how one climbs up or down this ladder. As you climb up, your requests are first placed in the hands of St. Joseph; St. Joseph hands them over to Mary, and Mary to Jesus. As you climb down, the responses come from Jesus; Jesus delivers them to Mary, and Mary hands them over to Saint Joseph. Jesus does everything for Mary, for He is Her Son; Mary, as His Mother, obtains everything, and Joseph, as a righteous man, husband, and father, can do all things."

In his decree *urbi et orbi* of December 8, 1870, officially proclaiming St. Joseph as the Patron Saint of the Universal Church, Pius IX alluded "to the sorrowful times" the Church was going through. Having recourse to such a protector was all the more justified. Three months prior to his proclamation, the Piedmontese troops had invaded the Papal States. The Pope was being held prisoner in the Vatican. A whole world was definitely falling apart. Saint Joseph was called upon by the events themselves to play his role of "Patron Saint of a Happy Death," that is, of being the indispensable expert in the trying moments of human existence.

One must acknowledge that Pius IX's pontificate is, as it were, invisibly accompanied by the growing presence of St. Joseph. There is nothing surprising in the fact that the Sovereign Pontiff affirmed on February 2, 1878 during his last audience, five days before he died, to a religious who was filled with admiration for his serenity: "Ah! That comes from the fact that today St. Joseph is better known. I am expressing my trust. If I am not, my successor will be the one to witness the Triumph of this Church, of which I officially chose Saint Joseph to be the Patron Saint."

(by Bl. Eymard—*Month of St. Joseph*, from pp. 80 & 107)

Thoughts from Fr. Jean Jacques Olier (founder of the Society of St. Sulpice and their first seminaries, as well as the pastor of St. Sulpice in 1657)—Saint Joseph, Patron of Priests. God dwells fully, and with His virgin fruitfulness, in His priests. Now, they more than any one else must model their conduct toward the children they beget to God on that of Saint Joseph. He led the Child Jesus according to the Spirit of the Heavenly Father, in mildness and prudence. So must we deal with all the members of Jesus Christ committed to our care, treating these other Christs with all the reverence of Saint Joseph. Like Saint Joseph, who knew he was infinitely inferior to Christ, and yet saw himself in authority, deputed in the Name and in the place of God the Father, let us be their superiors in God; but, in our consideration, their inferiors.

Because God (as He has shown me by His will) has entrusted St. Joseph with the special care of priests, we have chosen St. Joseph as a patron of our seminary. The Blessed Virgin also gave him to me as a patron, assuring me that he was the guardian of interior souls, and saying: "Outside of My Son, there is no one dearer to Me in Heaven or on earth."

Once, bringing Viaticum to a sick person, I repeated these words that had come to me: "You have been the guide of the just man." They reminded me that Saint Joseph had been the guide of our Lord, the Just One, and that I ought to represent him and carry the Son of God in the same spirit in which Saint Joseph had carried Him.

Thoughts from Saint Teresa of Avila.—To gain a favorable hearing with our Lord, I took Saint Joseph as advocate and protector and prayed very specially to him. His help was most strikingly shown. As a tender spiritual father and a loving protector, he quickly cured me of my sickness (while still so young, she was seriously paralysed) just as he had saved me from greater dangers of other sorts which were menacing my honor and my eternal salvation.

In his eagerness to make me happy, he has always answered my prayers far beyond my expectations. To this very day, I do not remember ever having asked him anything that he did not give me. What a picture I would have before my eyes if I could recall all the signal graces which God gave me, and all the dangers, bodily and spiritual, from which he delivered me through the intercession of this good saint. To the other saints, God gives the grace to help us in certain particular needs, but to Saint Joseph, I know by experience, He gives power to help us in all our needs.

Our Lord wants us to understand that just as He was obedient in this land of exile, recognizing in Joseph the authority of a foster-father and a master, so now He is happy to do his will in Heaven by listening to all his demands. Other persons whom I advised to pray to this incomparable protector have agreed with me; the number of his clients is growing and every day the happy effects of his mediation confirm my words.

Knowing now, by long experience, Joseph's power with God, I would like to persuade everyone to pray to him. I have seen persons with a real solid devotion to him progress steadily in virtue, for he helps in a very striking manner those who pray for help along the path of perfection.

I dare the skeptics to try praying to Saint Joseph, and they will see by experience the advantage of praying to this great Patriarch and honoring him with a special devotion.

(Favorite Prayers, from pp. 30 & 52)

In 1847, Pope Pius IX solemnly proclaimed St. Joseph "Patron and Protector of the Universal Church." And although St. Joseph is our father and our advocate in all necessities, he is especially considered the Patron of a Happy Death, a provider of financial help—particularly to the poor and to religious communities—the patron of families, of laborers, of the sick, of the poor, of the rich (to help them distribute their possessions charitably and to help them attain the riches of Heaven), of the suffering, of travelers, of exiles, of the afflicted, of the married, of virgins, of youths, of priests and of those aspiring to the priesthood, of those advanced in virtue, and those devoted to prayer; he is also a rescuer of sinners, consoler and liberator of the Poor Souls, terror of demons and conqueror of Hell. Pope Innocent XI made St. Joseph the Patron of the Jesuit Missions in China, and Pope Pius XI proclaimed, "We place the vast campaign of the Church against world Communism under the standard of Saint Joseph, her mighty protector.

In short, Saint Joseph is the Patron and Protector of all classes of Christians.

Once, on the Feast of the Annunciation, St. Gertrude had a vision during which the Heavenly Mother revealed to her the glory of Her spouse, St. Joseph, in order to awaken in the saint a greater love for him and to encourage her to have confidence in his intercession. Of this vision, St. Gertrude wrote:

"I saw Heaven opened and Saint Joseph sitting upon a magnificent throne. I felt myself wonderfully affected when, each time his name was mentioned, all the saints made a profound inclination toward him, showing by the serenity and sweetness of their looks that they rejoiced with him on account of his exalted dignity."

(by Filas— *Joseph, The Man,* from pp. 371, 546 & 565)

An encyclical of Pope Leo XIII states: "There can be no doubt that more than any other person, St. Joseph approached that super-eminent dignity by which the Mother of God is raised far above all created natures."

In the French *Dictionary of Catholic Theology,* we find: "Although no explicit assertion of Catholic theology exists to corroborate this interpretation, it seems that we can logically draw the conclusion this far, that in dignity, Saint Joseph surpasses not only the saints, but all angels as well."

One day, after Communion, St. Teresa of Avila wrote, "Our Lord commanded me to labor with all my might, promising that a monastery would certainly be built, that it should be called St. Joseph's, and that St. Joseph would keep guard at one door and our Lady at the other; that Christ would be in the midst of us. Once when I was in one of my difficulties, not knowing what to do and unable to pay the workmen, my true father and lord, St. Joseph, appeared to me and gave me to understand that money would not be wanting, and I must hire the workmen."

Of the 17 monasteries which she founded, Teresa dedicated 12 to Saint Joseph. After her death, the General Chapter of the Carmelite

Fathers selected Saint Joseph as Patron of the Order.

The basilica at Montreal, Canada, St. Joseph's Oratory, had its origin in the faith of a lay brother of the Congregation of The Holy Cross. Brother André, whose name in the world had been Alfred Bessette, entered the Congregation in 1870 and was assigned the humble post of doorkeeper at Notre Dame College in Montreal. "Some day," so he spoke with the certainty of faith, "God in His goodness would lift up a monument to St. Joseph on the steep western summit of Mount Royal, across the street from the college."

Without a doubt, it is presently the foremost shrine of St. Joseph in the world. The Oratory itself was founded in 1904. Some ten years later, the crypt structures were begun. The dimensions of the basilica unit are hard to imagine simply for their vastness. On the first level, about fifty feet from the ground, rests the sedate crypt church, three stories high and accommodating 2,000 persons. It is, however, dwarfed by the monumental basilica which rises behind it to a height of almost 400 feet, and capable of holding a congregation of more than 10,000 worshippers. Together with the majestic proportions of the basilica, the policy of constructing the Oratory gradually and according to the funds on hand was reminiscent of the decades required to erect the ageless cathedrals of Europe.

Brother André died in 1937 at the age of 92. He did not live to see the basilica finished, but he saw its future success assured, and with that, he was content. St. Joseph's Oratory would rise to the clouds, symbolizing the prayers of the millions of pilgrims who have traveled there to honor and imitate and beg the help of their patron. Brother André liked to call himself "St. Joseph's little dog," but the story of the monument he caused to be created merits for him the title of "Apostle of St. Joseph."

(by Filas—*St. Joseph, After*, from pp. 22, 79, 83 & 107)

Thus, in the developing Christian tradition, Joseph was looked upon in his biblical role, as head of the tiny group at Nazareth which represented the nascent Church. The concept of Joseph as protector of the Holy Family at Nazareth, and therefore protector of the Church, which grew out of that Family, was first enunciated by John Gerson in his writings and most explicitly in his speech at the Council of Constance in 1416. It was taken up ever more explicitly, coming to the fore when Pope Pius IX made Joseph *Patron of the Universal Church* in 1870.

In all Church writing on St. Joseph, none has ever surpassed in fullness the analysis of Joseph's position in the classic encyclical of Pope Leo XIII, *Quamquam Pluries*. This encyclical, published in 1889, is the source of the "golden text" in the history of the devotion of all the theology of St. Joseph to be expressed in our later commentary. It reads as follows:

"There are special reasons why Blessed Joseph should be explicitly named the Patron of the Church, and why the Church in turn should expect much from his patronage and guardianship. For he, indeed, was the husband of Mary, and the father, as was supposed, of

Jesus Christ. From this arise all his dignity, grace, holiness, and glory.

"The dignity of the Mother of God is certainly so sublime that nothing can surpass it; but none the less, since the bond of marriage existed between Joseph and the Blessed Virgin, there can be no doubt that, more than any other person, he approached the super-eminent dignity by which the Mother of God is raised far above all created natures.

"For marriage in the closest possible union and relationship whereby each spouse mutually participates in the good of the other. Consequently, if God gave Joseph as a husband to the Virgin, He assuredly gave him not only as a companion in life, a witness of Her virginity, and the guardian of Her Honor, but also as a sharer in Her exalted dignity by reason of the conjugal tie itself.

"Likewise, Joseph alone stands out in august dignity because he was the guardian of the Son of God by the divine appointment, and in the opinion of men, was His father. As a consequence, the Word of God was modestly obedient to Joseph, was attentive to his commands, and paid to him every honor that children should render their parent.

"Moreover, the divine household, which Joseph governed just as with paternal authority, contained the beginnings of the new Church. The Virgin most holy is the Mother of all Christians, since She is the Mother of Jesus, and since She gave birth to them on the Mount of Calvary amid the unspeakable sufferings of the Redeemer. Jesus is, as it were, the firstborn of all Christians, who are His brothers by adoption and redemption.

"From these considerations, we conclude that the blessed Patriarch must regard all the multitude of Christians who constitute the Church as confided to his care in a certain special manner.

"This is his numberless family, scattered throughout all lands, over which he rules with a sort of paternal authority, because he is the husband of Mary and the father of Jesus Christ. Thus, it is conformable to reason and in every way becoming to Blessed Joseph, that as once it was his sacred trust to guard with watchful care the Family of Nazareth, no matter what befell, so now, by virtue of his Heavenly patronage, he is in turn to protect and to defend the Church of Christ."

Joseph's fatherly patronage of the Church means his patronage of the entire human race. The reason is that the Church is destined for the whole human race, and since a certain special fittingness exists for certain saints to be mediators for specific groups or individuals, so in Joseph's case this special fittingness was also apparent. Joseph protects the entire Church, namely, the Church that embraces the whole human race as it potential members and as its actual responsibility.

This is why Joseph is the protector of everyone, everywhere, because he is the Patron of the Church everywhere. Since every member of the human race should be fully a member of Christ's Church, and since the Church must strive to bring all humans into union with it, according to its delegation received from Christ, therefore, Joseph is Patron of all in the human race.

Joseph's patronage is the order of grace continued when Joseph named the Child Jesus; when he assumed the responsibility of father; when he executed his duties prudently, deliberately, humbly. Such is the tenor of the Gospels in telling us what they do of the life and activities of the man. In God's providence, Joseph was not intended to stand at the foot of the cross like Mary. Nevertheless, since the spiritual martyrdom of Mary at the foot of the cross is accepted as a fact, accomplished by the offering of Mary's will to God, we can say that in a parallel though lesser way, Joseph, too, had his martyrdom of will long before, in his complete acceptance of God's designs concerning him.

May we respectfully paraphrase the final words of the Constitution on the Church, adapting the passage to refer directly to St. Joseph:

"May Joseph, exalted as he is above all the angels and saints after Mary, intercede before his Son in the fellowship of Mary and all the saints, until all families of people, whether they are honored with the title of Christian, or whether they still do not know the Savior, may be happily gathered together in peace and harmony into one People of God, for the glory of the most holy and undivided Trinity."

(by Gasnier—*Joseph the Silent*, from pp. 9 & 185)

In poetic language, Francis Jammes says: "O my dear ones, I promise you that he who goes about like one of the common herd, like one of us, with his tools on his shoulder and a smile in his beard...he will never abandon you."

As for the title of "Co-Redemptor" which certain men wish to attribute to St. Joseph, their efforts on this score are injudicious. "Co-Redemptor" as applied to St. Joseph is to be taken only in the way it is applicable to all those who chose to unite their merits and sufferings to those of Jesus Christ, in order, as St. Paul says, "to fill up those things that are wanting to the Passion of Christ."

For Joseph, of course, the title used in this sense would have a more exact meaning since he had guarded, nourished, and cherished the Divine Victim with the cross in view. He had by anticipation offered Him in the Temple as his own gift, and for Jesus' sake, he had endured sufferings whose propitiatory merits have profited all humanity redeemed by the Blood of Christ.

Our Ancestors, perhaps realizing better than we, God's interest in every least detail concerning us and our destiny, set themselves to study the name of Joseph. They noticed that all the letters in his name pointed to the saint's outstanding virtues: *J* for Justice, *O* for Obedience, *S* for silence, *E* for Experience, *P* for Prudence, and *H* for Humility. We might be tempted to smile at such childlike simplicity except for the fact that actually the virtues enumerated do have the characteristics of soul that Christian tradition has attributed to him.

It is not necessary, in order to extol Saint Joseph's greatness, to pile up titles of an exceptional order. It is enough remembering the self-effacement in which he took pleasure, to recall the Words of Jesus Himself. "Whoever, therefore, humbles himself as this little child, he is the greatest in the Kingdom of Heaven."

379.

(by Healy Thompson—*Life and*, from pp. x, 18 & 377)

With this sublime vocation and these incomparable privileges, the graces and virtues of Joseph fully corresponded; his merits were commensurate with his dignity; and therefore it is that he ranks next to Mary in the Court of Heaven and is seated in glory so nigh unto the throne of the Incarnate Word.

St. Joseph when, in Egypt, in Nazareth, in Jerusalem, he beheld Jesus, Who is the Sun of Justice, "subject" to him; his immaculate Spouse, Mary, Who is fair as the moon, yielding him obedience; and now in Heaven beholds the Apostles and Saints all doing him homage and paying him the profoundest veneration. Now, if such bright stars do reverence to Joseph, what homage, what veneration, do not we owe to him, miserable little lamps as we are!

There are two perfections which we are called upon specially to admire in Joseph; his most singular faith and his eminent supernatural wisdom. These were two rays, as it were, of the Divine Understanding descending into the mind of Joseph.

(by Griffin—*Saint Joseph & Third*, from pp. 56, 103, 271, 294 & 301)

Sacred Scripture is the principle foundation for devotion to Saint Joseph under the various patronages the Church has accorded to him. The slowness of the development of his devotion throughout history is traceable to the predominance of the non-scriptural, false images of him presented by the apocryphal writings. Joseph serves today as a patron and model for all people in general, and for many individual groups in particular. This chapter ends by listing some of the lights in which he may be seen, as grounded directly in Scripture, or as extrapolated from the Scriptural data and suggested for contemporary society.

1) *Model disciple, dedicating his whole life to the interests of Jesus.*—Joseph is an example of faith, righteousness, trust in God's providence, and prompt obedience to God's call.

2) *Patron of the Church.*—This title results from a combination of various elements: a) Paul's theology of the Church as an extension of Christ, the mystical body; b) an extension of John's and Luke's type of theology by which Mary, the Mother of Jesus, also in some sense becomes Mother of the Church; c) the Apostles' Creed: doctrine of the "communion of the saints," understood to mean that the deceased and saved continue to pray for their fellow Christians on earth.

As Joseph protected the physical body of the Child Jesus on earth, so does he continue to protect, through his intercessory prayer from Heaven, the mystical body of Christ, the Church. As the Mother of Christ is called Mother of the Church, so also Her husband, the guardian of Christ, is called the Protector of the Church.

3) *Patron of Husbands and of the Engaged.*— Joseph exhibits the deepest love for his Fiance and Wife, and the highest respect for women. He in no way seeks to use Mary, but rather to give himself to Her in accord with his God-given vocation. His call to live a virginal relationship with Her does not deter him from immediately and whole-heartedly taking Her as his Wife.

He is an example of true spousal love. For fiances, he is an example of sexual respect during engagement. For the married, who for a good reason must postpone another pregnancy, he is a model of the loving abstinence they must exercise during the fertile times, in order to practice natural family planning, rather than have recourse to artificial contraceptives, which may be easier, but which are not in harmony with their commitment in Christ.

His virginal relationship to Mary, however, does not indicate a lack of openness to offspring; Joseph is a model of acceptance of children in marriage, in his quick response to do so when so told by the angel. Mary and Joseph have a unique vocation to virginal marriage, because their love is already blessed with the greatest of offspring, the Son of God, with which no number of other children could ever compare.

4) *Patron of Fathers.*—Joseph models total self-sacrificing concern to provide for, protect, raise, educate, and be an example to the Child entrusted to him. He shows that authentic fatherhood consists in much more than physical generation. He constantly recognizes the subordination of his role to the primordial Fatherhood of God, always cooperating and never interfering with His designs.

5) *Patron of Family Life.*—With Jesus and Mary, Joseph is a model of unity, love, and

shared faith, showing the priority of family life over one's individual interests, and also the necessity of family life as a basis for learning to form community as Church.

6) *Protector of the Unborn and of Pregnant Mothers.*—After Mary, no one appreciates life in the womb more than St. Joseph. In faith, he recognized the Baby in Mary's womb as the Incarnate God, and was willing to make any sacrifice to care for that Life, and for the Mother called to bear It. In our age of rampant abortion, Joseph calls us as a society and as individuals to recognize the divine source of life and to always respect and defend it.

7) *Model of Workers.*—Joseph the Carpenter, who teaches his profession to Jesus, shows the dignity of work, which is measured not by earning power or prestige, but by the love and motivation with which it is done daily.

8) *Patron of the Marginalized, Emigrants, Refugees, and Those Discriminated Against.*—The father of Jesus experienced all these hardships in the persecution by Herod, and in the attitude of the ruling Judean authorities towards people from Galilee. He shows that one's dignity does not consist in social, political, or economic standing, but in one's inner integrity in being true to one's own calling. God favors and protects the lowly.

9) *Model of Humility, the Hidden Life, and the Sanctification of the Ordinary.*—Joseph's great sanctity is accompanied by no great words or deeds. The details of his life remain lost to history. Jesus' first 30 years belong to the "hidden life" at Nazareth. Joseph teaches us that holiness need not catch the world's attention. It consists, rather, in being lovingly faithful to the ordinary: family, work, religious

observance, the indications of circumstances, and God's revelation.

10) *Model of Contemplative Union with Christ.*— Besides Joseph's total availability to God's will, his daily life is dedicated to union with Christ. He is known as the "saint of silence," because no word of his has been preserved (except the name "Jesus," which he gave the Child). He is thus a model of the interior life and contemplative prayer.

11) *Patron of Apostles.*—Joseph's role, in large part, is to prepare Jesus for His life and ministry. All involved in apostolic ministry may learn from him those attitudes and virtues needed to bring Christ to others.

12) *Patron of a Happy Death.*—Total lack of mention of Joseph during Jesus' public ministry, even when Mary is present, leads to the assumption that he had already died. His acceptance of this death would be consistent with his quiet fulfillment of his role, followed by a gentle fading from the scene so as not to interfere with Jesus' proclamation of His Divine Sonship. His death in the arms of Jesus and Mary is the envy of every true Christian believer.

Joseph's role in the Scriptures will always be important for the life to the Church, because with him we celebrate our earliest origins as a Christian community. His union with Mary and Christ in the Mystery of the Incarnation means that he can never be far from us, Christ's Body.

John Paul II states: "It was from the marriage to Mary that Joseph derived his singular dignity and his rights in regard to Jesus. It is certain that the dignity of the Mother of God is so exalted, that nothing could be more sublime;

yet because Mary was united to Joseph by the bond of marriage, there can be no doubt that Joseph approached, as no other person ever could, that eminent dignity whereby the Mother of God towers above all creatures.

"Since marriage is the highest degree of an association and friendship, involving by its very nature a communion of goods, it follows that God, by giving Joseph to the Virgin, did not give him to Her only as a companion for life, a witness of Her virginity and protector of Her honor; He also gave Joseph to Mary in order that he might share, through the marriage pact, in Her own sublime greatness."

What contrasts are found in Joseph! He is the patron of celibates and those who are fathers of families; he is likewise the patron of the laity and of contemplatives, and patron of priests as well as businessmen. Over the centuries, Joseph has shown himself to be an advocate of the world's needy.

Joseph is the patron of those who meditate. Dr. Herbert Benson, in his recent book *Timeless Healing*, describes his own research and clinical work and that of others showing the remarkable healing value of spiritual meditation for two 15-minute periods daily in the treatment of hypertension, coronary artery disease, colitis, migraine headaches, and numerous illnesses.

Still others see Joseph as the patron of finance, as in the sale or purchase of property. While the practice of buying a statue of the saint to help the sale may seem frivolous to some, results have been productive.

In the *New Covenant*, we share a "flesh-and-blood" union with Christ, our brother, through the Blessed Eucharist. If Jesus is our "brother," then St. Joseph is also our "father."

To the thousands of men deprived of a healthy relationship with their fathers: Go to St. Joseph! To those seeking to overcome a negative father image: seek not further than St. Joseph for a potent cure. To the millions of children in fatherless families: Go to St. Joseph! You will find an earthly father who, like the Heavenly Father, is a father of the fatherless. The Heavenly Father has provided a link to Himself through the fatherhood of St. Joseph over the whole Family of God.

(by Hubert—*Knock, Vision of Hope*, from pp. 14 & 22)

At Knock, Mary is wearing a large, beautiful golden crown. She is a Queen. The special object of Saint Joseph's homage is, accordingly, Her Queenship. Again, certain features of the apparition point to this further truth, that Saint Joseph is venerating Mary as Queen of the Universal Church, that is the Church triumphant in Heaven, militant on earth, and suffering in purgatory. If St. Joseph is venerating Mary as Queen of the Universal Church, the harmonious design of the apparition as a whole leads with assurance to the conclusion that the glorious Patriarch himself appears as the Church's Patron and Protector.

Devotion to Saint Joseph is indeed a precious gift of Mary. It is a grace which reveals Her exquisite love for Her spouse and for those with whom She shares Her love for him. Full of gratitude for such singular proof of Mary's love, Joseph hastens to make Her a return of love, which is at once supremely affective and efficacious; by his powerful intercession with the Heavenly Queen, as well as by many hidden services, he will continue to be an efficient instrument in rendering the children of the Church like unto Her, Who is their Mother and their Queen.

Saint Joseph still likes to work quietly and unobstrusively, and because his patronage and charity are universal, all the children of the House of God share in his beneficent influence. In the blessed repose and peace of Paradise, the Heavenly artisan still labors with supreme energy and consummate skill to realize his dream of beauty—*the likeness of Mary*—in the Church and all Her children. His great work will not be completed until all the predestined partake of Mary's glory in Heaven and, through Her and in Her, of the glory of Jesus, Her Son.

(*by a sister, Joseph the Just,* from p. 1)

Great Saint Joseph, among all the saints most deserving of reverence, love, and confidence.

(by Levy—*Joseph, The Just Man,* from p. 81)

St. Alphonsus Liguori, the founder of the Redemptorists, burned with love for the Blessed Sacrament and for Mary, the Mother of Jesus, but he also inculcated into the hearts of his listeners a great confidence in the patronage of St. Joseph. He taught that the whole world acknowledges St. Joseph as the advocate of the dying, and this for three reasons; first, because being loved by Jesus not only as a friend but as a father, he possesses in Heaven a power of intercession greater than that of other saints; second, because he has special power over the demons who attack us on our deathbed, this privilege having been given him in recompense for the fact that he preserved the life of Jesus from the impious designs of Herod; and third, because of the assistance rendered him by Jesus and Mary at the hour of his death. In consequence, St. Joseph has received the privilege of obtaining for his devout clients, the inestimable grace of a holy and peaceful death in the sight of the Lord.

(by Llamera—*Saint Joseph*, from pp. 174 & 284)

Saint Joseph, as we have seen, is incorporated in the work of Redemption by the same divine decree which associated him with the Divine Maternity and the Incarnation of the Word, since our salvation was one of the primordial ends of these mysteries. God grants grace and sanctity to men according to the dignity and character of the mission to which He has destined them. Consequently, it is evident that the spouse of Mary, the Coredemptrix, had to be adorned with a most eminent sanctity, full of all graces and virtues, fitting him for his place with Jesus and Mary in the salvation of the world.

What was the degree and extent of Saint Joseph's growth in grace while he lived? The more obscure his life on earth, so much the more is he glorified in Heaven.

1) Each and every act of charity performed by Saint Joseph was, from his earliest infancy, intense, and his grace increased with each and every one of his works of virtue. Holy as he was, all his acts, at least virtually, were referred to God, so that he grew in grace not only by the acts of charity, born of his ardent love for God, but also by the acts of the other virtues, theological and moral.

2) Without fear of rashness, we may say that St. Joseph performed all his acts, even from his childhood, with all the strength of his habitual grace, for he never placed any of the obstacles, such as passion, defect, negligence, or distraction.

3) The virtues flow from grace just as properties flow from the essence and are, therefore, more perfect in proportion to the abundance of sanctifying grace in the soul. As the grace of St. Joseph was exceedingly abundant, we may easily believe that he was adorned with every virtue.

4) Similarly, he was filled with the gifts of the Holy Ghost and by them promptly moved, under the inspiration of God, in the execution of all his works.

5) The reason for this remarkable growth in sanctity was his association and continuous familiarity with Christ and Mary. Through Them, he obtained a profound knowledge of the mystery of the Incarnation and a perfect example of all the virtues. This daily contact was the permanent source of the infusion of grace in St. Joseph, as the authors unanimously declare. "Therefore," says Seldmayr, "St. Joseph possessed many more means for acquiring sanctity than did Saint

John the Baptist or the apostles, for during 30 years he enjoyed the presence, wisdom, love, and example of Jesus and Mary, in Whom there was no stain, but on the contrary, all the treasures of divine wisdom and holiness. Consequently, no one of sound reason would say that St. Joseph did not make use of these means of sanctification; but rather esteem him the greatest in sanctity after Jesus and Mary."

St. Bernardine de Busto says: "The holier the company, the more pleasing the conversation. He who converses with the good, will become good (Ps. 17:38). How much more the blessed Joseph, in daily communion with the holiest of the holy, the Son of God and His Mother, would grow in sanctity, and from good would become better, witnessing Their works and Their holy life! No one has ever had such a part in the life of the sweet Jesus and His blessed Mother."

Referring particularly to the Saint's earthly ministry with Jesus and Mary, he is a very special advocate—first, of the entire Catholic Church; second, of souls who are perfect or who aspire to perfection, particularly priests and religious; third, of Christian families, principally the poor; and fourth, of the dying.

(by Neuzil—*Our Lady of America*, from p. 27)

"I bring to souls, the purity of my life and the obedience that crowned it.

"All fatherhood is blest in me whom the Eternal Father chose as His representative on

earth, the Virgin-Father of His Own Divine Son.
Through me, the Heavenly Father has blessed all
fatherhood, and through me He continues, and
will continue, to do so till the end of time. My
spiritual fatherhood extends to all God's children,
and together with my Virgin Spouse, I watch
over them with great love and solicitude.

"Fathers must come to me to learn obedience
to authority: to the Church always, as the mouth-
piece of God, to the laws of the country in which
they live, insofar as these do not go against God
and their neighbor. Mine was perfect obedience
to the divine will, as it was shown and made
known to me by the Jewish law and religion. To
be careless in this is most displeasing to God and
will be severely punished in the next world.

"Let fathers also imitate my great purity
of life and the deep respect I held for my
Immaculate Spouse. Let them be an example to
their children and fellowmen, never willfully
doing anything that would cause scandal among
God's people. Fatherhood is from God, and it
must take, once again, its rightful place among
men.

"I desire souls to come to my heart that they
may learn true union with the divine will.

"God wishes me to be honored in union with
Jesus and Mary to obtain peace among men and
nations.

"The privilege of being chosen by God to be
the Virgin-Father of His Son was mine alone, and
no honor, excluding that bestowed upon my
Holy Spouse, was ever or will ever be as sublime
or as high as this. I desire that a day be set
aside to honor my fatherhood. The Holy Trinity
desires thus to honor me, that in my unique
fatherhood, all fatherhood might be blessed."

(O'Carroll—*The King Uncrowned*, from p. 102)

The Church's theologians are convinced that from the direct and indirect reference of the Sacred Scriptures, we can conclude that St. Joseph was predestined to a height of grace and glory exceeding that of any other creature except the Mother of God.

(O'Rafferty—*Discourses*, from pp. 9 & 11)

Among the saints, without a doubt, the greatest splendor is that of St. Joseph.

After the office of Mother of God for which Mary was selected, there is no office in Heaven or on earth greater than that for which St. Joseph was chosen, namely, that of spouse of Mary and guardian of Jesus. Therefore, since his office surpassed that of any other saint, patriarch or prophet, apostle or martyr, confessor or virgin, the grace conferred on him was superior to that bestowed on any other saint.

(*Our Lady of Knock*, from p. 12)

Provincial of the Holy Ghost Fathers, Very Rev. Patrick O'Carroll, C.S.Sp.,D.D.:— "St. Joseph, Patron and Protector of the Universal Church and model head of every family is depicted, in accounts of the apparition at Knock, as having his head slightly inclined towards our Lady, as if paying Her his respects. He appeared as one advanced in years, as lines of gray streaked his hair and beard. After our blessed Lady, he had the highest honor conferred on him, that of being the foster father of the Son of God and the spouse of His holy Mother. Saint Thomas says that God distributes His gifts as a preparation of the office He intends anyone to fill, and since, after our Lady's, Saint Joseph's was the most exalted, we may conclude that after his immaculate Spouse, he received the most copious infusion of divine favors. Thus, in that Heavenly Kingdom, he will rank after the Queen Herself, before any angel or any saint of either the Old or New Testament.

"**I**t is true that the saints in Heaven participate in the knowledge of God to the degree or measure in which they possessed sanctifying grace when their souls were leaving their bodies. Now the Church implies that Saint Joseph had an inconceivably great knowledge of God, since She constituted him Her Universal Patron and Protector. Saint Joseph has now to listen to the prayers addressed to him at all times and to see the needs of all the faithful, from the innumerable and complicated problems confronting the Sovereign Pontiff himself, down to the common and obvious difficulties of the poor struggler that has just been wrested from paganism on the mission field.

"**T**here were reasons why there could not be, in the early ages of the Church, too manifest a devotion to this great saint, but they now no longer hold, and hence, ever since the time of Saint Teresa of Avila, he, who in the Litany of the Church is addressed as the terror of demons, is becoming more and more known and appreciated.

"It is well to note the sources of his sanctity—his intimacy with Jesus and Mary. It was preeminently fitting that Jesus, Who is the Author of Grace, should simply fill him to overflowing with His choicest favors. Also reflect on his relation to our Lady, and bear in mind all I have said about Her special prerogative in the distribution of graces. He was the first to be devoted to Her—no other saint was so closely united to Her, and thus he received from Her hands all She could give and all She wished to give. Lastly, he is represented doing homage or inclined towards Her, here, in order to show that all the favors asked or granted through the prayers of the saints, must pass through and be received from our Lady."

(by Patrignani—*Manual,* from pp. 43, 55, 94 & 107)

The Angelic Doctor, Saint Thomas Aquinas teaches, that God has been pleased to give some saints a special power to protect under certain peculiar necessities, and others He has endowed with gifts of various kinds; but to Saint Joseph He has been more generous—He has made him, as it were, His plenipotentiary, His treasurer-general, that he may have it in his power to assist and relieve every description of person, whatever may be his necessity.

The other saints, it is true, have great power, but only to a certain extent. They intercede and supplicate as dependants, but they do not rule as masters; whereas, St. Joseph, to whom at Nazareth Jesus and Mary had lived submissive, as being the father of One and husband to the Other, now that he dwells in the House of God, where his titles, far from being obscured, shine out with incomparable brilliancy, may doubtless obtain all he desires from the King, his Son, and the Queen, his Spouse. His influence with Both is unbounded, and as Gerson says, "he rather commands than supplicates. Hence it may be seen, how powerful is the intercession of St. Joseph!"

"Saint Joseph is the most zealous champion against those who question My virginity," our Lady said to St. Bridget. St. Francis de Sales assures us, that St. Joseph's purity surpassed that of the angels of the first hierarchy; for, as he says, if the material sun can perfect the dazzling whiteness of the lily in a few days, who can conceive the admirable degree of perfection to which St. Joseph's purity was raised, when it was exposed, not for a few days only, but for the space of 30 years, to the rays of the Sun of Justice and of the Mystical Moon, which derived from that Sun all Her splendor?

Gerson once gave the Duke de Berri the following invitation: "My Lord, take St. Joseph for your special patron, your most powerful mediator, and best friend. Be not foolish as to neglect making interest, while time yet remains, with one who is considered the particular patron of dying Christians."

As the sentence of death has been pronounced on all, without exception, it follows that all and each, without exception, should endeavor to secure the interest and friendship of him who is all-powerful in procuring every assistance for his clients at that awful and decisive hour, to enable them to die happily. If a person engages in a lawsuit, on the event of which depends an immense gain or utter ruin, does he not call in the aid of some eminent lawyer, of one whose zeal for his interest he may safely depend?

Now every Christian at the hour of death, is about to hear an irrevocable sentence pronounced upon him, upon which will depend his eternal life or death, the rage and temptations of the devil at that critical moment—the remembrance of past sins—the uncertainty as to the real state of one's soul at that awful moment—the terror of the future—all combine in disputing, as it were, his claim to the Kingdom of Heaven, and in torturing his spirit with the dread apprehension of being condemned to the eternal loss of that God, Who loved him even so well as to die for him, Who alone can make him happy—to that Hell of fire where the worm dieth not, and the fire is never extinguished!

Why not, at that critical moment, call on some saint to plead his cause, and to obtain a favorable sentence for him at that awful tribunal, whence there is no appeal, should he once have the misfortune to be condemned? Who is there better qualified to perform this charitable office than Saint Joseph? He is acknowledged by all Christendom to be the special advocate of dying Christians; whence it is that congregations have been everywhere established and altars raised in his name, and that the feast of his blessed death is celebrated in many places.

Among the many motives for which St. Joseph has been constituted the particular patron of dying persons in preference to other saints, there are three which more especially engage us to consider him as such: 1st, St. Joseph is the adopted father of our Judge, whereas the other saints are only His friends; 2nd, his power is more formidable to the devils: 3rd, his death was the most singularly privileged, and the happiest ever recorded in the annals of mankind.

St. Teresa of Avila, after struggling for three years with the most violent and irremediable maladies, which deprived her of rest and of all hope of recovery, at length had recourse to St. Joseph, who restored her miraculously to health.

The holy foundress was one day in great anxiety, because she actually had not money enough to pay the workmen's wages, and could not devise any possible means of procuring it. St. Joseph, on this occasion, appeared to her, and offered, not only to become answerable for the debt, but also to be her treasurer; he assured her that she should not want for money, and induced her to make an agreement with the men, and to go on with the work. The saint had not a fraction, but, nevertheless, she complied with Saint Joseph's request. He was not wanting on his part, and supplied her with money in so many extraordinary ways, that those who witnessed them deemed them altogether miraculous.

(Pesquera—*She Went in Haste*, from p. 252)

Concerning St. Joseph: He is the greatest of the saints in Heaven.

(by Petrisko—*St. Joseph and the Triumph*, from p. vii)

Forward by Fr. Richard Foley. S.J.—St. Joseph is second only to Our Lady as the complete all-round patron in Heaven. This is to say, besides being supremely holy, he is an ideal friend and advocate when we approach him in our different needs.

In the first place, St. Joseph is patron of Christ's worldwide family, the Church. And this is because of his headship of the Holy Family. This further explains why he is the Heavenly protector of every individual human family. Again, as the man closest to Jesus and Mary, he is the model of all who strive after closer Christ-likeness.

One very special need that commonly prompts young ladies to invoke St. Joseph's intercession is that he will help them find a nice husband. And, in turn, who more fittingly and effectively will assist, with his prayers, any young man in search of the right life-partner than "he who cherished Mary with a husband's love," as the liturgy describes him.

Another vital area over which St. Joseph is principal patron is the world of work, and with very good reason, too. For it was as breadwinner for the Holy Family that he plied his trade at Nazareth. In the process, he taught us to sanctify our daily labors, of whatever kind they may be.

One of commonest and most important needs for which St. Joseph's prayers are requested, is the grace of a happy death. Underlying this is the ancient tradition that he himself died at Nazareth in the presence of Jesus and Mary, surely the most privileged ever situation for anybody leaving this world. Hence the unique value of Saint Joseph's patronage in our last moments.

Enjoying as he does such an extra-special status, and playing such a many-sided role in salvation history, St. Joseph has been adopted as their special patron by many a future saint. For they understand, better than most, how intimately he was locked into the life and lifework of the Redeemer and His Mother. Indeed, St. Teresa of Avila even suggested that none of us can afford the luxury of not having a devotion to Mary's spouse and foster-father of the Word-made-Flesh.

(by Poranganel—*St. Joseph*, from pp. 35, 41 & 47)

It is because of the omnipotent intercession of Blessed Joseph, St. Lawrence tell us, "He who chooses St. Joseph for his patron and protector is most fortunate; Joseph will protect him in this world, and accompany him to the next.

St. Lawrence, speaking about the dignity of Joseph, tells us that he was of noble birth, being the descendant of David, in addition to his triple position of being the husband of Mary, legitimate father of Jesus, and the head of the Holy Family of Nazareth. The Heavenly Father entrusted Joseph with His richest treasures of infinite value, namely His Eternal Son and His virgin Mother, for protection, care, and sustenance. Lawrence speaks of Joseph, "Oh how wonderful and divine is the dignity, as well as the authority, of this man, Joseph!"

We have seen that St. Joseph's dignity is due to his fourfold position: as the spouse of the Mother of God, the virginal father of Jesus, the head of the Holy Family, and the patron of the Universal Church. Because of these exalted positions, St. Joseph's dignity is far superior to that of other saints and angels.

(by Robert—*Guardian of God's Lilies*, from p. 26)

It is a common error among the ignorant and even among the worldly-wise, to believe that Saint Joseph was only an ordinary workman. He was a man of eminent dignity, of most perfect virtue; and he enjoys great power and singular grandeur in Heaven.

(by Rondet—*Saint Joseph*, from pp. 27 & 69)

St. Teresa of Avila, at the age or 26, was cured of a serious illness after praying to St. Joseph, and she became an enthusiastic advocate of devotion to him; she declared that those who invoke his aid receive not only temporal good things, but, better still, the gift of prayer. Teresa dedicated her first convent at Avila in Joseph's name, and two-thirds of her other foundations had the same dedication.

If Jesus spoke truly when He said, "Where I am, there also shall My servant be" (John 12:26), surely he who, after Mary, was closest to Him on earth, who was so dutiful and faithful in his service of Him, must have a place nearest to Him in Heaven.

(by Sparks—*Dominicans*, from pp. 16 & 168)

St. Antoninus concurs with St. Ignatius, St. Jerome, and St. Ambrose that Jesus was born of an espoused Mother so that the devil might be deceived. God willed that the Virgin Mary have a husband for the protection of the Child lest the devil be particularly vehement against Him. This traditional reasoning could well bolster the invocation in the Litany of St. Joseph: "Terror of Demons," and this is significant in the understanding of St. Joseph's Patronage over the Church.

Though Cardinal Gotti does not use the word *protodulia*, he readily concedes that to St. Joseph is due the *summus duliae cultus*. Dulia is a witnessing to the honor and excellence of someone. The excellence of St. Joseph seems to be the highest after that of Christ and Mary. Only lately has the Church begun to celebrate the excellence and dignity *quamvis maxima*— of St. Joseph, and of the parents of the blessed Virgin, St. Joachim and St. Ann.

(*The Glories of Saint Joseph*, from pp. 74 & 185)

Countless are all the graces gained through the intercession of St. Joseph, especially in favor of married couples who, wishing to see their home gladdened by the presence of a child, address themselves to him with confidence and ask him to grant them the grace of fertility.

Regarding the famous staircase of 1873 in Santa Fe, New Mexico, on the last day of a novena to Saint Joseph made by the sisters there, a gray-haired man leading a donkey and carrying a tool chest stopped at the Academy and offered to build the stairs.

The construction of the stairs lasted about six months. Certain sisters who were present at the work site remarked that the mysterious worker had used only a saw, a T-square, and a hammer. They remembered seeing tubs of water filled with pieces of soaking wood. When Mother Magdalene looked for the worker to pay him, he was nowhere to be found. A reward was offered; no one claimed it. Even the local lumber yard gave no proof of purchase of the wood used.

The completed work is a circular staircase of 33 steps consisting to two complete spirals, at 360°, without any central support. It rests above against the loft and below on the floor, where the entire weight seems to be supported. Woodpegs take the place of nails.

During the course of the years, architects and builders from numerous foreign countries have inspected this architectural wonder. They all marvel to see how the stairs still remain standing. Certain people thought that it would fall apart as soon as it was used, but, in spite of daily use, the staircase remains in place, even after more than a century.

At the Academy, Sister Mary, then 13 years old, was one of the first to mount these stairs with her friends. However, being frightened, they came down on their hands and knees. We can easily understand how, having no railing for support, they were afraid.

Several experts in building materials affirm that the curved stringers had been installed with precision. The wood is spliced in seven different places on the inside and in nine different places on the outside, with each piece forming a perfect curve. Moreover, this wood is of a hard variety and is not native to New Mexico. Its origin is still a mystery.

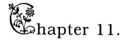hapter 11.

Devotions to St. Joseph

(by Ann—The Heart of Saint Joseph, from p. 35)

Prophetically, a learned writer and preacher of the 16th century, Isidore of L'Isle, lifted his voice in praise: "God raised up and glorified Saint Joseph for the honor of His Own Name, establishing him as Head and Patron of the Church Militant. His glory is far from being at its height. As, before the Last Judgment, all nations must know the Name of, and venerate and adore, the only true God, so also must all admire the long-hidden, yet inestimable gifts whereof Saint Joseph was the recipient. Yes, all gifts shall be granted unto him.

"In that favored time, the Lord will give a more subtle intelligence to the minds and hearts of His elect; they shall scrutinize the heart of St. Joseph, to admire therein the loving marvels of grace, and they shall find an admirable treasure, such as the Patriarchs of the Old Law never either discovered or suspected.

"That magnificent outpouring of light and glory shall be the special work of the Holy Angels. Thus shall he, who is first amongst the saints of Heaven, take on earth that first rank, which is his due!"

(*Ante-Nicene*, from p. 392)

Jesus speaks to Joseph—And whosoever shall make an offering on the day of thy remembrance, him will I bless and recompense in the congregation of the virgins; and whoever shall give food to the wretched, the poor, the widows, and orphans from the work of his hands, on the day on which thy memory shall be celebrated, and in thy name, shall not be in want of good things all the days of his life.

And whosoever shall have given a cup of water, or of wine, to drink to the widow or orphan in thy name, I will give him to thee, that thou mayst go in with him to the banquet of the thousand years. And every man who shall present an offering on the day of thy commemoration will I bless and recompense in the Church of the virgins; for one I will render unto him 30, 60 and a 100.

And whosoever shall write the history of thy life, of thy labor, and thy departure from this world, and this narrative that has issued from My mouth, him shall I commit to thy keeping as long as he shall have to do with this life. And when his soul departs from the body, and when he must leave this world, I will burn the book of his sins, nor will I torment him with any punishment in the day of judgment; but he shall cross the sea of flames, and shall go through it without trouble or pain.

And upon every poor man who can give none of those things which I have mentioned, this is incumbent: viz., if a son is born to him, he shall call his name Joseph. So there shall not take place in that house either poverty or any sudden death forever.

(by Chorpenning—*Just Man*, from pp. 31, 39, 48 & 135)

Describing St. Teresa of Avila's devotion to Joseph, Gracian reports that "she carried with her to all her foundations a statue of this glorious saint." Teresa placed 12 of the 17 monasteries that she founded during her lifetime under St. Joseph's patronage by naming these houses for him.

One of the principal reasons Teresa undertook her reform of Carmel was so that she and her nuns could devote themselves to prayer in an enclosed (cloistered) monastery, without having their attention diffused by the distractions that were common in the unenclosed houses of their Order. The purpose of this prayer was apostolic and missionary; it was for the Church that was being attacked by the Protestant reformers, and for the millions of souls in the New World that were being lost for want of Christian instruction.

In this context, St. Joseph, who lived in intimacy with Mary and Jesus, takes on another role: teacher of prayer. Teresa asserts: "Anyone who cannot find a master to teach him prayer should take this glorious saint for his master, and he will not go astray." Thus Joseph became the prototype of the contemplative life.

Teresa's reform of Carmel, and making Joseph the guardian of her foundation, underscored the saint's role as father, not only in her life, but henceforth in the life at Carmel. Traditionally, the Carmelites were dedicated to the Virgin Mary under the title of "Our Lady of Mt. Carmel." However, as Teresa remarks, "I don't know how one can think about the Queen of Angels, and about when She went through so much with the Infant Jesus, without giving thanks to St. Joseph for the good assistance he then provided to Both of Them."

Teresa must not have been surprised, then, when she received the divine command to name her first reformed monastery for the guardian of Christ and husband of Mary. "One day after Communion, His Majesty earnestly commanded me to strive for this new monastery with all my powers, and He made great promises that it would be founded, and that He would be highly served in it. He said it should be called St. Joseph, and that this saint would keep watch over us at one door, and our Lady at the other...that Christ would remain with us." Now, the Order of the Virgin Mary also becomes the Order of St. Joseph, and Teresa's monasteries become the dwelling place of the Holy Family.

This Order recognizes as the founder of its Reform the glorious St. Joseph, because it was with his assistance that Mother Teresa carried out this Reform. After Teresa's canonization (1622), some monasteries wanted to change their patron from St. Joseph to St. Teresa. Teresa appeared to Venerable Isabel de Santo Domingo, and sternly admonished her: "Tell the Provincial to remove my name from the monasteries and to restore the name of St. Joseph."

St. Bernadine of Siena (1380-1444) observed that the father/son relationship between Joseph and Jesus continues even in Heaven.

(by Chorpenning—*The Holy Family*, from p. 6)

Why this sudden interest in St. Joseph and the Holy Family? The answer is to be found in the crises confronting the medieval and modern family. External assaults precipitated an internal crisis of affection within the family.

(*Devotions to St. Joseph*, from pp. 7 & 23)

Devotion of the Seven Sundays—An excellent means to obtain special favors through the intercession of St. Joseph is to honor his Seven Sundays. This devotion may be practiced at any time of the year, but fervent devotees of St. Joseph like to venerate him especially on the seven Sundays preceding his Feast. Then they more confidently hope to obtain some particular favor: often the favors they receive are greater than they had expected. St. Teresa tells us that St. Joseph frequently obtained for her much greater favors than those for which she had petitioned.

The Seven Sundays in honor of St. Joseph are observed in the following manner: Holy Communion is received in his honor on seven consecutive Sundays, and on each Sunday the prayers in honor of the seven sorrows and the seven joys of St. Joseph are recited.

It is related that two Franciscan friars once suffered shipwreck during a voyage across the ocean. By clinging to a plank, they kept themselves above water for three days, but were so violently tossed and buffeted by the waves that they were in grave danger of being drowned. Having always faithfully venerated St. Joseph, they fervently invoked his aid in their extreme peril. Their confidence was soon rewarded.

The fury of the storm abated, the sky became clear and the sea calm, and their joy was unspeakable when they suddenly beheld a creature of celestial beauty, who greeted them kindly and guided them safely to shore. When they reached land, the two religious cast themselves at the feet of their rescuer to thank him, for they supposed him to be an angel.

But the celestial visitor replied: "I am Joseph; if you wish to do something pleasing to me, never let a day pass without saying the Our Father and the Hail Mary seven times in honor of the seven joys that consoled me during the days I spent on earth in the company of Jesus and Mary." After these words he vanished.

Dear devotees of St. Joseph, if you desire to serve him according to his wishes, prefer this devotion to every other in his honor, since he himself designated it and declared how pleasing it is to him. Comply with his wishes in this regard, and rest assured that this devotion will be an excellent means to obtain precious graces and favors through his intercession.

We can best recognize our friends by their sympathy for us in our joys and sorrows, for it is here that true charity manifests itself. And for this reason, Holy Church so frequently reminds us of the joyful and sorrowful mysteries in the lives of Jesus, Mary, and Joseph.

Those who are seeking a special request may also have seven Masses said in honor of St. Joseph, or assist at seven Masses, give alms or fast seven times, make seven visits to a chapel or to an image of the saint. A novena may be made by daily saying the prayers of the seven sorrows and seven joys of St. Joseph; or this devotion may be performed for 30 days, and ended with the reception of the Sacraments.

It is very pleasing to St. Joseph, and a great act of charity in his honor, to aid those souls in purgatory who during life practiced special devotion to him. In our various necessities, we might promise St. Joseph that if he comes to our aid, we will have one or more Masses said for the Poor Souls or offer Holy Communion for them.

Prayer of St. Clement Mary Hofbauer

St. Joseph, my loving father,
I place myself forever under your protection.
Look on me as your child, and keep me from all sin.
I take refuge in your arms,
so that you may lead me in the path of virtue,
and assist me at the hour of my death.

(by Filas—*Joseph Most Just*, from p. 11)

Devotion to St. Joseph was reserved for our times because our times need him as the Saint of Social Justice and the Saint of the Family.

(by Gasnier—*Joseph the Silent*, from p. 189)

We must not regret not having any words spoken by Joseph, for the lesson he teaches is precisely the lesson of silence. He knew the Father had confided a secret in trust to him, and the better to keep it so that no slightest inkling of it might leak out, he buried himself in silence. He did not want anyone who saw him to think him other than a simple workman trying to earn his daily bread, so that no sign or word of his might prove an obstacle to the manifestation of the Word.

This quiet self-effacement expressed not only what he considered his utter nothingness before God, but a homage rendered to divine magnificence. He remained breathless in wonder at the sign of what God had done to a poor worthless creature such as he. He felt himself so overwhelmed by glory that only silence could express the depth of his gratitude, his utter annihilation in the presence of this mystery taking place around him. He needed more and more, deeper and deeper silence and recollection in order to meditate on the graces, the mysteries hidden in his heart.

Joseph teaches us that true greatness consists in serving God and our neighbor; that the only real productiveness springs from a life indifferent to show and glitter, and that the really thrilling exploits are the conscientious and loving accomplishment of one's duties, no matter how humble. They will please God who, seeking nothing but His good pleasure, submit to His design. They will fear but one thing, that of not serving Him as faithfully as possible.

(by Griffin—*Saint Joseph & Third*, from p. 296)

Prayer, mysterious as it is, is on the increase as stated in the cover story "The Mystery of Prayer," in the March 31, 1997 issue of *Newsweek* magazine, relating that: "Most Americans say prayers every day."

(by Griffin—*Saint Joseph, Theo.*, from pp. 40 & 49)

Devotion, as a principal component of the virtue of religion, is the highest of all forms of devotion. It means a perfect willingness to fulfill the will of God in all things; the readiness to perform all our duties and obligations towards God, no matter what the cost may be. It is concerned with honoring and serving God as He *deserves* to be honored and served.

A man filled with devotion to God is moved to serve Him with a zeal that amounts to perfect self-dedication. This is the goal towards which we must all aspire. Blessed is the man who serves his God with his whole heart, his whole mind, his whole strength, and his neighbor as himself! Every Christian is called to this type of holiness according to the words of Christ: "Be perfect as your Heavenly Father is perfect."

When we consider Saint Joseph, the first thing that naturally comes to our minds is the fact that he was the most *devoted* man who ever lived. No other human being was ever as devoted in his service to Christ and to Mary as the holy Patriarch of Nazareth. In this lies his chief accomplishment and his highest praise.

Devotion to a particular saint always means that the saint in question is held in high personal regard. Not only do we have particular reverence for the saint, but we are spiritually fascinated by his life, works, and virtues. Somehow we are able spiritually to enter into his life; we seem to understand and grasp something of his unique spiritual genius. Not only that, but we want to be influenced by this saint, because the way he lived and practiced virtue on earth is viewed as a thing of compelling beauty.

Pope John XXIII, in his talk to Roman workers, said: "All the saints in glory assuredly merit honor and particular respect, but it is evident that Saint Joseph possesses a just title to a more sweet, more intimate and penetrating place in our hearts, belonging to him alone... Here we are able to estimate completely all the greatness of Saint Joseph, not only by reason of the fact that he was close to Jesus and Mary, but also by the shining example he has given to all virtues."

Though the Church from the beginning was aware that Mary was given to be the spiritual

Mother of all, it is a fact that the consciousness of Saint Joseph as the spiritual father and protector of every Christian was only gradually arrived at. In the last 100 years, the Church had taken ever more cognizance of the role of Saint Joseph. Quite obviously, this devotion is a grace that has been reserved for this present age.

Why Devotion to Saint Joseph is Highly Recommended

1) Showing Joseph honor and respect and veneration are means of rendering glory and gratitude to Almighty God for the merciful graces He poured out upon this saint.

2) Saint Joseph was a model in the heroic practice of all the virtues. The example of virtuous living that he gave in the exact fulfillment of the duties of his state of life is worthy of our reflection.

If devotion to Joseph is so important, it may be asked, why did it not flourish in the Church until more recent times? The only answer that can be given to this question is that in the providence of God, it was necessary for Joseph to remain in obscurity in order to protect the mystery of the Incarnation and the virginity of Mary. Also, devotion to Joseph was reserved to our age because of its special aptness to the times in which we live.

So convinced was St. Teresa of Avila from her own personal experience, that she did not hesitate to challenge anyone who doubted her words: "All I ask, for the love of God, is that anyone who does not believe me will put what I say to the test, and he will learn for himself how advantageous it is to commend oneself to this glorious Patriarch Joseph and to have a special devotion to him."

(by Gorman—*Life With Joseph*, from pp. 13 & 40)

As Saint Peter Julian Eymard pointed out: "Devotion to St. Joseph is one of the choicest graces that God can give to a soul, for it is tantamount to revealing the entire treasury of our Lord's graces. When God wishes to raise a soul to greater heights, He unites it to St. Joseph by giving it a strong love for the good Saint."

Four fundamental virtues of St. Joseph should be applied to our own spiritual life:

1) Fidelity to grace: doing the Father's will as perfectly as possible; keeping all God's laws.

2) Fidelity to the interior life: constant awareness of the Presence of God dwelling within the soul; striving to know, love, and serve God.

3) Devotion to Mary: commitment to Mary leads Her to obtain in return an abundance of the choicest graces and favors for Her devotees.

4) Devotion to Jesus: union with, love for, and total commitment to Christ.

415.

(by Joseph—*Reflections on Saint Joseph*, from p. vii)

More then three centuries ago, a saintly French priest, Louis Lallemant, S.J., designed for himself and his spiritual children a special form of devotion to Saint Joseph. Into it he wove the elements of meditation, self-discipline, and concentration upon the great mysteries of the Faith associated with the Incarnation of the Word of God. Two features of this devotion are remarkable; its simplicity, and its profundity. Any child can practice it in its simplest form and make spiritual progress; the most learned theologian will be attracted to the devotion as a perfect opportunity for growth in spiritual stature. The form of this devotion is easily out-lined: four times a day one makes an imaginary visit to Saint Joseph. This visit can be made any place at all—at home, on a bus, while walking or waiting for an appointment. No specific prayers are required for this devotion.

During each visit:

a) One recalls Saint Joseph's grace-filled actions.

b) One asks for help to imitate his fidelity in a similar manner.

c) One asks God for a specific favor being sought through St. Joseph's intercession.

On the *first visit* each day, one recalls Joseph's fidelity to grace, and thanks God for the sublime way Joseph always responded.

On the *second visit* each day, one recalls Joseph's fidelity to the interior life.

On the *third visit* each day, one recalls Joseph's devotion to our Lady.

On the *fourth visit* each day, one recalls Joseph's devotion to the Divine Child.

Within the past few years, thousands of Saint Joseph's clients have been honoring him by the practice of this devotion. Favors of both a material and a spiritual nature have been so numerous, that it seems Saint Joseph has merely to present a request to his Divine Foster Son and it is granted. This should cause no one surprise. As the Christ of Nazareth offered prompt obedience to His foster father throughout the years of His hidden life, so now in Heaven, He listens to each request of Saint Joseph, as if it were command.

By one pope after another, his Heavenly glory has been proclaimed and extolled. Confidently, then, may his clients expect from him a prompt and powerful intercession on their behalf.

(by Llamera—*Saint Joseph*, from p. 155)

St. Joseph is higher than the angels in dignity. Because he is higher than all creatures except the Virgin, the comparison must begin with the angels. The difference between these two ministries is readily apparent, for "the office of the angels," says Carthagena, "is the guardianship of men, but Joseph was entrusted with a more excellent charge—the care, not of a mere man, but of Christ the Lord, Who was both God and Man, and also of His holy Mother.

(by Neuzil—*Our Lady of America*, from p. 31)

"**I** am the protector of the Church and the home, as I was the protector of Christ and His Mother while I lived upon earth. Jesus and Mary desire that my pure heart, so long hidden and unknown, be now honored in a special way. Let my children honor my most pure heart in a special manner on the First Wednesday of the month by reciting the Joyful Mysteries of the Rosary in memory of my life with Jesus and Mary and the love I bore them, the sorrow I suffered with Them.

Let them receive Holy Communion in union with the love with which I received the Savior for the first time, and each time I held Him in my arms. Those who honor me in this way will be consoled by my presence at their death, and I myself will conduct them safely into the Presence of Jesus and Mary.

(by O'Rafferty—*Discourses*, from pp. 13 & 241)

Our worship of God and the saints is again divided into worship of *latria*, which is given to God alone, and is called adoration; worship of *dulia*, which is given to the saints, and is called veneration; worship of *hyperdulia*, which is given to the blessed virgin Mary, and is the very highest kind of veneration. To St. Joseph, we give the highest form of worship of *dulia* or simple veneration, that is to say, greater than that given to any of the other saints. It is only right that we should dedicate one month of the year to St. Joseph to show our devotion for him. When we honor St. Joseph with all the devotion and enthusiasm we possibly can, we but follow the example of the Church, the example of Mary, and the example of Jesus.

In the first place, when we honor St. Joseph, we follow the example of the Church. There is no saint whom the Church honors so much as she does St. Joseph. The Church dedicates to St. Joseph one day of the week, Wednesday, and one whole month of the year, March. Thousands upon thousands of churches and chapels have been erected in his honor. And in those erected to the honor of the other saints, we always find an altar or at least a statue of St. Joseph. His intercession is invoked in times of need and whenever the Church wishes to obtain special favors from God. All this goes to show that Holy Church honors St. Joseph more than she does any other saint.

Indulgences of Devotions to St. Joseph

An indulgence is the remission of the temporal punishment due to sin. Indulgences are both partial and plenary. A partial indulgence is the remission of part of the temporal punishment due to sin; a plenary indulgence is the remission of all the temporal punishment due to sin. Temporal punishment is due to venial sins and to mortal sins already forgiven. To gain an indulgence, it is necessary to be in the state of grace and to perform the works prescribed. To gain a plenary indulgence, the usual conditions are: Confession, Communion, a visit to some church or public chapel, and prayers for the intentions of the Holy Father.

The devotion to St. Joseph is enriched with many indulgences both partial and plenary. To any public Novena in honor of St. Joseph, not only in preparation for his Feasts, but at any time as well, a plenary indulgence is attached; private novenas are enriched with partial indulgences. Certain prayers in honor of St. Joseph, especially when said daily for a month, are enriched with a plenary indulgence; for certain other prayers a partial indulgence is granted. Any prayers in honor of St. Joseph may be used for a Novena.

(by Patrignani—*Manual*, from pp. xix & 177)

Wednesday devotion.—This practice consists in offering this day to God for the extension of the devotion to St. Joseph, and for the spiritual good of the participants. To spread devotion to St. Joseph, the associates should, above all things, endeavor to make the holy Patriarch known. Those who adopt this devotion may confine themselves to the Consecration of the day and some works of piety. In the places where the associates have the free disposal of their time, they assemble on Wednesday to assist at the Holy Sacrifice of the Mass.

Practices for Each Day:

1) *Image of St. Joseph*

Venerate his image; and with this view, let it occupy a distinguished place in your oratory; for in every family, the portraits of the most illustrious benefactors, patrons, or relatives, constitute the most valuable part of the furniture. Imitate in this respect the devout St. Francis de Sales, who would have no other picture in his Breviary but St. Joseph's; also Fr. Louis Lallemant, who would have St. Joseph's likeness always about his person, and even in the grave.

2) Prayer at Mass

Insert the name of Joseph in your prayers at Mass.

3) Patronage of St. Joseph

Entrust your family, home, and work to the care of the saint to whom the Eternal Father confided all that was most dear Him, namely, Jesus and Mary.

4) Remembrance of St. Joseph

Frequently think of St. Joseph in the course of the day, especially when the striking of the clock warns you to venerate the great mystery of the "Incarnation." Also, when you hear a siren sounding or bell tolling to announce the agony of a dying person, as is usual in many places, think then of him who is the special patron of the agonizing, and repeat the following, or a similar aspiration: "O holy Joseph, worthy spouse of the Mother of Life, pray for the soul who is now agonizing, and remember me when I am in my last agony!"

5) Invocations of St. Joseph

Frequently invoke the three sweet names of Jesus, Mary, and Joseph, in imitation of the blessed Gaspar Bon, who lived and died with these sacred names in his heart and on his lips.

6)   Imitation of St. Joseph

Since the most solid devotion to our holy patrons consists in striving to imitate their example, you should endeavor to practice each day some particular virtue for which St. Joseph was remarkable.

7)   Honor the seven privileges of St. Joseph

These are: 1) spouse of Mary, 2) adopted father of Jesus, 3) a most pure virgin, 4) vicar and lieutenant of the Eternal Father, 5) chief and protector of the Holy Family, 6) happiest of men in life and in death, 7) after our Lady, the most exalted of all the saints in Heaven.

8)   Cultivate a special devotion to the seven dolors and seven joys of St. Joseph

St. Joseph himself taught this practice to three Franciscan friars. The Church, by numerous indulgences, as testified Her approbation of this devotion.

(by Robert—*Guardian of*, from pp. 27 & 161)

The graces we should especially ask Saint Joseph to obtain for us are: the gift of piety, the spirit of prayer, and a happy death. It is through the gift of piety and the spirit of prayer that we acquire that interior life which is so indispensable for our perfection, and the grace of a happy death, which is its reward.

Blessed Peter Julian Eymard wrote: "Our Lord has given me a singular grace. He has inspired me to dedicate myself in an especial manner to Saint Joseph as to my father, leader, and protector."

(by Stein—*The Tapestry*, from pp. 20, 26, 29, 31, 93, 102, 119 & 171)

St. Anastasia Church in Rome contains a precious relic, St. Joseph's pallium or mantle, venerated because it must have enveloped the Divine Infant when clasped in Joseph's arms. An inscription in Latin on a stone attests to the antiquity of the relics, as there is also the blessed Virgin's Veil and a portion of Wood from the Cross: thus the Holy Family always remains together.

When St. Jerome was called to Rome during the Pontificate of St. Damascus, he celebrated Mass during the three years at the altar of St. Anastasia Church, where St. Joseph's precious relic is preserved.

In the Syrian calendar, the seventh Sunday before Christmas was the Feast of the "Revelation to Joseph, spouse of the blessed Virgin."

At Nazareth, about 200 feet from the Basilica of the Annunciation, there is still located St. Joseph's workshop, which is now also a Catholic Church.

Christ honors Joseph, in fulfillment of God's own command: "Honor thy father and thy mother." St. Joseph was the father of Jesus in the most perfect manner possible, and this he was in three ways: by love, by care, and by authority.

Devotion to the saints consist chiefly of three things: admiration of their greatness, imitation of their virtues, and invocation of their help. But of these three, the most important is imitation of their virtues. St. Augustine tells us that "true devotion consists of imitating the one we honor."

March 19, the Solemn Feast of St. Joseph, was listed in several churches as far back as the 10th century. Church history tells us the oldest church bearing St. Joseph's name in Italy, was a parish church in Bologna about 1129. It claims the distinction to have included the name of St. Joseph in the Litany of the Saints in the year 1350.

St. Albert said that the marriage of Mary and Joseph was ordained in order to make men regard St. Joseph as their father, even as they recognize Mary as their Mother.

Truly in all things, St. Joseph is the people's friend:

> Go then to Joseph, and do all that he shall say to you.

> Go to Joseph, and obey him as Jesus and Mary obeyed him.

> Go to Joseph, and speak to him as They spoke to him.

> Go to Joseph, and consult him as They consulted him.

> Go to Joseph, and honor him as They honored him.

Go to Joseph, and be grateful to him as They
were grateful to him.

Go to Joseph, and love him as They
loved him, and as They love him still.

However much you love Joseph, your love will
always fall short of the extraordinary love which
Jesus and Mary bore to him. On the other hand,
the love of Joseph necessarily leads us to Jesus
and Mary.

As we close out the 19th century, we find an
atmosphere within the Papacy ready to give the
recognition to Saint Joseph that has been
proclaimed in varying degrees for more than
1800 years. We should note that there is no
saint, other than the blessed Mother, Whom the
Church honors more than St. Joseph, dedicating
every Wednesday and the entire month of March
to him.

Cap-de-la-Madeleine

Another example of St. Joseph deals with
the blessed Mother and construction of the great
Canadian Shrine dedicated to the blessed Mother
at Cap-de-la-Madeleine located at Three Rivers,
Quebec, Canada. It was maintained by the Sisters
of the Holy Names of Jesus and Mary, whose
foundress, Blessed Marie-Rose Durocher (1811-
1849), was a relative of Blessed Brother André.

During the winter of 1878 to 1879, it was
desired to build a larger church. Stone for this
building was on the opposite side of the river. All
hope to continue construction was lost when,
during March, the river was no longer frozen. The
saintly pastor, Fr. Luke Desilets, made a vow: he
would preserve the old church and dedicate it to
the holy Virgin, if She would obtain a bridge of
ice before the end of winter.

On March 14 and 15, some blocks of ice began to form and come together. Sunday, March 16, the Vicar made a promise to the whole parish that a High Mass of Thanksgiving would be given in honor of Saint Joseph on the morning of Wednesday, March 19 (Saint Joseph's Feast Day), if they would be able to reach the other side of the river within a day.

The first delivery of stones happened during the night of March 18, at the hour when the priests commenced to say the Office of St. Joseph. During the entire Octave of the Feast of St. Joseph, they transported stone. The last journey was made on the Octave Day itself. They then saw with amazement that the bridge of ice rapidly disengaged. Once again, St. Joseph was there to assist his beloved Bride.

Blessed Mother Katherine Drexel

About 1894, while on a trip to Virginia, Blessed Mother Katherine Drexel, who had great devotion to St. Joseph, and Sister Mercedes arrived in Richmond at about 1 a.m. They had made no previous arrangements, since they planned to spend the night in the train station. When they arrived, they found the station closed.

An elderly man approached and asked if they were the ladies the sisters in Duval Street had sent him to meet. He took them to St. Joseph's Convent. On arriving at the convent, the man deposited their bags on the porch and left. Mother Katherine rang the door bell. The end result: finally gaining admittance, she realized no one was expecting them. Mother Katherine felt St. Joseph had intervened for their protection.

The devotion to the Cord of Saint Joseph took its rise in Antwerp, Belgium in 1657, due to a miraculous healing effected by the wearing of this precious girdle. An Augustinian nun was cured after her physicians had declared her death to be inevitable. This was related by the Bollandists and published in 1810.

The Cord of St. Joseph was worn, not merely for bodily ailments, but also as a preservative of the virtue of purity. On September 19, 1859, the new Formula of Blessing and permission for its solemn and private use was approved by the Sacred Congregation.

The Cord should be of cotton, wool, or linen, ending at one extremity in seven knots, indicative of the joyous, sorrowful, and glorious mysteries of the august Patriarch. It is worn as a girdle and ought to be blessed by a priest possessing powers to engird one with it. It should be noted that while Brother André was alive, he was responsible for making the Cords of St. Joseph for the community. While doing so, he fashioned the end threads into a tassel of his own design.

(by Rondet—*Saint Joseph*, from p. 159)

St. Alphonsus Liguori exhorts us to never let a day pass, then, without recommending ourselves to St. Joseph, who has more power with God than any other saint except the blessed Virgin Mary. Every day we ought to offer some particular prayer to him, and during the nine days before his Feast, let us redouble our prayers, and fast on the day preceding it. If we ask for the gifts that are for our good, he will not fail to obtain them for us.

I urge you to ask for three special graces in particular: forgiveness of your sins, love for Jesus Christ, and a good death.

(by Stramare—*Saint Joseph*, from pp. 63 & 140)

In the late 1800's, Pope Leo the XIII stated: "Since it is of great importance that his cult penetrate deeply in Catholic morals and practice, we wish the Christian people to receive from our own voice and authority every possible incentive." He therefore attached to his encyclical a special prayer to St. Joseph, (To you, O blessed Joseph...), ordering that it be added to the recitation of the Rosary every year in perpetuity, during the month of October. He also recommends dedicating to the holy Patriarch the month of March, with daily exercises of piety in his honor, and to observe at least a triduum of prayers preceding the Feast of St. Joseph.

The Magisterium proclaims that it is "very useful for the faithful to become accustomed to praying devoutly and trustfully to the Virgin Mother, as well as to St. Joseph in union with Her." It is noteworthy, moreover, that this truth is also expressed by deeds, if we consider as no mere coincidence that the Patronage of St. Joseph was proclaimed on December 8, 1870, a day consecrated to the Immaculate Conception of his Spouse, and that the encyclical *Quamquam Pluries*—now in its hundredth anniversary—is dated August 15, Feast of the Assumption. Besides, the observance of the insertion of the name of St. Joseph in the Canon "as a pleasing remembrance and fruit of the Council itself" was made by John XXIII on December 8, 1962, Feast of the Immaculate Conception of the blessed Virgin Mary.

Instinctively, all those who tend seriously toward Christian perfection consider St. Joseph as the master of their interior life, just as parents, and those who have the task of educating youth, choose him as their special patron. Consequently, they entrust their spiritual life to St. Joseph and take him as their model in their behavior, with the assurance that he is the saint most perfectly suited and able to form them into children of the Heavenly Father, that is, into images of Jesus.

Pope John Paul II adds that even today, we have perduring motives to recommend every man to St. Joseph; his patronage is ever necessary for the Church, not only as a defense against all dangers that threaten her, but also, and indeed primarily, as an impetus for her renewed commitment to evangelization in the world, and re-evangelization in those lands and nations where religion and Christian life are now put to a hard test.

Besides trusting in Saint Joseph's sure protection, the Church also trusts in his noble example, which transcends all individual states of life and serves as a model for the entire Christian community, whatever the condition and duties of each of its members may be.

429.

(The Glories of Saint Joseph, from pp. 11 & 84)

Besides dedicating the month of March to St. Joseph, Holy Church shows her supreme love and veneration for her Heavenly patron by the annual celebration of two Feasts in his honor.

On March 19, she solemnly commemorates the death of St. Joseph, which, according to Tradition, occurred on that day. On this Feast, he is venerated in particular as the Spouse of the Virgin Mary and the Patron of the Universal Church, and his protection is invoked by the faithful, in order to obtain the grace of a happy death.

On May 1 of each year is celebrated the Feast of St. Joseph the Worker, which was established by Pope Pius XII in 1955, in order to Christianize the concept of labor and give to all workmen a model and a protector. By the daily labor in his work-shop, offered to God with patience and joy, St. Joseph provided for the necessities of his holy Spouse and of the Incarnate Son of God, and thus became an example to all laborers. "Workmen and all those laboring in conditions of poverty will have reasons to rejoice rather than to grieve, since they have in common with the Holy Family daily preoccupations and cares" (Pope Leo XIII).

Pious custom also dedicates Wednesday of each week to the honor of St. Joseph and, in the past, indulgences were granted for any pious exercises performed on the first Wednesday of the month.

Do What He Tells You!

St. Teresa of Avila had left Valladolid, Spain, to found a monastery at Beas, in Andalusia, when, while crossing the Sierra Morena, the wagon drivers lost their way in the passes. Foolishly, they advanced along a path so narrow that soon they could go neither forward nor backward. Teresa and her companions were left hanging over precipices and cliffs, down which they could all fall at the slightest movement.

"My daughters," said the saint, "let us pray to God that, by the intercession of St. Joseph, He may deliver us from this danger."

At that moment, the voice of an old man shouted to them: "Stop! If you go any further, you are doomed!"

"But how can we get out of this terrible situation?" they asked. "Lean your wagon to this side," came the reply, "and turn back."

They followed these directions, and to their great surprise, the guides at once found themselves on an excellent road. Full of gratitude to their deliverer, they ran to thank him to the place from which the voice had spoken. Teresa watched them and, seeing them running at full speed searching in vain, said to her daughters: "Really, I do not know why we let these good men go on running, for what we heard was the voice of my Father, St. Joseph, and they will never find him!"

Jesus, Mary, and Joseph were three. Nevertheless, they seem to be only one—one in a unity so marvelous, a unity which of three made only one, and nevertheless left them three. Pay, therefore, frequent honor to that trinity, that was visible for us on earth: Jesus, Mary, and Joseph. Engrave in your heart in letters of gold those three Heavenly names, utter them often, write them everywhere: Jesus, Mary, Joseph. Repeat them several times a day, those sacred names, and may they still be on your lips when you draw your last breath (St. Leonard of Port-Maurice).

St. Joseph as father is placed at the head of this little Family, small in number, but great by the two great Personages it contains: the Mother of God and the Only Son-of-God made Man. In this household, Joseph commands, and the Son of God obeys. "This subjection of the Son of God," says Gerson, "while proving to us the humility of the Savior, shows us the high dignity of Saint Joseph. And what greater dignity, what higher elevation could there be, than to command the One Who commands all the kings?" (St. Alphonsus de Liguori).

(*The Spiritual Doctrine*, from p. 10)

Father Louis Lallemant was gifted with an extraordinary grace for inspiring everyone with a devotion to Saint Joseph; and his advice to persons who desired to enter on the ways of spiritual perfection was, to take as their model of humility, Jesus Christ; as their model of purity, the blessed Virgin; and as their model of the interior life, St. Joseph. It was after these divine patterns that he labored at his own perfection; and it was easy to perceive how happily he had wrought them out in his own person.

Every day, in honor of St. Joseph, he observed four short exercises, from which he drew wonderful profit. The two first were for the morning, and the other two for after dinner. The first was to raise himself in spirit to the heart of St. Joseph, and consider how faithful he was to the inspirations of grace; then turning his eyes inward on his own heart, to discover his own want of fidelity, he made an act of humiliation, and excited himself to perseverance.

The second was, to reflect how perfectly St. Joseph reconciled the interior life with his external occupation. Then, turning to observe himself and his own occupations, he perceived wherein they fell short of the perfection of his model. By means of this exercise, he made such progress, that towards the close of his life he remained in an uninterrupted state of interior recollection; and the attention which he paid to external things, instead of weakening his union with God, served rather to strengthen it.

The third was, to accompany in spirit St. Joseph, as the spouse of the blessed Virgin, and to meditate on the wonderful knowledge which he had enjoyed of Her virginity and maternity, in consequence of the humble submission with which he received the announcement of the angel respecting the mystery of the Incarnation. By this exercise he excited himself to love St. Joseph for his love of his most holy Spouse.

The fourth was, to figure to himself the adoration and homage of love and gratitude which St. Joseph paid to the holy Child Jesus, and to beg to participate therein, that he might adore and love the Divine Child with all the sentiments of the deepest reverence and the tenderest love of which he was capable. He wished to carry with him to the grave some tokens of his devotion to his great saint, and requested that an image of his beloved patron might be put with him in his coffin.

It was observed on many occasions that St. Joseph never refused him anything he asked;

and whenever he wished to induce persons to honor St. Joseph, he used to assure them that he did not possess a single grace which he had not obtained through St. Joseph's intercession. He promised them, that they should obtain everything they asked through the intercession of this great saint, if they would exhort others to be devout towards him, and to do something more than ordinary on one of his Feast Days.

(by Toschi—*Saint Joseph in Lives*, from pp. 15, 19, & 23)

Father Eusebio Kino (arrived in Mexico in 1681) writes that after Mass with the crew was celebrated "in honor of St. Joseph to be able to reach quickly a good port of refuge, a propitious wind blew from the east and carried us along."

In a subsequent Franciscan period, we will see mention of St. Joseph's image driving away locusts at San José.

Among the devotions at La Canada: "The 19th of each month, Mass was sung in honor of St. Joseph."

(by Van De Putte—*Following Saint Joseph,* from p. 23)

*O*fficial Action of the Church in Promoting Devotion to Saint Joseph:

1479—(March 19) Feast of Saint Joseph is introduced at Rome by Pope Sixtus IV.

1621—(May 8)—The Feast of Saint Joseph is made a Holyday of Obligation for the whole world by Pope Gregory XV.

1714—(February 4)—A Proper Mass and Office are approved for the Feast of Saint Joseph by Pope Clement XI.

1726—(December 19)—The name of Saint Joseph is inserted in the Litany of the Saints by Pope Benedict XIII.

1870—(December 8)—Saint Joseph is made Patron of the Universal Church by Pope Pius IX, who also reinforces March as his month (the month of Saint Joseph) and approves his Confraternity.

1884—(January 6)—The Leonine Prayers are decreed to be recited after all Low Masses, and they incorporate a prayer that invokes Saint Joseph, among others.

1889—(August 15)—The prayer to Saint Joseph "To you, O Blessed Joseph..." is approved by Pope Leo XIII, and recommended to be recited each day in October after the Rosary (see page 440).

1909—(March 18)—The Litany of Saint Joseph is approved and indulgenced for public worship by Pope Pius X.

1920—(July 25)—A special document ("Motu Proprio") on "Saint Joseph and Labor" is issued by Pope Benedict XV in commemoration of the 50th anniversary of the declaration of Saint Joseph as Patron of the Church.

1921—(February 23)—An invocation in honor of Saint Joseph is inserted by Pope Benedict XV in the Divine Praises: "Blessed be Saint Joseph, Her most chaste spouse."

1937—(March 19)—Saint Joseph is named the guardian of the spiritual battle against Communism by Pope Pius XI.

1955—(May 1)—Pope Pius XII institutes the Feast of Saint Joseph the Worker to replace the Solemnity of Saint Joseph, and to compete with the Communists' celebration of May Day.

1961—(March 19)—Saint Joseph is selected by Pope John XXIII as the Protector of the Second Vatican Council.

1962—(November 13)—The name of Saint Joseph is inserted in the Canon of the Mass by Pope John XXIII.

This impressive advance of devotion to you, dear Saint, clearly demonstrates that we are living in the "Age of Saint Joseph."

(by Van Speybrouck—*Father Paul,* from p. 238
& back cover)

Fr. Paul said to a person from Oostcamp, "In an ecstasy, a saint has seen the body of Saint Joseph preserved intact in a tomb, the site of which is yet unknown. The more the glorious spouse of the most blessed Virgin is honored, the sooner will the finding of this body take place, which will be a day of great joy for the Church."

Fr. Paul of Moll is undoubtedly an extraordinary saint. One of his most famous predictions is that when devotion to St. Joseph is sufficiently widespread, his body will be found incorrupt.

(by Vaughn—*Who is St. Joseph,* from p. 63)

This prayer is claimed to be over 1900 years old. In 1505, it was sent from the Pope to Emperor Charles, when he was going into battle. Whoever shall read this prayer, or hear it, or keep it about themselves, shall never die a sudden death, or be drowned, nor shall poison take effect on them. Neither shall they fall into the hands of the enemy, nor shall be burned in any fire, nor shall be overpowered in battle.

Say it for nine mornings for anything you may desire. It has never been known to fail.

Prayer to St. Joseph
-over 1900 years old-

O St. Joseph, whose protection is so great,
so strong, so prompt before the Throne of God,
I place in you all my interests and desires.

O St. Joseph, do assist me by your
powerful intercession, and obtain for me
from your Divine Son all spiritual blessings
through Jesus Christ, our Lord;
so that having engaged here below
your Heavenly power, I may offer my thanksgiving
and homage to the most loving of fathers.

O St. Joseph, I never weary contemplating
you and Jesus asleep in your arms.
I dare not approach while He reposes
near your heart. Press Him in my name,
and kiss His fine Head for me,
and ask Him to return the kiss
when I draw my dying breath.

O St. Joseph, Patron of Departing Souls,
pray for us. Amen.

(Imprimatur, September 25, 1950
Hugh C. Boyle, Bishop of Pittsburgh)

The Novena below, goes back to Father Louis Lallemant, S.J. (1588—1635), and has proven to be highly efficacious. It seems to be pleasing to St. Joseph and helpful to souls. *No special prayers need to be said.* It consists in turning to St. Joseph four times a day (it does not matter when or where, but only one point is to be taken at a time) and honoring him in the four points of:

1) His *fidelity to grace.* Think of this for a minute; thank God, and ask through St. Joseph to be faithful to grace.

2) His *fidelity to the interior life.* Think of this for a minute; thank God, and ask through St. Joseph to be faithful to an interior life.

3) His *love of our blessed Lady.* Think of this for a minute; thank God, and ask through St. Joseph to be faithful to love of our blessed Lady.

4) His *love of the holy Child.* Think of this for a minute; thank God, and ask through St. Joseph to be faithful to love of the holy Child.

439.

Prayer To St. Joseph for Purity

(Raccolta #435, Pope John XXIII)

St. Joseph, father and guardian of virgins, into whose faithful keeping was entrusted Innocence itself, Christ Jesus, and Mary, the Virgin of virgins, I pray and beseech you through Jesus and Mary, Whose Love made yours secure, to keep me from all uncleanness, and to grant that my mind may be untainted, my heart pure, and my body chaste; help me always to serve Jesus and Mary in perfect chastity. Amen.

To You, O Blessed Joseph

*(The new Enchiridion of Indulgences has,
excepting ejaculations, just two items on St. Joseph:
the Litany and the following prayer.)*

To you, O blessed Joseph, do we come in our tribulation, and having implored the help of your most holy Spouse, we confidently invoke your patronage also. Through that charity which bound you to the Immaculate Virgin Mother of God, and through the paternal love with which you embraced the Child Jesus, we humbly beg you graciously to regard the inheritance which Jesus Christ has purchased by His Blood, and with your power and strength to aid us in our necessities.

O most watchful Guardian of the Holy Family, defend the chosen children of Jesus Christ; O most loving Father, ward off from us every contagion of error and corrupting influence; O our most mighty Protector, be propitious to us, and from Heaven assist us in our struggle with the power of darkness; and as once you rescued the Child Jesus from deadly peril, so now protect God's Holy Church from the snares of the enemy and from all adversity; shield, too, each one of us by your constant protection, so that supported by your example and your aid, we may be able to live piously, to die holily, and to obtain eternal happiness in Heaven. Amen.

Litany of Saint Joseph

Lord, have mercy.
Christ, have mercy,
Lord, have mercy.

Christ, hear us.
Christ graciously hears us.

God, the Father of Heaven,
 have mercy on us.
God the Son, Redeemer of the world,
 have mercy on us.
God the Holy Spirit,
 have mercy on us.
Holy Trinity, One God,
 have mercy on us.

Holy Mary, pray for us.*   (*Pray for us, repeated
St. Joseph,   after each invocation)
Renowned Offspring of David,
Light of Patriarchs,
Spouse of the Mother of God,
Chaste Guardian of the Virgin,
Foster Father of the Son of God,
Diligent Protector of Christ,
Head of the Holy Family,
Joseph most just,
Joseph most chaste,
Joseph most prudent,
Joseph most strong,
Joseph most obedient,
Joseph most faithful,

Mirror of patience,*
Lover of poverty,
Model of artisans,
Glory of home life,
Guardian of virgins,
Pillar of families,
Solace of the wretched,
Hope of the sick,
Patron of the dying,
Terror of demons,
Protector of Holy Church,

Lamb of God, You take away the sins of the world,
    spare us, O Lord!
Lamb of God, You take away the sins of the world,
    graciously hear us, O Lord!
Lamb of God, You take away the sins of the world,
    have mercy on us.

He made him the lord of His household,
    and prince over all His possessions.

Let us pray: O God, in Your ineffable Providence,
You were pleased to choose Blessed Joseph to
be the spouse of Your Most Holy Mother; grant,
we beg You, that we may be worthy to have him
for our Intercessor in Heaven, whom on earth we
venerate as our Protector; You, Who live and reign
forever and ever. Amen.

443.

Powerful Prayer

O Glorious St. Joseph, you who have power to
render possible, things which are impossible,
come to our aid in our present trouble and distress.

Take this important and difficult affair under your
particular protection, that it may end happily.

O Dear St. Joseph, all our confidence is in you.

Let it not be said that we have invoked you in vain,
and since you are so powerful with Jesus and Mary,
show that your goodness equals your power. Amen.

A Man of Treasure

by Fr. Hugh F. Blunt

Three wise men came, their gifts to bring
Unto the little new-born King;
Gold, frankincense and myrrh they gave,
Making His crib a treasure-cave.

Happy were they to make Him glad;
Such gifts, they thought, He never had.
They little guessed that Joseph, poor,
Had brought such very gifts before.

A heart of gold, incense of prayer,
And myrrh of all the pains He bare.
Good wise men, see a wiser one,
Who calls the God you worship—Son!

Hymn To St. Joseph

by F. Kevin Condol

If I could walk, as you have walked
    Beside the Little Boy,
Who made the world, made you and me,
    I'd ask no greater joy.

Oh, when you held His little Hand,
    I wonder did you think
Of nails and thorns and lance and cross—
    The chalice He would drink.

And did you watch Him as you worked
    And, as the shavings curled,
Remember how, without a tool,
    His wee Hands made the world?

While in one arm you hold Him fast,
    Embrace me with the other,
That I may never stray from Him
    Nor from our loving Mother.

Bibliography

Agreda, Ven. Sister Mary of Jesus of. *"Mystical City of God."* Ave Maria Institute, Washington, NJ 07882, 1971.

Ann, F.M.S.C., Sister M. Barbara. *"The Heart of Saint Joseph."* *The Maryfaithful,* March-April, 1999, pp. 34-37.

"Ante-Nicene Fathers, Volume VIII—Translations of The Writings of the Fathers Down to A.D. 325." Edited by Rev. Alexander Roberts, D.D. and James Donaldson, LL.D. Wm. B. Eerdmans Publishing Company, Grand Rapids, MI, 1995, (American reprint of the Edinburgh Edition by T & T Clark Publishing Company).

Aumann, O.P., Jordan. *"Compendium of Spirituality, Volume 1—Universal Patronage of St. Joseph,"* by Basil Cole, O.P., pp. 117-126. Alba House, New York, Society of St. Paul, 2187 Victory Blvd., Staten Island, New York 10314, 1995.

Baij, O.S.B., Abbess Maria Cecilia. *"The Life of Saint Joseph."* The 101 Foundation, Inc., P.O. Box 151, Asbury, New Jersey 08802-0151, 1997, (Written in the 1700's).

Binet, S.J., Père. *"Divine Favors Granted to St. Joseph."* TAN Books and Publishing, Inc., Rockford, Illinois, P.O. Box 424, 61105, 1973.

Biver, Comte Paul. *"Père Lamy."* TAN Books and Publishing, Inc., Rockford, Illinois, P.O. Box 424, 61105, 1973.

"Birgitta of Sweden—Life and Selected Revelations." Edited by Marguerite Tjader Harris. Paulist Press, 997 MacArthur Boulevard, Mahwah, New Jersey 07430, 1990.

Burkey, O.F.M. Cap., Blaine E. *"The Theology of St. Joseph in the Writings of St. Lawrence of Brindisi."* Cahiers de Joséphologie, Vol. XXI, No. 1, Center of Research and Documentation, Saint Joseph's Oratory, Montreal, 1973.

Chorpenning, O.S.F.S., Joseph F. *"Just Man, Husband of Mary, Guardian of Christ—An Anthology of Readings from Jeronimo Gracian's Summary of the Excellencies of St. Joseph (1597)."* Saint Joseph's University Press, Philadelphia, Pennsylvania, 1993.

Chorpenning, O.S.F.S., Joseph F. *"The Holy Family Devotion—A Brief History."* Center of Research and Documentation, Saint Joseph's Oratory, Montreal, 1997.

Cirrincione, Msgr. Joseph A. *"St. Joseph, Fatima And Fatherhood."* TAN Books and Publishing, Inc., P.O. Box 424, Rockford, Illinois, 61105, 1989.

Cristiani, Leon. *"The Father of Jesus."* St. Paul Publications, Derby, New York, 1967, (Original: *"Saint Joseph."* Société of Saint Paul, Paris, France).

"Diary of Blessed Sister M. Faustina Kowalska." Marians of the Immaculate Conception. Association of Marian Helpers, Stockbridge, Massachusetts, 01263, 1996, (first published in 1987).

De Domenico, O.P., Dominic. *"True Devotion to St. Joseph and the Church."* St. Gabriel Press, 3050 Gap Knob Road, New Hope, Kentucky, 40052, 1996.

Deiss, C.S.Sp., Lucien. *"Joseph, Mary, Jesus."* The Liturgical Press, Collegeville, Minnesota 56321, 1996.

de la Potterie, Ignace. *"Mary in the Mystery of the Covenant,"* Alba House, New York, Society of St. Paul, 2187 Victory Blvd., Staten Island, New York 10314, 1992.

"Devotions to St. Joseph." Daughters of St. Paul, St. Paul Books & Media, 50 St. Paul's Avenue, Jamaica Plain, Boston, MA 02130, 1978.

Doyle, S.S.J., Fr. Joseph M., *"Espousals of Mary and Joseph."* Text of Homily. President's Office, St. Augustine High School, 2600 A.P. Tureaud Avenue, New Orleans, LA, 70119-1299, January 23, 1999.

Doze, Andrew. *"Saint Joseph: Shadow of the Father."* Alba House, New York; Society of St. Paul, 2187 Victory Blvd., Staten Island, NY 10314, 1992.

Emmerich, Ven. Anne Catherine. *"The Life of Jesus Christ and Biblical Revelations."* Edited by Very Reverend Carl E. Schmoger, C.SS.R. TAN Books and Publishing, Inc., P.O. Box 424, Rockford, Illinois, 61105, 1986, (originally published in 1914).

Emmerich, Ven. Anne Catherine. *"The Life of the Blessed Virgin Mary."* Translated by Sir Michael Palairet. TAN Books and Publishing, Inc., P.O. Box 424, Rockford, Illinois, 61105, 1970, (originally published in 1954).

Emyard, Bl. Peter Julian. *"Month of Saint Joseph."* Emmanuel Publications, 5384 Wilson Mills Road, Cleveland, Ohio 44143, 1948.

"Favorite Prayers to St. Joseph." Compiled from Traditional Sources. TAN Books and Publishing, Inc., P.O. Box 424, Rockford, Illinois, 61105, 1997.

Filas, S.J., Francis L. *"Joseph and Jesus—A Theological Study of Their Relationship."* The Bruce Publishing Company, Milwaukee, WI, 1956.

Filas, S.J., Francis L. *"Joseph Most Just—Theological Questions About St. Jospeh."* The Bruce Publishing Company, Milwaukee, WI, 1956.

Filas, S.J., Francis L. *"Joseph: The Man Closest To Jesus."* The Complete Life, Theology and Devotional History of St. Joseph. Daughters of St. Paul, St. Paul Books & Media, 50 St. Paul's Avenue, Jamaica Plain, Boston, MA 02130, 1962.

Filas, S.J., Francis L. *"St. Joseph—After Vatican II."* Conciliar Implications Regarding St. Joseph. Cogan Productions, 1134 Youngstown Avenue, Youngstown, Arizona 85363, 1981.

Fitzmyer, S.J., Joseph A. Saint Joseph's Day Lecture. *"Saint Joseph in Matthew's Gospel."* Saint Joseph's University Press, Philadelphia, Pennsylvania, 19131-1395, 1997.

Fox, Fr. Robert J. *"Saint Joseph—His Life As He Might Tell It."* Booklet excerpted from *Saints and Heroes Speak.* The Blue Army of Our Lady of Fatima, Washington, NJ 07882, 1977.

Gasnier, O.P., Michael. *"Joseph The Silent."* P. J. Kenedy & Sons, New York, 1962.

Gill, S.J., Henry V. *"Saint Joseph—A Short Life Based on the Gospels."* M. H. Gill and Son, Ltd., 50 Upper O'Connell Street, Dublin, Ireland, 1946.

Gorman, Rev. Paul J. *"Life With Joseph."* The Leaflet Missal Company, 976 W. Minnehaha Ave., St. Paul, Minnesota 55104, 1988.

Griffin, O.C.D., Michael D. *"Saint Joseph And The Third Millennium."* Traditional Themes and Contemporary Issues. Teresian Charism Press, 1525 Carmel Road, Holy Hill, Hubertus, Wisconsin 53033, 1999.

Griffin, O.C.D., Michael D. *"Saint Joseph—A Theological Introduction."* Centre de recherche et de documentation, Oratoire Saint-Joseph, Montreal, Canada, 1996, (originally printed in 1972).

Hubert, O.F.M. Cap., Fr. *"Knock, Vision of Hope."*
Roscommon Herald, Boyle, Ireland, 1959.

John Paul II, Supeme Pontiff. *"Guardian of the Redeemer."*
Daughters of St. Paul, St. Paul Books & Media,
50 St. Paul's Avenue, Jamaica Plain, Boston,
MA 02130, 1989.

Joseph, C.S.J., Sister Emily. *"Joseph, Son of David."* St.
Anthony Guild Press, Paterson, New Jersey, 1961.

Joseph, C.S.J., Sister Emily. *"Reflecting On Saint Joseph."* St.
Anthony Guild Press, Paterson, New Jersey, 1959.

"Joseph the Just," A Sister of Saint Joseph, Benziger
Brothers, New York, 1937.

Keyes, Frances Parkinson. *"St. Anne, Grandmother of Our
Saviour."* Hawthorn Books, Inc. New York, 1955.

Levy, Rosalie Marie. *"Joseph, The Just Man."* Daughters of
St. Paul, St. Paul Books & Media, 50 St. Paul's
Avenue, Jamaica Plain, Boston, MA 02130, 1955.

Llamera, O.P. Boniface. *"Saint Joseph."* B. Herder Book Co.,
15 & 17 South Broadway, St. Louis 2, MO, 1962,
(published as *Teologia de San José* in Madrid in
1953).

Meinardus, Otto F. A. *"The Holy Family In Egypt."* The
American University in Cairo Press, 113 Sharia Kasr
el Aini, Cairo, Egypt, 1986.

Molinari, S.J., Paul, and Hennessy, C.S.J., Anne. *"The
Vocation and Mission of Joseph & Mary."* Veritas
Publication, 7-8 Lower Abbey Street, Dublin 1,
Ireland, 1992.

Neuzil, Sister Mildred Mary. *"Our Lady of America."* Our Lady
of America Center, 700 N. Susan Drive, P.O.
Box 445, Fostoria, Ohio 44830, 1993.

O'Carroll, C.S.Sp., D.D., Michael. *"Joseph, Son of David."* M. H. Gill & Son Ltd., 50 Upper O'Connell Street, Dublin 1, Ireland, 1963.

O'Carroll, C.S.Sp., D.D., Michael. *"The King Uncrowned—A Study of Saint Joseph."* The Mercier Press Limited, Cork, Ireland, 1947.

O'Rafferty, Father Nicholas. *"Discourses On St. Joseph."* The Bruce Publishing Company, Milwaukee, WI, 1951.

O'Shea, C.C., Denis. *"Mary and Joseph—Their Lives and Times."* The Bruce Publishing Company, Milwaukee, WI, 1949.

"Our Lady of Knock." 101 Foundation, Inc, P.O. Box 151, Asbury, New Jersey, 08802-0151, 1993.

Patrignani, S.J., Father Anthony Joseph. *"A Manual of Practical Devotion to St. Joseph."* TAN Books and Publishing, Inc., P.O. Box 424, Rockford, Illinois, 61105, 1982, (Written in 1709).

Pesquera, O.F.M., Father Eusebio Garcia de. *"She Went In Haste To The Mountain—Book One."* St. Joseph Publications, 17700 Lorain Avenue, Cleveland, Ohio, 44111, 1981.

Petrisko, Dr. Thomas. *"Saint Joseph and the Triumph of the Saints."* St. Andrews Productions, 6111 Steubenville Pike, McKees Rocks, PA 15136, 1998.

Poranganel, Varkey. *"St. Joseph—Envoy of the Heavenly Father at Nazareth."* Mar Mathews Press, Muvattupuzha, Kerala State, India, 1987.

Robert, Brother Cyril. *"Guardian of God's Lilies."* The Marist Brothers, St. Ann's Hermitage, Poughkeepsie, New York, 1945.

Rondet, S.J., Henri. *"Saint Joseph."* P. J. Kenedy, New York, 1956.

Sabat-Rivers, Georgina. Saint Joseph's Day Lecture. *"Sor Juana Inés de la Cruz and Sor Marcela de San Félix: Their Devotion to St. Joseph as the Antithesis of Patriarchal Authoritarianism."* Saint Joseph's University Press, Philadelphia, Pennsylvania, 19131-1395, 1997.

Sparks, O.P., Father Timothy, and Basil Cole, O.P. *"Dominicans on Saint Joseph."* TAN Books and Publishing, Inc., P.O. Box 424, Rockford, Illinois, 61105, 1997.

St. Bridget of Sweden. *"Revelations of St. Bridget—On the Life and Passion of Our Lord and the Life of His Blessed Mother."* TAN Books and Publishing, Inc., P.O. Box 424, Rockford, Illinois, 61105, 1984.

Stein, Susan T. *"The Tapestry of Saint Joseph."* Apostle Publishing, 401 Parlin Place, Philadelphia, Pennsylvania 19116, 1991.

Stramare, O.S.J., Fr. Tarcisio. *"Saint Joseph—Guardian of the Redeemer."* Apostolic Exhortation of John Paul II, Text and Reflections. Guardian of the Redeemer Books, 544 West Cliff Drive, Santa Cruz, CA 95060, 1997.

Suarez, Federico. *"Joseph of Nazareth."* Sinag-Tala Publishers, Inc. P.O. Box 536, Greenhills Post Office, Manila 3113, Philippines, 1985.

"The Glories of Saint Joseph." Compiled by the Monks of St. Joseph's Abbey. Traditions Monastiques Press, 21150 Flavigny-sur-Ozerain, France, 1997.

"The Spiritual Doctrine of Father Louis Lallemant of the Society of Jesus." Edited by Alan G. McDougall. The Newman Book Shop, Westminster, Maryland, 1946.

Thompson, M.A., Edward Healy. *"The Life and Glories of Saint Joseph."* TAN Books and Publishing, Inc., P.O. Box 424, Rockford, Illinois, 61105, 1980, (Originally published in 1888).

Toschi, O.S.J., Rev. Larry M. *"Joseph in the New Testament."* Guardian of the Redeemer Books, 544 West Cliff Drive, Santa Cruz, CA 95060, 1993.

Toschi, O.S.J., Rev. Larry M. *"Saint Joseph in the Lives of Two Blesseds of the Church—Blessed Junipero Serra, Blessed Joseph Marello."* Guardian of the Redeemer Books, 544 West Cliff Drive, Santa Cruz, CA 95060, 1994.

Valtorta, Maria. *"The Poem of the Man-God."* Centro Editoriale Valtortiano srl, 03036 Isola del Lira, Italy, 1987.

Van De Putte, C.S.Sp., Rev. Walter. *"Following Saint Joseph."* Catholic Book Publishing Co., New York, 1980.

Van Speybrouck, Edward. *"Father Paul of Moll."* TAN Books and Publishing, Inc., P.O. Box 424, Rockford, Illinois, 61105, 1980, (Originally published in 1910 by the Benedictine Convent of Clyde, MO).

Vaughn, Herbert Cardinal. *"Who Is St. Joseph?"* The Reparation Society of the Immaculate Heart of Mary, Inc., 100 East 20th Street, Baltimore, Maryland, 21218, 1949.

Patrons:

Edward Desloge
Sarah Bridget Mullan
Karen A. Young

(Cover: Mysterious rose petal. perhaps from Heaven.
Recipient wishes to remain anonymous.)

Trinity presenting crown to Saint Joseph,
domed ceiling fresco, St. Joseph Parish, Qala, Gozo, Malta.
Photograph taken by Fr. Larry Toschi, O.S.J.